The peter pilot just looked terrified as I continued to reduce power. I could feel the branches breaking under me. I keyed the mike. "How much more?"

"Four feet."

I glanced down at the chin bubble. Branches were pressed against it. I hoped it would hold. I could hear the whistling snap of bullets pressing within inches of the aircraft. The bird dropped the final two feet as more branches gave way.

I thought, "Come on. Come on, get in the damn rigs."

I had not heard any hits in the fuselage. I knew that we must have taken some in the blades. It was taking forever for the team to get in the rigs. I heard the sharp whistle of more rounds.

The belly man said, "We got thumbs up. Go!"

I started to climb while I felt as if every gook in the universe was shooting at me.

WINGS OF THE EAGLE

A Kingsmen's Story

W. T. Grant

IVY BOOKS • NEW YORK

Ivy Books
Published by Ballantine Books
Copyright © 1994 by William T. Grant

Library of Congress Catalog Card Number: 93-94987

ISBN 0-8041-1062-X

Manufactured in the United States of America

First Edition: May 1994

10 9 8 7 6 5 4 3 2 1

DEDICATION

This book is dedicated to my lovely wife Jackie who, for the last twenty-six years, has held down the toughest job in the army, An Army Wife. Thank you for standing by me through war, rumor of war, and playing at war. Thank you for your waiting through late nights and long days and all the time away from home. Thank you for your fears when the phone rang and when it didn't ring. Thank you for two wonderful children, and thank you for being my best friend. And thank you for always wanting me to write this book.

ACKNOWLEDGMENTS

I want to thank all those to helped me "get it right." Several of my fellow Kingsmen have spent many hours answering my questions and relating stories to make this book as accurate as possible. I sent out a lot of letters asking for help. As usual, the Kingsmen's response was above and beyond the call. Among those who gave so much time:

WILLIAM C. "WILD BILL" MEACHAM
JAMES A. "SIR JAMES" THOMPSON
EUGENE L. "H$_2$O" GILLENWATER
KENNETH D. "TEENYBOPPER" ROACH
BARRY SCHREIBER
TED "WILD TURKEY" CROZIER*

*NOTE: Colonel Crozier is not a real Kingsman, but we like to let him think he's one of the boys.

Then there are the LRPs of F Company, 58th Infantry, who not only got me in all that trouble so I would have stories to tell but, years later, came back and helped me piece those stories together.

RILEY "BULLDOZER" COX
KEN "I WANNA HOVER" EKLUND
KENN MILLER
HONEST JOHN BURFORD
TONY "TI TI" TERCERO
TIM "GREEN LANTERN" COLEMAN
LARRY "LET ME WALK POINT" CHAMBERS

These are the ones who spent a considerable amount of time answering all my questions. There are others who were not able to contribute quite as much, and I thank them as well. There is one LRP whom I have deliberately left off the list because his contribution goes far beyond helping me get the story straight. Gary A. Linderer's contribution started by writing his own two books and showing me it could be done. From the day I called him to renew our friendship, he has pushed, prodded, and nagged me to see this book through to completion. He has guided the writing and the research; he has provided encouragement when I wanted to quit. Thank you, Gary.

The last but certainly not the least thanks have to go to the one who helped me through all the stupid things I did. He guided my flying and my decisions. He made some of my screwups look like triumphs and allowed me to walk away looking like an ace of the skies. For all us drunks and dumb animals, thanks God.

We were all glad to hear that because it was very close in the club already, and we wanted to get the bar opened.

The major continued. "We will be lifting the second of the five oh deuce and the second of the three two seventh infantry battalions into the valley."

He paused to uncover the map on the easel. "The LZs will be here at A Leui strip and here at Ta Bat strip."

I leaned over and looked at Jim Riden on the other side of the room. He just smiled back. It seemed the brigade commander had liked the recommendations that Jim had given him.

"The purpose of the operation is to interdict supply lines that the enemy has established through the valley going south."

All the Arc Lights were not doing the job. No matter how good the technology is, it still takes the infantryman to finish the job.

"The operation will be conducted slightly differently than we are used to. The lifts will be done in flights of five. All operations will be flown at low level to avoid antiaircraft weapons on the other side of the border. This will be a maximum effort by all three lift companies. We will be putting up everything we have that is flyable, and so will the other companies."

That comment drew a few snickers from the audience. There were those who felt there was a major difference in the maximum effort of the Kingsmen and certain other lift companies.

"At ease, gentlemen! Enough of that." Then he smiled and said, "We will all do the best we are capable of." It was not often that he let us see through his solid military bearing to the person that was inside.

He had Rick brief the crew and aircraft assignments. We would be staging out of FSB Birmingham. The commander would lead the first flight himself. When Rick had finished, the CO took the floor once more. He stared down at the floor as he spoke. "There is just one more thing I have to cover. Signal Operations. We are now part of the 101st Airborne Division and must operate from the division SOI. We are B Company, 101st Aviation Battalion, and our call sign for the period of tomorrow's lift is Snakey Inkwell."

That drew great guffaws from the assembly of pilots. Everyone was laughing so hard we could not even hear the commander continue.

"Please quiet down, gentlemen." But the laughing continued. Finally he lost patience and yelled, "Shut the hell up!"

The room was suddenly silent. The Old Man straightened his

shirt and went on. "I'm serious about this. I do not want to hear the word Kingsmen or any other personal call signs on the radio tomorrow. That will be all, gentlemen."

The bar opened quickly and the next day's call sign soon started taking a beating. Someone yelled from the back. "Stinky Finger Two-Four Bravo, this is Stinky Finger Four-Seven Alpha. Send me a fucking beer."

The laughter was back, and the division directive to use the SOI was as good as dead. If it had not come so soon on the tail of telling us to change the patch we wore . . . But there was just no way we were going to give up our pride in being Kingsmen.

As the evening wore on, Sir James climbed up on a chair and said, "Gentlemen, may I have your attention please! I have just received this notice from division headquarters." He held up a piece of paper as though he was reading from it. "If you bastards don't use your new Stinky Asshole call sign during the lift tomorrow, we are going to send all your smelly asses to Vietnam."

Lou Pulver stood up and yelled, *"Opera Non Verba,"* and threw the contents of his beer mug at Thompson. Everyone yelled, *"Opera Non Verba,"* and soon the air in the club was filled with beer, bits of crackers, and the contents of ashtrays.

Monday, 5 August (226 days to go). Operation SOMERSET PLAIN. Somehow it seems appropriate that the assault of the A Shau Valley should begin on a Monday. Not that it made any difference in Nam what day it was; it was just that it seems fitting that a big job should start on Monday. The wake-up came early. The sky was just beginning to lighten as we finished our preflights and got strapped in for the crank. I was flying in Chalk Three of the lead flight.

The CO called the tower, "Eagle Tower, Snakey Inkwell Four-Seven, flight of five for departure to the west."

The whole crew burst out laughing. We were laughing so hard that Dave Poley had trouble lifting the aircraft out of the revetment. The crew chief and gunner forgot to clear us when the aircraft lifted to a hover. At first everyone stuck to the SOI, but there was total confusion. Nobody could tell who anybody was. We landed at the airstrip on FSB Birmingham. The oiled strip was covered with thirty-five slicks and over twenty Charlie-model guns. In all, more than 110 rotor blades were drumming the air. The red-orange clay dust hung in the air like a fog on the planet Mars. The grunts were ready, and the anticipation of the assault had begun to build. I once again started to have thoughts of helicopters ripped from the sky by walls of antiaircraft fire. This was the biggest operation that any of us had participated in.

The Kingsmen would be going into the A Leui strip near the village of A Sap. We loaded up and followed Major Addiss into the air, staying at treetop level and heading west toward FSB Veghel. After Veghel, we turned south and crossed into the valley through a low saddle at one hundred and ten knots. All three radios were alive from the time we left Birmingham. The Fox Mike bubbled with the conversation of the grunts, the UHF had the slicks, and the VHF was tuned to the gunships. One had to develop an ear that could sort out all the different conversations. After a while, one could tell the difference in each radio by the tone and thereby knew which one to answer. Left on its own, the mind learned to sort out all the voices and heard only those that mattered.

The guns had made no attempt to use the SOI, at least not that I heard. I could hear Killer Three-Five and Killer Three-Six talking as we rounded the turn at Veghel. The tactical call signs caused total confusion, and nobody had any idea who anyone was. By the time the first flight was crossing the last ridgeline into the valley, even Major Addiss had to give up and went back to calling himself Kingsmen Six. There was almost constant chatter on the radio.

"Killer Three-Five, this is Killer Three-Six on Victor. Are you with the flight?"

"Roger."

"The flight is inbound."

On UHF. "Killer Three-Six, this is Stinky ... uh ... uh ... Snakey Inkey ... Oh hell. This is Kingsmen Six, inbound with the first flight."

"Roger, Six. I have you at the ridgeline."

Then on FM. "Cease fire. Cease fire the artillery. Cease fire. Cease fire the artillery."

On VHF. "Okay, those lifts will be coming from the river."

"Never mind the rockets, never mind the rockets. Cease fire the artillery."

"There's the flight."

"Man, there's still artillery in that place."

They were having trouble getting the artillery prep shut off. Even crazy Dave Poley was concerned with this one. He had not said much during the flight out to the valley. When we crossed the saddle into the valley, I braced myself for the fire that I knew would be coming. It didn't come. The approach to the strip was fast, and we touched down, still moving forward. The Huey slid about six inches, and the grunts were gone in a flash.

Victor again. "Killer One-Seven, breaking right."

"I see where they're going in down there now."

"The first one is on the ground."

As soon as we stopped sliding, Poley had the aircraft light on the skids again.

"Two-One, are you with us?"

"Roger."

"We're going to climb out here and set up an orbit. Watch out."

On UHF, "Kingsmen lead lifting."

The flight built airspeed quickly and was out of the valley. The flying was fast and furious; it was like flying LRPs.

When we landed at Birmingham, Dave gave me the controls. After the first successful lift, I felt more confident. Nobody had gotten blasted out of the sky. As we headed back out, we could hear the radios come alive again.

"Killer Six, Killer Three-Five. We are receiving fire from southeast of the LZ."

"Where is it?"

"Heading of two one zero, one klick from the LZ."

There were Charlie-model gunships everywhere. I had never seen such intense gun cover. Most of them were just circling with nothing to do. They would pick up the incoming flights and escort them to the LZ. There were so many, that at times they got in each other's way.

"Gunships, this is Killer Three-Six. We took fire on heading of two one zero out of the Lima Zulu, about a thousand meters."

On Uniform. "Kingsman One-Two, this One-Six. Over."

"What was that?"

"Ah . . . someone put a rocket in there."

"Ah, those aren't rockets those are mortars."

"Killer Six, this is Killer One-Two. Over."

"There are mortars on the west side of the LZ."

"Three-Five, this is Three-Six. I just went by you."

Then on Fox Mike. "Soapy Zebra One-Two, this Kingsman Eight. The Lima Zulu is cold." Soapy Zebra was the call sign for the C & C bird.

The chatter continued on the radios as we flew lift after lift into the valley. Many calls went unanswered. The enormity of the operation was staggering.

"Zebra One-Two, this is Killer Six. We are receiving fire from the ridgeline just to the west of the LZ."

"Is that the big terrain feature immediately west?"

"That's affirmative."

"Roger."

"What range from the LZ are you receiving fire? Do you know, Killer Six?"

"A thousand meters."

"Ah . . . Killer Six, this is Soapy Zebra One-Two. They're putting tac air, tac air. Remain clear . . ."

"We've got a gunship down. We've got a gunship down at nine o'clock."

"Roger."

"My minigun just jammed. I'm going to back off and orbit over here."

"Roger the FO . . . ah . . . correction, the FAC is calling down tac air now."

"One-Two, this is Three-Six. Appears we got a gunship down. Do you have knowledge?"

"Roger. I've got the gunship in sight."

"Roger. We have one down in the LZ. Should be no problem. Ground elements should be able to get to him right away. Over."

"Ah . . . roger."

"See if you can contact my One-Six element and see if he's in the area now. Over."

"Black Widow Six, this is Soapy Zebra One-Two. Over."

"This is One . . . uh, this is Six. I think we're out of order on the Black Bandit element over."

"Black Bandit Recovery One, Bandit Yellow One. Can you make the recovery at this time? Over."

"Soapy Zebra One-Two, Bandit One . . . uh . . . Negative at this time."

"Killer Three-Six, this is Killer Three-Five."

"Bandit, what is your location?"

"I'm approaching the hillside to the northwest."

"Go ahead, Three-Five."

"We've been circling to the west side of the LZ. Our miniguns are out, and we've got one gunship down."

"Say again, please."

"He wants you to patrol the west side of the LZ, and his miniguns are out, and they have one gunship down."

"Black Widow, what is your location?"

"My white element is inbound."

"Roger. We'll pick up the west side on the next pass."

The Black Widows were taking the second load of grunts in. No one was waiting for his turn to talk on the radio, everyone just jumped in wherever they could. Aircraft were everywhere. The only thing that prevented us from having a midair collision was that we knew what we were supposed to do. All those aviators did this every day; we knew our business. Although the operation was bigger than we were used to, the scenario was familiar.

"Killer Three-Five, Three-Six. Did you monitor the west side?"

There was a pause with no response, then, "Killer Three-Five, Three-Six moving to the west side."

"Ah, roger that."

"Killer One-Six, this is Killer Six. Are you in orbit west side? Over."

"This is Killer One-Seven. Roger. Over."

"Roger which ship is down? Killer Two-One?"

"Ah, this is One-Seven . . . I'm not sure; he got shot a while ago . . . ah, before I was here."

"Roger, Killer Two-One, you receiving Killer Six? Over."

"Black Widow Six, this is One-Two. We are inbound to get that bird."

"Roger. You can go ahead and recover. We have security around the bird now."

"Okay, this is Killer Six. I think things are pretty quiet right now. I'm gonna head back because the miniguns are out. You assume control, Three-Six, and I'm goin' back for fuel, Three-six."

"Killer One-Six, this is One-Seven. Was that a 2d Platoon aircraft?"

"Roger that."

Later on I heard that Killer Six had gone head-to-head with a .51-caliber machine gun. Both windshields were shot out and several instruments. They got the fifty, but Six had several bad cuts on his face from glass flying around the cockpit. When he went back to FSB Birmingham, he jumped out of the shot-up Charlie-model gunship with blood running down his face and soaking his shirt. Offered a medevac, he said, "Get me another aircraft; I'm going back out!" The kind of stuff John Wayne movies were made from. There were those that felt that there were smarter ways to take on a fifty and that there were more than enough gun pilots on station to cover the mission. Killer Six was probably just trying to let everybody know that he had the kind of courage his warrants displayed every day.

"Killer One-Six, Three-Six on Victor."

"Receiving fire from the hills west!"

"Three-Six, Three-Five."

"One-Six, Three-Six. Our VHF is out. You're receiving fire from the hills to west. Back off a minute ... mmm ... see if you can locate it. We have no minigun. Over."

"Uh ... I see it, thanks. Roger."

Then very calmly came, "Three-Six, this is Three-Five."

"Three-Six, go."

"Uh, this is Three-Five. I had to adjust my fire. I took fire in the right pod, and it caught fire, and I had to jettison it. Over."

He sounded pretty cool for someone who just had a pod of high-explosive rockets catch fire on the side of his aircraft.

"Where's that fire coming from?"

"The southwest side of the runway."

"Gunships, this is Killer Three-Six. Let's set up one chain, right-hand orbits about one five zero off the LZ; anyone that has the target go ahead and hit it."

"This is One-Seven. Understand you want a right-hand orbit."

"Roger. Let's get 'em all over that one side. Any gunship that knows where that fire is coming from break off a fire team and go get it."

"This is One-Seven. I'm breaking off over the LZ now."

"Roger. And Three-Six is behind One-Seven."

"Three-Six, Three-Five. It's the southwest side of the runway." There was just a short stretch of the dirt strip still visible amongst the bomb craters. "I dropped the pods right near it."

"One-Six, I see Widow Mender is with the downed ship. He just landed." Widow Mender was the call sign for C Company's maintenance.

"It's okay. We've got a lot of ships with us now."

"Okay, I have the smoke off of Three-Five's pods when they hit."

"Okay."

"Pods mark the spot?"

"Uh, yeah. He had to drop 'em."

"One-Seven this is Three-Six. Off the end of the runway, the two pods are smoking. As you come around, let's dump a little on it this time."

"Understand. To the right of the runway."

"Uh . . . roger."

"Okay, I'll slap a little on 'em."

"Yeah, put forty Mike Mike down in there."

The plan seemed to be working. Since the Cav had gotten blasted back in April going in at altitude, we were going in on the treetops. The guns were flying at fifty feet above the trees, doing their job protecting us. Also the low altitude was shielding us from the fire that was coming from the hills to west of the LZs.

"Three-Zero, Three-Three. You got me now?"

"Three-Zero, Three-Three is with the flight that has just crossed the ridgeline."

"Three-Zero, Three-Six is with the flight that just passed FSB Zon."

"Killer Six, this is Soapy Zebra One-Two. Have you got a hot LZ?"

The C & C was sticking to the tactical call sign, most likely because he had the brigade commander on board.

"Uh, this is Killer Six. Keep on coming in. Negative fire."

"Zebra One-Two, Eagle lead is off, and it is pretty cold down here."

It was true, the LZs were all cold. Only the guns were taking fire.

The C & C aircraft had started out at about two hundred feet. About the time that our flight was crossing the ridgeline into the valley, there was an airburst that had been aimed at the C & C bird. He soon gave up and performed his job with a ridgeline between him and the dreaded A Shau Valley.

"Killer, this is Kingsman Six. Inbound at the ridge."

"Roger, Kingsman. Keep to the low lying terrain. We got a 37-millimeter we believe firing from your nine o'clock position. We had an airburst up here shortly ago."

The guns were monopolizing the radios, but with good reason. The slicks had been thoroughly briefed on their routes and loads for the mission ahead of time. Since the guns were doing such a good job of keeping the gooks off our backs, our flights went as planned. When things go as planned, there is little need for conversation during a lift. The gunships had to respond to situations as they developed, therefore requiring a lot of talk on the radios.

Killer Six spent much of his time in the air, doing duty as a traffic cop. At one point, three light fire teams were circling with nothing to do.

"Killer Six, this is Killer Three-Six. Over."

"This is Killer Six. Say again on UHF, negative VHF."

"Killer One-Five got a light team on the right side of the LZ. We are in good shape at this time."

"Roger. You still have ordnance. Over."

"Roger that."

"Roger any other Killer in the area. Over."

"This is Killer Three-Six. I have two lights just north of the Lima Zulu, comin' in on the west side. Over."

"Roger. Well, come on down south of the Lima Zulu. You might get something. It's all quiet up there."

"Roger."

"I don't have any guns left, I'm down here to the south area. If I can get somebody to come down here, we'll all see what's down by this road where we had the fire before. Over."

"Roger. I'll bring my light straight across the LZ."

Then came, "Receiving fire. Receiving fire."

Again still fairly calm, "Receiving fire, Three-Eight is receiving fire."

"Who is receiving fire?" Killer Six was asking.

Then came the most horrifying radio transmission that I heard during my entire tour. The voice came back several octaves higher. "I'm on fire! I'm on fire! God!"

Each pilot flying a combat mission in Vietnam was aware that he had in the aircraft two hundred some gallons of fuel that was meant to burn. Fear of getting shot was not as bad. It was quick. Fire was an agonizing way to die. As a result of Vietnam, new helicopters have come equipped with crashworthy fuel cells. Older aircraft like the Huey have been updated with them. In Nam, hard landings could, and often did, result in postcrash fires. Today, to open up a fuel cell, one generally has to hit the ground so hard that the impact itself is not survivable.

Killer Six, unable to hear the transmission on VHF, was talking about his guns being jammed. A calmer voice came on the radio. "Killer Three-Eight, I'm on fire, I'm going down."

"You're on fire, put it down."

Then an apparently inadvertent transmission, "We're on fire, shit!"

A Charlie-model with the aft end engulfed in flames could be seen descending through about fifteen hundred feet.

"Killer One-Five is going to cover the downed ship."

"To the west of the LZ. He's going down."

Then Killer Six's voice with the obvious, "Put it on the ground. Put it on the ground."

It got so hot in the back of the aircraft that the crew chief and gunner crawled out on the skids. As the stricken bird neared the ground, they leaped to escape the flames. The Charlie-model's hurry to get on the ground caused an impact so hard the mast snapped off with the rotor system. The AC immediately undid his seat belt, and the second bounce launched him through the overhead greenhouse window. The fact that he fit through made all the harassment he got about being small from his fellow aviators worthwhile. The peter pilot later swore that he did not know how he got out, but when he looked back, the aircraft was on its side, and the windshield in front of his seat was gone. With his door turned to the ground, he must have just run right through the windshield without even thinking about it. The crew chief escaped with some burns and bad bruises from his jump. In his haste to leave the flames, the gunner did not unhook his monkey strap. Attached to the bird he was dragged along until the aircraft rolled on him and trapped him in the flames.

The assault ended with not one slick being shot down. None were even hit. The guns had three birds shot down. Two were reparable, the last burned to the ground. The one door gunner was killed. All of those wounded suffered only minor wounds. In all, the lift had been a grand success, especially given the Cav's previous experience with the valley. That day saw the birth of the low-altitude tactics that we still use today.

That night I wrote to Jackie and told her about the operation. I figured that it would be in the papers, and I wanted her to know that I was not one of the ones shot down. Right after the lift, I came down with food poisoning. It had been going around for a few days. We had been calling it A Shau fever since everyone was coming down with it right before the big lift into the valley. I was glad I made it till after the assault. I spent the night calling to Ralph. I couldn't even keep down the antinausea pills the flight surgeon was handing out like candy. Each time I went to puke, all I could see was our big, fat mess sergeant dripping sweat into the food. I told Jackie that if I got sick again, I would empty my .38 into that fat son of a bitch.

Even A Shau fever didn't keep crews out of the air. The Kingsmen put up every aircraft for the mission. Even the first sergeant flew, replacing one of the gunner's who really was too sick to fly.

* * *

Tuesday, 6 August (225 days to go). Capt. William "Wild Bill" Meacham came down to my hootch and asked me to fly him down to Da Nang for his R & R flight to Hawaii. He explained that I would have to spend the night in Da Nang since someone else was returning from R & R the next day, and I was to fly back with him. This would mean that we would have to suffer through having to take showers that had hot and cold water, both available on the same day, and endure toilets that flushed. After taking about three seconds to think the matter over carefully, and considering all the possibilities, I said, "We ain't left yet?"

After throwing a few items in the AWOL bag and grabbing my flight gear, we headed out to preflight. One of the joys of flying to Da Nang was the climb to thirty-five hundred feet to cross the Hai Van Pass. An amazing thing about being away from the World was that one could learn to appreciate some little things in life, like a six-degree drop in temperature.

The flight was uneventful, but crossing the Hai Van and looking out across Da Nang Bay made me realize that Da Nang was so different from Camp Eagle and our life back there that it was like being on another planet. If there was so much difference in just a few miles, how would it ever be possible to go home again? Was it possible that the World even existed out there anymore?

After the usual high-speed run down the beach under the approach path at Da Nang Main Air Base, and then climbing back to a hundred feet, the familiar runway of Marble Mountain came into view. We landed and hovered into the Black Cat's parking area. As we hovered in, it dawned on me that Bill had let me do all the flying, which was unusual. He normally wanted his share of the stick time. While we were still at idle and waiting for the two-minute cool down, the crew chief and gunner were already filling out the log book and getting the forms ready for the next day. They were well aware that the sooner they got their work done, the sooner they could enjoy a short vacation from the war. Besides, having the daily done then meant that they would not have to do it the next day with a hangover. Bill and I had no such problem; our work was done on shutdown. We checked with the crew to see if they needed help getting settled, but they had local friends and could take care of themselves.

The first order of business was to arrange for a room for the night. The Black Cats had several two-man rooms available for visitors. When you lived like that, and had so many poor relations, you had to expect a lot of visitors. The next item on the agenda was a hot shower. Now it was hot as hell there, just the way it was at Eagle, but one could not ignore the fact that a hot shower on demand was not something to be overlooked. Besides, the club was air-conditioned and was next on the list of places to go. Of course, it was quickly followed by the navy's Stone Elephant club at Da Nang and the air force O club at Da Nang AB. The fighter pilots coming in wore tailored powder blue flight suits, with white silk ascots that had the Gunfighter patch sewn on them. These were flight suits not for flying but for wearing to the club. A short time later, Wild Bill sat down at a table with some air force lieutenants, while a group of us stayed at the bar talking to some of the fighter pilots. The conversation I was having would prove valuable in the future. A captain was telling me how once they took off in their F-4s with a full load of armament and fuel, they had to expend either the ordnance or the fuel to land again.

While the F-4 had the thrust to hurl it into the air with all that weight, its brakes and drag chutes needed more runway than Da Nang Main had to offer to stop it while fully loaded. What this meant was that most of the time there were some aircraft circling over Da Nang, burning off fuel so they could land again. This guy told me that even as rapidly as the F-4 sucks down jet fuel, the pilot could dump ordnance much faster. Besides, blowing things up was much more fun than boring holes in the sky. It didn't take long to pull out my little notebook to jot down the Gunfighter's internal frequency. All I had to do was find a target, get clearance to fire it up, and then call. If my new friend was circling and still had the fuel to get to the target area, he would be more than glad to swing by and shoot up a target for us. Since our AO was only minutes away for these jet jockeys, they didn't need a whole lot of fuel.

I explained to him that we had a hard time getting air strikes on call. By the time the request went all the way through channels, the opportunity was usually lost before they could get the fighters launched. It amazed me! These guys were always looking for targets, and we had the targets, but our leaders couldn't find a way to put us together. Many times, it would take an hour or more to get air support that wasn't already on standby. When we were working LRPs, there just wasn't that kind of time. If we needed fire support, we needed it now! This captain and I had just reduced the procedure to a thirty-second radio call.

In practice, an air-strike request generated by us had to go through our operations, then to our battalion, then to our group, then to division, then to some mysterious liaison office, then to the air force, then to their group, then to their squadron, then to their operations as a mission request. Their operations would usually respond that they had no aircraft on standby and the only ones loaded with armament had just landed and needed to be refueled. Of course, all the little lifers along the way would have to make sure their asses were covered before they sent it forward. And that was only if everything went according to plan and one of the ass coverers didn't turn it down because it didn't have the proper twenty-four-hour lead time. I couldn't help but wonder how many bad guys got away or how many GIs got killed because of the lack of coordination.

About then, the good Captain told me he was going to hit the sack and left. Not long after that, Meacham and I and our companions were asked to leave. We quietly returned to the Black Cat club, but it shut down early. So the only option left was the Marine officers club on the other side of the airfield. Sleepy Bear wanted to go to bed, but we convinced him to drive us over. Once we were there, it wasn't hard to talk him into a nightcap. (It was a long walk back.)

Suddenly, it was as bright as day. My eyelids slammed shut involuntarily; I struggled to force them open. It was so bright, my vision was blurred, and I couldn't focus. Someone had put a wooden barricade in front of me. I was lying on my left side. I rolled over. A large heavy object was loose in my head. It crashed to the right side as I turned. I was in a room that measured about ten by ten. "Where the hell am I," my brain screamed. My eyes finally began to focus. The object bouncing around in my skull was my brain. There was a large shape across the room. It appeared to be camouflaged. I finally recognized it as Wild Bill in a bunk, with poncho liner over him. Then everything came flooding back.

I hissed, "Meacham, wake up!" It hurt. My head felt like it was trapped in a size-five flight helmet.

I tried again, "Meacham, wake up!" It still hurt.

He didn't move.

"Meacham, wake up!"

He groaned, "What do you want, damn it?"

"I just want to say fuck you, Bill!" Content, I then slipped back to sleep.

9 August (222 days to go). I flew resupply in the A Shau all day. When I got back, a letter from Jackie was waiting for me. I opened the envelope, and a piece of zebra-stripe material fell out.

Dave Poley saw it and said, "What's that?"

"I don't know."

"Your Camaro probably has a zebra-stripe interior now."

"It better not have."

It turned out to be a sample of material that Jackie had made some throw pillows out of. That was a relief. I sometimes felt absolutely helpless not being able to be part of her life and be involved in the things we should be doing together. Other times, it all seemed so far away. It was like a life I just dreamed up, and the only reality was the war that would go on forever.

That night, I was assigned duty as the OD. Officer of the day. The Kingsmen had responsibility for two bunkers on the perimeter. Each bunker had two guards that switched off-on shifts throughout the night. A CQ and a runner were assigned to monitor the radio and land line in operations. One of the pilots was assigned the duty of supervising the whole operation. It was tough duty to pull, after having to fly that day and then stay up all night as the OD. The OD was given the next day off, since you wouldn't be worth a shit as pilot. Operations would get the most they could out of you on the day of the duty, since you had the next day off. They saw no sense in letting someone "get over" on them. It was even tougher on the enlisted guys. They would have to pull the day's flight. Then, because they were allowed to sleep between guards shifts, they would be put on the flight schedule in the morning. They would, many times, spend hours working on their bird after a day's flying. As hard as the crews worked on flying and maintaining the aircraft, they were still hit up with KP and guard duty. The worst part of the job of OD was making sure that everybody stayed awake.

It was shortly after midnight, and I decided it was a good time for a visit out to the bunkers. After I crossed the perimeter road, I paused for a few minutes to let my eyes become accustomed to the darkness. Staring out into the night soon had every shadow turning into a sapper slowly trying to sneak up and blow up all the helicopters in their revetments. *Well, not while I was on duty damn it!*

At the first bunker, no one challenged me. I stood a moment and waited. There was no movement. I tried to see into the darkness. Was there any sign of trouble? I knew that I had made enough noise in my approach that I should have been challenged by the guards. I slid the .38 from its holster and moved it to my left hand. The right hand undid the snap on the big K-bar and slid it from the sheath. I wished that I had a rifle. I crouched, moving slowly, just as Burnell and Brubaker had instructed me. I crept up to the bunker and found the guard sitting on top, leaning against a pole that stuck up from the back side. His hands were clasped behind his head, with the elbows sticking straight out. There was a cigarette dangling from his mouth. He did not move as I inched closer. I thought about stories of sappers sneaking up and cutting guards' throats and leaving them in their positions. There were no marks on him. The son of a bitch was asleep!

I put the weapons away and just stood there staring. How could anyone fall asleep on guard duty in a combat zone? As I stared in disbelief, I slowly realized that this crew chief had probably put in a fourteen-hour day on the flight line and then had to pull guard. I knew that I could not let this go. We were responsible for the safety of the entire company. On the other hand, if I wrote this up he would end up in LBJ—Long Binh Jail. Still I had to do something . . . Then I realized that the cigarette in his mouth was lit and was an unfiltered Pall Mall. If I just stood there a while, it would burn all the way down. Yup, that would do it. I carefully lifted his M-16 from his lap. I figured I would be safer that way, and I took over his watch of the perimeter. He could not have been asleep long because the cigarette was almost at its full length. I had to wait several minutes till it burned its way down. He woke to a burning sensation on his lips and a silhouette standing over him with his own weapon. I could see in his eyes that he knew his life was over.

Relief washed over his face when the voice that spoke to him was New York accented English, not Vietnamese. "You realize how important it is that we stay awake out here, don't you?"

His reply was sheepish like that of child caught raiding the cookie jar. His eyes cast down. "Yes, sir."

"You're not going to fall asleep on me again, are you?"

"No, sir."

I tossed the weapon back to him and left. I was quite pleased with myself. I had made the point without having to turn him in. Of course, I had forgotten to tell him that I had no intention of entering the incident in the log. I smiled to myself on the way back to the company area. He would worry all night about what would happen to him in the morning. It would keep him awake and punish him without having the army send him to prison.

The next day, I saw him. His lips were blistered, and I immediately felt sorry for him. He came over to me and thanked me. "Sir, I want to thank you for not turning me in."

"Don't worry about it. The main thing is that we get the job done."

"Yes, sir, but you did me a big favor. The lifers woulda' sent me to LBJ."

"It wasn't your fault, we expect you to work pretty hard around here. Still, we can't allow ourselves to slack off."

"Yes sir. Thanks again."

I could see in his eyes that his fear of LBJ was even greater than the fear that was there when he thought I was an NVA soldier standing over him in the night.

LIEUTENANT DIPSTICK

It was during August that Lieutenant Dipstick arrived. He quickly set about the task of proving to everyone that he was everything that lieutenants are supposed to be. Right off the bat, he laid claim to every additional duty that was not taken. He then went around asking some of the warrant officers to give him some of the ones they had. It was obvious that he was working on making his OER (officer efficiency report) look good.

Dipstick was all that we expected of an RLO. There were warrant officers and there were real live officers. Warrant officers were expected to be the technical experts when it came to flying. Commissioned aviators were branched infantry, armor, artillery, etc. The army demanded that they spend tours with their basic branch and saw their flying abilities simply as additional skill. The army's attitude presented some problems. Since, as commissioned officers, RLOs were considered the leaders, they were frequently assigned as aircraft commander and flight lead, i.e., because of their rank, not because of their ability. Many were aware enough of the situation to allow the warrants to help them out. Some were smug enough to think that their position and army policy made them qualified and skilled. Most often, the problem was no bigger than some good natured kidding on both sides.

Upon returning from flying one day, Gene Gillenwater and I left operations together and walked back to the tent. When we got there we saw Dave Poley standing on the porch that had been built on the back end of the tent. He was standing in front of the refrigerator. Suddenly he drew his weapon and took aim at the fridge. We ran to his side, and Gene said, "Dave, what the hell are you doing?"

Someone had put a hasp on the door and locked it with a padlock. Dave was aiming at the lock.

"I'm gonna shoot off this lock, then I'm gonna shoot that fucking lieutenant."

"Dave, you'll screw up the refrigerator."

Dave put his pistol away. There was a sign taped to the front of the fridge that read, SEE LT DIPSTICK FOR REFRIGERATOR SOP. It seems the lieutenant had found a container of milk in there that had gone sour. Real milk was a scarce commodity, and we would make it last as long as we could. The milk had been Dave's, and he was using a little at a time in his morning coffee.

"I still think that I'll shoot the FNG son of a bitch," he mumbled as he walked away.

Not only had Dipstick committed the crime of acting like an RLO, but he had committed the unpardonable transgression of a new guy, messing with something that belonged to a veteran. He wouldn't easily be forgiven.

Dipstick accumulated additional duties as fast as the rest of us accumulated flight time. Some felt that he was not particularly interested in flying. There were some who believed that he was trying to keep busy enough so that he wouldn't have to go out and get shot at.

Monday, 12 August (219 days to go). Scott Wilson and I had become good friends, much against army policy. We spent many nights in his hootch, talking of home and family. I would take a couple of six-packs of beer or a bottle of booze, and we would spend hours just talking. Occasionally, another crew chief or gunner would join us. When we were alone, Scott and I were on a first-name basis. When the sun rose the next morning, Wilson was always the professional soldier. Scott was not by any means a career soldier. He looked forward to his ETS, which came at the same time as his DEROS. His aircraft was always clean and well maintained, and though his moustache was never in accordance with the regulation, he was one of the best crew chiefs in the company.

It was his professionalism and devotion to duty that caused him to end up a civilian in the A Shau Valley. It was not uncommon for someone's orders to get screwed up and arrive late. Generally, it was corrected early enough for the soldier to go home on time. In Wilson's case, the screwup was compounded by his DEROS and ETS being on the same day. Being a good soldier, he made no more stink about the late orders than was required. Consequently, he ended up still at Camp Eagle five days past his ETS. Technically that made him a civilian. The army's position was that you are not out of the army until they see fit to discharge you. There was no way they would discharge someone in country and chance having a private citizen killed in Vietnam.

Wilson was just sitting around the company area waiting for things to get straightened out. He had quit flying and was getting bored sitting around. When the operations clerk came around trying to round up a crew for a routine ash-and-trash mission, Scotty thought, "Why not?" and volunteered. He even got to crew old magnet ass 350, his bird, one last time. The routine mission got a little uncomfortable for Scott when the battalion commander they were supporting announced that he wanted to visit a unit in the A Shau. The routine mission ended when 350 collected several more hits and went down in the valley. There was Scott Wilson, civilian, on the ground in the last place in Vietnam he wanted to be. He swore that night that if they kept him in country a hundred more years till his orders came, he wouldn't get on another helicopter.

Saturday, 17 August (214 days to go). I found out that there were plans to transfer me to the 163d General Support Company. It was the unit that did all the flying for the commanding general and all the division staffers. I was filled with panic. It would mean no more LRP flying. Worse yet, it meant that I would be back flying VIPs. I went to my platoon leader and told him that I did not want to go. He told me that it was too late. I was going to the 163d and there was nothing I could do about it. I could not accept that, and I asked to see Major Addis. Captain Senita denied my request.

I went to see Wild Bill, and he told me the only way was to convince the gaining commander that he did not want me.

"Junior, what you've got to do is tell the commander of the 163d what you are really like. You know, tell him the truth. Tell him that you are a smartassed, drunken troublemaker."

"Think it will work?"

"I don't know, but it's your only chance. There is one drawback."

"What's that?"

"Well, if it works, they're liable to be really pissed off at you here. If it doesn't work, you start off with your new commander pissed at you."

The next chance I got, I went over to the 163d and asked to see the CO. When I entered his office, I saluted and said, "Sir, I'm WO1 William T. Grant, and I have orders to report here on the twenty-fourth."

The major said, "I'm aware of that. You're a little early, aren't you, Grant?"

"Well, sir, I thought it only fair that you should know why the Kingsmen are so eager to get rid of me."

"And I suppose that you plan to tell me all about it?"

"Yes, sir!"

"Well, get on with it, mister."

"Well you see, sir, it's because I get all drunked up in the club and start fights."

"Is that all?"

It wasn't going to be as easy as I thought. He was not buying any of it.

"No, sir. I hang around with the enlisted guys and drink with them. Not only that, but I hang around with LRPs and act like them."

"I see. And why is it, that you being such a shitty officer and all, you are warning me about yourself?"

There was smile creeping into the corner of his mouth.

"Well, sir, I figured that this being a VIP support company you wouldn't want a pilot like me around. I would probably still hang around with LRPs, even if I wasn't flying them anymore."

"I certainly couldn't have any of my officers acting like that. I guess I'll just have to tell Major Addiss that I heard that you're a troublemaker and that I don't want you."

"Thank you, sir."

"You realize that this will not make you popular with the higher-ups."

"Yes, sir."

"I hope those LRPs know what you're putting on the line here." The smile was much broader now. "Now get out of my office, you troublemaker."

"Yes, sir. And thanks again, sir."

He was shaking his head as he picked up his pen and went back to what he was doing when I came in.

Operation SOMERSET PLAIN held one of my worst memories of the war. We were flying routine support missions, and we got a call to pick up some bodies at one of the units. When we arrived, an NCO came over and apologized because they did not have any body bags. It was only then that I realized we would be hauling American KIAs. Worse yet, they had been killed three days ago. The unit had been in contact, and the only aircraft that had come in brought rations and ammo and back-hauled wounded. Somehow three KIAs got set aside for three whole days. There is just no way to describe how bad a body that has been laying in the sun for three days smells. It was all the crew could do to keep the last meal down during the flight back to Eagle.

Wednesday, 21 August (210 days to go). The end of Operation SOMERSET PLAIN. Jim Thompson and Lou Pulver were flying together for extraction of the soldiers in the valley. The operation had netted 181 NVA KIA and 4 prisoners. The troopers had destroyed several base camps, captured weapons caches, and obliterated roads. The valley was mined and ringed with artillery.

Wednesday, 28 August (203 days to go). Jackie's birthday. My day started so early that I got an hour of night time logged before the sun came up. That meant about a 0330 wake-up call. After flying for about four hours, I came back to the company area to find it was time to get our new hootches. The Seabees would build them for us, but we had to tear down the tents and rip up the floors. They were the basic Vietnam-style military hootches, of plywood and with two-by-four framing. The walls extended halfway up, and the upper half was only a frame. The intention was to have a corrugated steel roof with screening for the upper half of the wall. The upper half of the wall would have hinged plywood that would open from the bottom and form an awning to keep out the elements. The problem was they did not have the roofing material, so they just put the tents back over the top. It wasn't a real building, but it was an improvement. I inherited the corner that was Jim Riden's in the tent. It was just to the left as one entered the back door. The corner was prized because a corner gave your area a little definition. Each aviator owned two sheets of plywood floor, giving him an eight-by-eight living space. We worked till about 2030 that night getting settled. A long day without much flying.

Lieutenant Dipstick had the next area on that side of the tent. My wall locker and the desk/dresser that I had made of ammo crates made a wall in between us. It was not long before the L T chewed me out for my wall locker extending two inches into his area. He and I were destined not to get along.

Dipstick's area in the tent was always neat and spotless. His bunk was made so that someone could bounce a quarter on the tightly stretched and tucked blanket. He had even purchased a straw mat for the floor next to his bed. Many of the warrants speculated that he had a teddy bear hidden in his locker that he brought out after everyone else was asleep. One day while he was out flying, some of the warrants, myself and Poley among them, carefully moved all his belongings down to the FNG tent on the far end of the officers' row. His bunk, straw mat, and all were set up in the exact manner in which he had left them. His new area was even in the same part of the tent as it had been in the old tent. When Dipstick returned from flying, he walked into the hootch and was shocked to find an empty space where his stuff had been. The warrants in the tent were sitting there reading books. (This made Dipstick suspicious right away. He knew in his heart that warrant officers could not read.)

"Where is my stuff?" he demanded.

Poley was our prearranged spokesman. "What stuff?" he asked, with a puzzled look on his face.

"You know damn well what stuff, Mr. Poley. My bunk. My locker. All my stuff."

"Why, L T, your stuff is in the FNG tent right where it has been since you got here."

The rest of us pretended to still be reading.

"It is not. It is supposed to be right there." He pointed to the empty space.

"L T, maybe you oughta go see the flight surgeon. I think maybe you are experiencing some combat fatigue."

Dipstick walked out and went to the new-guy tent. The observer we had stationed there said that he walked in, stared at his stuff, scratched his head, and sat down like he was not quite sure if he was crazy or not. It took him a couple of days to decide to move back.

29 August (202 days to go). A mission came down to pick up four new aircraft in Nha Trang. The maintenance bird took four pilots, a TI and mechanic to pick up the helicopters. The four pilots were Jim Thompson, B. J. Hoyt, Lou Pulver, and Rod Heim. The technical inspector checked all four aircraft and found them satisfactory. The flight of five refueled at Qui Nhon. After careful examination of the maps, they figured out that it was 185 nautical miles back to Eagle in a straight line. If the flight cut inland and flew at a hundred knots all the way, they could easily make it on one fuel load. The flight took off and headed north again, with Sir James flying Chalk Four, and the maintenance bird in trail. As the flight cut through the tall mountain passes just to the west of Chu Lai, they started receiving fire. Thompson heard and felt the *thunk, thunk, thunk* of the aircraft taking multiple hits.

"Flight, this is Lead. We are receiving fire."

Jim keyed the mike, "This is Four. I'm taking hits."

"Four, this is Trail. As soon as you find a spot put it on the ground. We'll pick you up."

"No, no, that won't be necessary. Everything is still in the green. I'll keep going till something breaks."

"Trail, roger."

The flight continued. They bypassed Chu Lai. They called Marble Mountain tower for transition on the east side of the airport traffic area. Jim began to get a little nervous when they flew across the Da Nang Bay instead of around it. The normal routine was to fly around the bay. Flying over water was not one of our favorite things to begin with, but with an aircraft that had taken hits, it was downright scary. They made it back to the Castle. When Jim rolled the throttle back to flight idle, something broke. The bird spit out all the transmission oil like it was vomiting. On the postflight inspection, Thompson found that he had also taken five hits in the tail-rotor drive shaft. Had he known how badly damaged the Huey was, he would have certainly landed at Chu Lai rather than fly another seventy-three miles.

At the close of August, three new WO1s arrived. There were new guys arriving all the time, but these guys were special. The Dave, Gene Gillenwater, myself, and couple of other guys were sitting on the sandbags out back of the tent, having a cold one after the day's flying. Dave spotted them first. They were not hard to pick out; they were wearing flight jackets. It was hot as hell, and they were wearing flight jackets! They were obviously cherries. They wore brand-new jungle fatigues and looked around like tourists taking in all the sights. As they got closer, we could see the patch on the breast of their flight jackets. The patch depicted a coiled cobra spitting rockets, and had the word COBRA embroidered in red letters at the top. When they were close enough The Dave asked, "Are you FNGs lost?"

One of them said, "No, we're looking for the tent we are supposed to sleep in until they assign us to a platoon."

Poley responded, "Four down on the left. It's the FNG tent."

Another one, named Barry Schreiber, perked up. He thrust his shoulders back and stuck out his chest so we could see the patch.

"We won't be here long; we're Cobra pilots!"

They had been among the first to be transitioned into the new gunship after graduation from flight school. Our reaction was that we all burst out laughing. The Dave was actually rolling on the ground. The new guys looked confused. They knew that we were supposed to be really impressed with their qualification in the hottest thing with rotor blades.

The Dave finally said, "W. T., go show 'em." Then he burst out laughing all over again.

I said, "Come with me."

When they started to take their duffle bags, I told them, "Leave those here, we'll be right back."

I could not keep from giggling as I balanced on the sandbag wall to cut through the tent rows. After we got through the enlisted row, we could see the aircraft on the other hillside. Since Barry was the cocky one, I threw my arm around his shoulder. I extended my arm out in front of me pointing at the hill across the way.

"What do you see out there, new guy?"

"Slicks. Slicks are for kids."

I started laughing again. "And what do you see at the bottom of the hill?"

"More slicks."

"Look harder."

"They are slicks."

"No, they are Charlie-model gunships. The *only* kind of gunships in the division."

The grin vanished from his face instantly. The realization that he would not become the fierce killer of the skies had hit hard. Barry soon proved that he was fast learner. He quickly became an excellent peter pilot; of the three, he was the last to leave the Kingsmen to go to the gun company.

* * *

CHAPTER 7
SEPTEMBER 1968

Sunday, 1 September (199 days to go). I finally broke two hundred days. After the day's flying, I listened to my stereo to escape the war for a short period of time. I thought of Jackie as the Turtles sang our song.

Wednesday, 4 September (196 days to go). The fourth brought us a visitor. Her name was Bess. She was a typhoon. The rains had started on the evening of the third. The rain was heavy, even by monsoon standards. The tent that leaked with every rain storm resembled a shower point on the inside. Outside, the visibility was reduced to about three feet. There would be no flying for a while. At least there was no worry of Charlie paying us a visit. Even Chuck was not interested in coming out to play in that kind of weather. Wild Bill Meacham and I were to fly south to Phuoc Vinh on the fourth. The 17th AHC had a section located there to support the 101st units in that area. Meacham was to take over the section from Capt. Dave Greenlee who was due to go home shortly. My assignment was to fly down to Phuoc Vinh with Bill and fly back with Greenlee. The flight was postponed until Bess was through with us. We had loaded the aircraft and were ready to leave as soon as the weather broke.

By late in the afternoon on the fourth, Bill and I got together and decided that since all our stuff was in the bird, we might as well be there, too. Inside the aircraft, we would be drier than in the tent. That afternoon, the winds hit 120 miles per hour. The aircraft rocked and swayed in the wind, and at times, we thought that it would surely blow over. Tom Turk and the gunner slept on the baggage in the back. Strapped in with the shoulder harness locked so that we could sleep sitting up, Bill and I slept in the front. For me, it was the final proof that a man could learn to sleep anywhere if he was tired enough.

During breaks in the downpour, we could see our fellow Kingsmen wrestling with tents to keep them from completely falling down. It was amazing that the tents were still standing at all. It was even more amazing that none of the aircraft were destroyed or severely damaged during the storm.

5 September (195 days to go). Bess passed, and the weather was clear blue and twenty-two, meaning no clouds and unlimited visibility. We took off bright and early on the fifth and logged 7.2 hours on the way south, with four fuel stops. I had anticipated spending a couple of days in Phuoc Vinh while Dave Greenlee broke Wild Bill in. That was the way I had been briefed. The problem was that no one had considered consulting Dave Greenlee. He was not due to DEROS until the twentieth and had no intention of going back north and spending two weeks flying in I Corps. His intention was to leave Phuoc Vinh with only enough time to fly up to Eagle, sign out, then head back south to catch his freedom bird. That left me in Phuoc Vinh with two weeks of nothing to do. It was like getting to go AWOL, with two captains giving me permission. My first question was, "Where's the club?"

The flight crews lived in quarters that looked like a Spanish villa, a square, single-story structure with a tile roof. There were about ten rooms on each side of the square. The club was in the south wing. I was to share a room with Wild Bill Meacham in the west wing. The room was less than fifty feet from the door to the club, so I would not even have to save myself much crawling energy. The club was nicely decorated. It had a padded bar and comfortable bar stools. The stools had padded arm rests that made keeping your balance easier. I knew that this was going to be a really tough assignment.

I had a great time playing with the minds of some of the REMFs. Whenever I was in the latrine and one would come in, I would go into the stall and squat down in front of the commode. I would then flush the toilet and watch the water go down like I had never seen such a sight and was fascinated by it. It was fun to see them grossed out by my behavior.

One night (after leaving the club about midnight), we were woken up to the sound of explosions about 0200. I heard machine-gun fire mixed with the explosions. As we pulled our pants on, Meacham said, "Shit, junior, it sounds like we're being overrun!"

I replied, "Fuckin' A."

I stuffed my feet in my boots and one arm through my shirt. I wasn't going to face the Commie hordes half-naked. I grabbed my pissant little .38 revolver and followed Wild Bill out the door. We moved in crouch along the low retaining wall that surrounded the courtyard. I looked over the wall. There were no VC in the courtyard. The commotion was coming from the direction of the flight line. The only way to leave the villa was through breezeways at the four corners. When we reached the end of the corridor, Bill covered me as I crossed the breezeway. It was all clear. We moved to the end of the hall. The path beyond was clear. A sergeant came running by, and Bill stopped him. "What's going on?"

The sergeant replied, "Charlie-model burned up at the hot fuel point."

After a surge in pressure in the refueling system, the hose had popped out from the fuel port and sprayed fuel up the side of the aircraft to the hot engine, which set the fuel on fire. The aircraft burned to the ground. The ammunition and rockets cooked off during the fire, making it sound like a major attack.

Sunday, 8 September (192 days to go). Jim Thompson and Rod Heim both had the day off. It had been a maximum-effort day for the Kingsmen. Jim and Rod had the company area pretty much all to themselves. Operations got a last-minute mission and rounded up the two ACs to fly together. But there was no crew chief or door gunner available. After scrounging around, company operations came up with two cooks to go along as gunners. The mission was a snatch and interrogation. It was a fairly easy and low-risk mission. The way it worked was the aircraft would take along an infantry battalion commander and a Vietnamese officer. The aircraft would fly around a designated area, looking for people on the ground, and the Vietnamese officer would say, "VC," or he would say, "No VC," deciding on the spot the fate of the person we had found. One or two would be selected, the aircraft would land to grab the suspect, then take him back to Eagle for interrogation. All the aviators wondered how the VN officer could tell. My theory was the Vietnamese officer was a local VC chief who knew all the local VC. All we had to do was pick up those he identified as "No VC," and the local bad guys would be quickly rounded up.

Heim and Thompson readied the bird for the mission, loaded up the two cooks, and took off. After an hour or so of flight, the ARVN found a likely suspect. Sir James landed the aircraft next to him, and he looked up and started to run when he saw them. This was considered a sure sign of guilt, or fear. The NCO who the battalion commander had brought to guard the prisoners was *slowly* climbing out the aircraft, and it was clear that he had no intention of trying to catch the suspect. The Lieutenant Colonel reached over and slapped the right-side gunner on the shoulder and said over the intercom, "Shoot him!"

The gunner just stared at him blankly.

He repeated, "Shoot the bastard!"

The gunner looked at the colonel with the same blank expression, then he looked to the pilots for help as he stammered, "Ah . . . ah . . . sir I ah . . . ah don't . . . ah . . . know how."

They all just stared at him in disbelief. The colonel didn't know the "crew" were cooks. And it had never occurred to Jim or Rod that the cooks did not know how to operate the 60s.

Tuesday, 10 September (190 days to go). I had four days off in a row. Four days without flying. At first it had seemed like a great idea to spend almost two weeks in Phuoc Vinh with nothing to do but party; I was far too accustomed to long, hard days. Part of my problem was that most of the time I spent in the club, it was just me and the bartender. Once in a while, one of the local staffers would drop in, but REMFs were not much fun, and they wanted nothing to do with a snot-nosed young W1.

I was heading for the club that day, having just had lunch. I got to the door, and with my hand on the doorknob, it hit me that I didn't want to go in. I turned and went back to the room and got my helmet and chicken plate and headed for the flight line. There had to be a helicopter seat I could sit in somewhere. In operations, they told me that I didn't have any flight records, so I couldn't fly. In March, that story had worked just fine; I had been in Vietnam too long to buy that bullshit. Now my reply was different. "Bullshit. I don't want flight time, I want to fly."

"But you're not part of this unit."

"It don't mean nothin', just give somebody the afternoon off. They can even have credit for the flight time."

"I don't know, Grant. I don't think Captain Greenlee would approve."

Greenlee and Meacham were out flying together. My next comment surprised even me. "Well, I heard there is a recon platoon here and they set up ambushes each night. How about I go out with them on their ambush tonight."

The guy looked at me like I had just stepped out of a flying saucer. If his eyes opened any further, the eyeballs would have fallen on the floor. Much to my relief it worked.

"Look why don't you go down to the maintenance hangar and see the maintenance officer. I think he has a flight down to Cu Chi today. Maybe you can go with him."

When I got to maintenance, the MO was glad to see me. Maintenance officers (MOs) spend most of their time flying with just a mechanic. When another pilot was actually willing to go along on a flight, they were generally thrilled. They normally did not fly many combat missions because the line pilots kept them so busy fixing broken aircraft. Many times, they did not even get to socialize with the rest of us. Because we spent the days getting the birds shot full of holes, overtorquing them, and generally beating the shit out of them, the MOs frequently worked late into the night. The MOs, mechanics, and TIs did a fantastic job of keeping us supplied with equipment to tear up.

When I asked about the opportunity to fly, he said, "Sure, I've got a flight down to Cu Chi to drop one off and pick another up. I'll be glad to have you come along if you're interested."

"I just want to go flying."

"You may not be as interested once you see the bird we're flying. It's got a lot of holes in it."

"It will be interesting to fly one with some holes in it for a change."

He laughed at my remark. The introductions had established that I had been flying up north for a while. He naturally assumed that I was well accustomed to taking hits. As we preflighted the aircraft, I found that it had taken fourteen hits, making twenty-eight holes, counting exit wounds. In looking over the Huey, it was apparent that the fire had come from both above and below the aircraft.

The MO explained, "There is a bridge between here and Cu Chi that people seem to think it's cool to fly under. I'll show it to you on the way there. Yesterday, one of our studs thought it would be fun to fly under the thing on the way home. There were four shooters, two in the river bed, two up under the bridge. That's how they got him from above and below. It's a good thing the motherfuckers couldn't shoot worth a damn."

Just then, one of the maintenance NCOs walked up to the aircraft. The MO asked, "Hey, Sarge, did you find out what was wrong with the seat?"

"Yes sir! Ain't nuthin' wrong with that seat."

The AC who was flying when the bird got shot up had trouble with his seat. He could not get it to go down to the position he normally set it in. The unusual thing about it was that they had taken a hit through the chin bubble. The round had gone through the cyclic and struck the lower front of the armored seat. The bullet then ricocheted down through the floor of the aircraft. The seat had stuck one notch above where the AC usually set it. The TI had measured the height of the strike on the seat, then after he moved the seat, he ran a string through the holes to the seat. Had the seat been in its normal position, the bullet would have struck the seat cushion and caught the pilot dead center in the crotch. The AC had cussed the seat. He had the crew chief beat on the seat, still it did not budge. When I got in the aircraft and pulled the handle, the seat dropped all the way to the bottom. Looking at the holes in the chin bubble and cyclic made my nuts hurt all the way to Cu Chi.

I got to make a parts run with the MO to Cu Chi on the eleventh. The two flights did not get me much time, but they at least killed some time.

Back at the Eagle, Sir James and B. J. Hoyt were on the LRP mission. They landed on the Acid pad, shut down, and were briefed for some VRs. As they were headed out to the aircraft, Sergeant First Class Burnell came up to Jim and asked, "Do you fly crazy?"

"What?"

"Do you fly crazy? Mister Hoyt is a lunatic. He flys crazy; I don't want to fly with him."

Jim flashed his usual ear to ear smile and said, "Why, no I don't fly crazy. Hop in."

Jim made a palm-up gesture toward the cargo door. Burnell climbed in, and Jim headed around to other side of the aircraft, grinning to himself. "Who me? Fly crazy? No way!"

The flight took off and headed west at tree-top level. Jim spotted a couple of trees ahead and decided that he would fly between them. He missed. The aircraft clipped a branch with a gun mount, and pieces of branches went everywhere, including inside the cargo compartment. Burnell threw a royal fit. On the next flight, he flew with Hoyt.

13 September (187 days to go). Captain Greenlee announced that the very next day we would pull pitch for Camp Eagle. That night as we sat in the club, Wild Bill suggested that we go over to the Vultures' club and make some new friends. That place was a lot more fun than the club at the villa.

Saturday, 14 September (186 days to go). Dave Greenlee and I logged the same 7.2 hours on the way home that Wild Bill and I had on the way to Phuoc Vinh. The realization struck me that I had begun to think of Camp Eagle as home. There had been a very drastic change in me. I was finding the comforts of Phuoc Vinh were something that I despised. There were times at Eagle when I felt guilty about having a bed to sleep in and a cold shower. The grunts were out there sleeping on the ground in the rain. There was a lot of difference in the way the war was being fought from one place to another.

I was unpacking my stuff when Gene Gillenwater came by.

"Hey, W. T., welcome back."

"Hi Gene. What's happenin' bro? Did you fuck up all of I Corps while I was gone?"

"I took my AC ride."

"Congratulations."

"I took the call sign One-Zero. No one has ever had it before."

"Well, everyone has always said that you are a numba ten pilot."

I stopped what I was doing and shook his hand. Gene kind of hung his head and said, "I heard some rumors . . . that they are considering not giving you an AC ride."

"Why?"

"Look, I'm not telling you this stuff to hurt your feelings. I mean er . . . I'm your friend, and I think you ought to know."

Gillenwater was not one who had trouble stating his feelings normally. I turned toward Gene and gave him a hard look. "Why Gene?"

" 'Cause some of them think you're not aggressive enough."

"What the fuc . . . Who?"

"I don't know for sure. It's because you just ride along and do what you're told. Some of the ACs think you don't know anything."

"Bull-fucking-shit. That's the way the army wants us to behave. Go along with the system and keep your mouth shut. I've
just been playing their fuckin' game, and now they think I'm a
shithead for it?"

"That's about the size of it. I know that you have your shit
together, but not all of them do."

"Did they fuckin' ask Riden before he left? Did they ask
Meacham? Did they ask Poley?"

"You know The Dave is in your corner, but he's nuts. Riden's
gone, and Meacham's down south."

"I ain't taken' this shit. This is because I got outta goin' to
the 163d and because I fly LRPs. We'll just see about this shit."

"Wait a minute, W. T., don't do something stupid."

"They want a big mouth; they got a big mouth."

"Where ya goin'?"

I smiled and said, "To tear out Senita's jugular vein."

"Be cool."

I said over my shoulder as I left the tent, "What are they going to do, send my fuckin' ass to Vietnam?"

I stormed into the platoon leader's tent. "Captain, I need to
see you right now!"

I didn't wait for his response. "Sir, what's this bullshit I hear
that they don't want to make me an AC?"

I still did not wait for an answer. "I know what the hell is going on out there, and I'm just as good as anybody else. I just
don't believe in submitting my opinions to the AC when he's
supposed to be in charge. I thought that's what the army wanted
from us. You want to know what's goin' on in my head, then
just ask. Better yet I'm going to tell you." By then I was so furious that I could feel the tears welling up in my eyes. I would
be damned if I was going to let them fall. "I can handle any
mission out there. I've already proven that I can handle LRPs
and FOB which are some of the toughest missions to fly. Some
of the ACs that are bad mouthing me don't have the balls to fly
those missions themselves. If you've got any doubts, just put me
in the left seat, and I'll fucking show you . . . sir!"

I figured that I had better put the sir on the end of that one.

"Do you have any questions, sir?"

Mike Senita just smiled and said, "No, Grant, I don't have
any questions."

"Thank you for your time. Good-night, sir."

"Good-night, Grant."

I wasn't too sure of his reaction. Maybe since he was from

Brooklyn, he'd just been waiting to see some New York fire in me. I figured him as an all-right guy, but he was an RLO and pretty much played by the army's rules.

Back at the hootch, Poley had returned from the day's flying. As I went back to my unpacking, he came over with his head down, looking like a little boy about to 'fess up to his daddy.

"The Dave broke your fan while you were gone." He pulled the fan from behind his back and handed it to me. I looked down at it. One of the blades was broken off about halfway along its length. When I looked back at Poley, he looked really upset, like he expected me to be very mad at him. I was much too pissed about the aircraft commander situation to be upset about the fan.

"Doan mean nothin'. I said you could use it while I was gone, didn't I?"

"That's not all. Your stereo is fucked up, too." I stopped unpacking and looked at him. He continued, "There was a generator surge. Light bulbs popped that were not even turned on. Fans that were turned off started turning. Your stereo was playing at the time. I'm really sorry, W. T."

I threw my bag down in disgust. "Was the whole company out to fuck me while I was gone?"

Poley just looked at me strangely; he didn't know about the conversation with Gene Gillenwater. I went over to my Akai and turned it on. The tape reels worked and the VU meters indicated that there was music playing. Nothing would come out either the big speakers or the ones built into the tape deck. I got the headphones out of my locker and plugged them in. The music blasted into my ears as I put them on. The problem was something in the tape deck; the speakers were okay. (When I got it home to a Stateside stereo shop, they replaced the four main output transistors, and it still works.) At least I would be able to listen to my music alone and to rely on the automatic shutoff so I could go to sleep listening to the music.

Later, I borrowed some tools and cut the remainder of the broken blade off the fan. I also cut the blade off the opposite side, making the four-bladed fan a two-bladed fan. A little filing on the stumps for balancing, and it worked just fine. The decreased weight allowed the motor to turn the blades faster. The increased speed made up for the lack of blades, and the volume of air was as great as ever.

* * *

Monday, 16 September (184 days to go). I took and passed my AC check ride.

The weather was pretty bad down south. Wild Bill was out flying and trying to get back from a mission to Cu Chi. Not being as familiar with that area as he was with northern I Corps, Bill got lost. He called Phuoc Vinh GCA and asked for assistance. The radar was down. That was another unusual phenomenon that occurred in Nam. Radar only broke during bad weather.

"Phuoc Vinh tower, this is Kingsman Two-Five, on Fox Mike."

"Kingsman Two-Five, Phuoc Vinh tower. Go ahead."

"Tower, I got kind of lost out here, could you give me a couple of long counts so I can FM home back to the field."

The tower began talking so Bill could find his way home. As no one else was flying in the lousy weather, the controller was bored. The clouds were sitting at about fifty feet. The tower operator told Bill about his wife. He told Bill about his home town. Meacham continued to follow the signal. Flying partially by reference to the instruments, his attention was divided both inside and outside the aircraft. He failed to notice the airfield perimeter pass under the Huey. The controller did not fail to notice the rapidly approaching helicopter. Meacham noticed the controller leaping from the tower, as he took evasive action to keep from hitting the tower. Bill now knew how accurate FM homing could be.

Poley was flying LRPs, with Pearce as the other AC. They were called out for a hot extraction with McGuire rigs. Poley went in first. When they were over the team, they tossed out the ropes. Three team members hooked up and were pulled out quickly. Next, Pearce took his place over the team, as Poley headed for FSB Birmingham. Sergeant First Class Brubaker was the belly man. He called out that the three LRPs were in the seats and ready to go. The aircraft started taking heavy automatic-weapons fire. About the time that the LRPs were twenty feet off the ground, Brubaker's head suddenly snapped back, and he rolled over. The visor on his flight helmet was shattered and covered with blood.

The door gunner called out, "Doc's dead. I'll take the belly."

He leaped over the seat post and lay on the cargo floor. When he looked out, he saw only two LRPs on the ropes. Down below on the jungle floor, he saw the last LRP lying on the ground.

"We lost one. He's still alive. I can see him moving."

By then, they were clearing the trees. There was nothing they could do. Their third rope was dangling uselessly with no seat.

Pearce called Poley, "One-Nine get back here as quick as you can. We still got one on the ground."

Poley was already setting his LRPs down on Birmingham. He told the belly man to cut two of the ropes and haul the third back in. The lone LRP was Johnny Quick. We discovered later that a single round had cut the rope he was on. It was that rope, its burden released, that had snapped up and hit Brubaker in the face. Doc was not dead, he had just ended up with a nasty cut on his forehead. Poley managed to get back and rescue Quick before a bunch of pissed-off bad guys figured out that he was the only one left holding them off.

Tuesday, 17 September (183 days to go). I was scheduled with Dave Poley on the LRP mission. I was surprised, since I should have been working as an AC. We inserted a team in the hills southeast of Nui Khe to hunt for rocket launchers. When we got back to the Acid pad, I found out that I had not been scheduled as an AC because I had to be checked out on McGuire rigs before I could be turned loose. Sergeant First Class Burnell was to be the belly man. I would find out later that this was Burnell's first time working the belly since he had been dragged along the ground by a pilot from another unit, through a row of concertina wire and slammed against a bunker. He received multiple cuts and bruises and three broken ribs.

We made the takeoff and swung around outside the perimeter, with three men on the ropes. Burnell talked me to a fifteen-hundred-foot hover over the pad. Then he proceeded to give me six-inch corrections all the way to the ground. It took forty-five minutes to set the team down.

Hovering is the hardest thing to do in a helicopter. To do it with the great precision that is required by McGuire rigs is quite a workload. By the time Burnell was finished with me, I was completely drained. My shirt was as soaked with sweat as if I had run twenty-five miles. As I set the aircraft on the pad, the ropes were pulled out to the sides by the team. I looked over to see Poley laughing his ass off. He keyed the mike and said, "Whatcha think, Bernie? Will he do?"

Realizing that Poley was pulling his chain as much as mine, Burnell said, "I don't know, maybe we'd better do it again."

"Fuck you both, very much," I said.

Since I was in the left seat, I said to Dave, "Shut this thing down, Mr. Peter Pilot." I then hopped out of the seat and walked away, snickering. That afternoon, we inserted a team in the hills, just to the east of FSB Brick.

That evening, I was assigned my aircraft—66-16348. I wondered if it had been selected because it was almost as cherry as I was; 348 had only been hit twice since it had been in Nam. There was one patch on the fiberglass cowling that surrounded the transmission. The bullet had touched nothing else but the one side of the cowling. The other hit had been in the tail boom, about halfway along its length. That hole had been covered with a heart-shaped patch. Someone had come up with a rose color metallic paint to cover the heart; 348 and I would be well matched.

I wandered up the hill to the revetment. I conducted my first preflight inspection of my assigned aircraft alone. I went over every inch of the aircraft. I wanted to know every rivet. I made note of each oil spot and every scratch and nick. We knew all the aircraft in our platoon well; that knowledge might mean life or death. This was different. This was my own aircraft. There I was, a twenty-year-old hot-rodder that had just been given his own 1,495-horsepower hot rod. The crew chief of 348 was Juan Sablan, a quiet kid from Guam. His nickname was Sugar Bear. It came from his being built short and stocky. He was a competent crew chief, but some folks wondered about him because he was so quiet. I soon found out that he could do the job as well as anybody; he just did not make a lot of noise about it.

Wednesday, 18 September (182 days to go). That morning, it was with great pride that I carefully set 348 down on Acid pad. While waiting on the two-minute cooldown to elapse, I looked around the F Company area. I found that things had a new look through the eyes of an aircraft commander. I would now have to back up all the talk I had thrown at Captain Senita only four days ago.

The other AC was Kingsman One-Two, Horace Pearce. After shut-down, we strolled up the hill to the F Company TOC (tactical operations center). Captain Eklund briefed us: There were two teams in the field. One was the team Poley and I had inserted the day before; the other was Sergeant First Class Brubaker's team. Doc's team had been in for a full five days. Since I was replacing The Dave on the mission, and the other crew was all new, both would be my responsibility. Zoschak's team had heard some movement during the night, so there was enemy activity in the area. Captain Eklund said that we would also do some visual recons and LZ selection for future missions. The VRs would be conducted in the area south of FSB Vehgel and east of the A Shau Valley, where it was suspected that base camps had been established.

We flew our recons in the morning and were back on the pad in time for lunch. Zoschak's team was still monitoring a trail, and things were quiet. In the afternoon heat, we lounged around in the aircraft, waiting for a nightfall or the call that would mean a hot extraction. It was around 1630 when L T Williams called us up to the TOC. The team had once again reported movement. We sat by the radio listening tensely.

Then it came. "Normal Credit Three, this is Normal Credit One-Seven . . ." Pearce and I were on our feet and headed for the door, the voice was not whispered; we knew what the rest of the transmission would be. ". . . we have been spotted; we are in contact. We are moving to our primary LZ."

The downhill run on the rocky soil was always treacherous. As we charged downhill, arms waving straight out from our sides to keep our balance, our crews sprang to life, untying rotor blades and opening doors. In less than two minutes, both birds were clawing their way into the air. I rolled 348 over to 115 knots. Hoping to see the guns on the way out, I looked to my left as we rounded the north side of the Eagle. I couldn't see them anywhere.

I squeezed the trigger on the front of the cyclic all the way down. "Credit One-Seven, Kingsmen One-Eight. Hang in there we are on the way."

"One-Eight we are unable to get to the LZ. We will have to come out on the strings."

"Roger. Break. One-Two, you monitor?"

"Roger, One-Eight."

The team was pinned down by an NVA force of unknown size. The guns were still en route. When we arrived onsite, I decided that we should go ahead with the extraction rather than wait on the guns.

"One-Seven this is Kingsmen One-Eight. Gimme smoke."

"Roger. Smoke's out."

I started to slow the bird's airspeed for the ridgeline. The coordinates we had told me the team was where I saw purple smoke rising from the trees. "I have goofy grape."

"Goofy grape it is."

Right on target. I continued to slow, coming to a hover over the rising smoke. As soon as the aircraft stopped, I could hear the distinctive crack of AK-47s shooting at us on full automatic. Zoschak called us off.

"One-Eight, get out of here. They have us pinned down."

I lowered the nose, and the bird began to accelerate. As the two slicks got clear, the guns called.

"One-Eight, this is Hootchmaid. We've been monitoring, mark our targets." I don't think even R. L. Smith knew his real call sign.

"This is Credit One-Seven. Smoke's out, everything twenty meters out is yours."

"Roger. Sit back and enjoy the show. I got lemon yellow."

"Roger. Lemon. Waste 'em."

Almost instantly, the hillside erupted with black smoke and orange flame. That should have dampened Charlie's enthusiasm. I lined up on final again. We hovered over the team, and the belly man kicked out the three McGuire rigs. The shooting started again.

Zo called, "Lower. Lower."

"What?"

"Lower damn it. We can't reach the ropes."

I said on the intercom, "Coming down."

"No, sir, we'll be in the trees."

"Clear the tail rotor. Coming down!"

"Sir, swing the tail about three feet to the right."

I complied.

"Clear down, left."

"Clear down, right."

The peter pilot just looked terrified. Later, I wondered if it was me or Chuck that scared him. I could feel the pressure of the tree branches against the belly of the Huey. I continued to reduce power, I could feel the branches breaking under me. I keyed the mike. "How much more?"

"Four feet."

On the intercom. "How's the tail rotor?"

"Clear, sir. Go for it."

I glanced down at the chin bubble in front of me. Branches were pressed against it. I hoped it would hold as I reduced power even more. As we settled, the leafy branches slowly crawled over the nose of the aircraft and up to the windshields. I could hear the whistling snap of bullets passing within inches of the aircraft. The bird dropped another two feet as more branches gave way.

"Tail rotor?"

"Still clear, sir."

"Watch the main rotor; it's getting close."

"Clear left."

"Clear right."

"Clear front."

As we sat in the trees, I could hear the sharp reports of the CAR-15s of the team responding to enemy fire.

"Come on. Come on, get in the damn rigs," I thought.

I had not heard any hits in the fuselage. I knew that we must have taken some in the blades. The radio broke squelch.

"Normal Credit Three, this is Normal Credit Two-Four."

It was Brubaker. His team was about two thousand meters to the west.

"Credit Two-Four, this is Three. Standby we have a team in contact."

"Well, I'm in damn contact too . . . pant . . . pant, we are being . . . chased by a . . . pant . . . pant . . . company-size force. We are *di di mau*ing for our secondary LZ. Repeat . . . pant . . . secondary LZ."

"Well, Grant, you wanted to be a fuckin' LRP pilot. Welcome to the party," I thought. It was taking forever for the team to get in the rigs. I heard the sharp whistle of more rounds go by.

The belly man said, "We got thumbs-up. Go."

I pulled in power as the peter pilot called out the torque; 348 climbed straight up. We only climbed about five feet when I felt the weight of the three LRPs pull against the ropes. One hundred and twenty feet to go. I continued to climb, while I felt as if every gook in the universe was shooting at me.

After what seemed like an eternity, the belly man called out. "They are clear of the trees."

I lowered the nose and broke to the left. I headed toward FSB Birmingham.

"One-Two, One-Eight. I'm headed to Birmingham. I'll drop this load and head out to pick up Doc's team." This brand new AC's voice was at least a full octave higher than it had been that morning.

"Credit Two-Four, Kingsmen One-Eight. Are you going to make it to the LZ?"

"Beats the shit . . . pant . . . outta me . . . pant . . . the gooks don't think so, damn it."

"Are you gonna need strings, damn it!"

"No, damn it!"

"Okay, damn it."

Damn it, if those LRPs didn't have a sense of humor. Doc was playing word games on the run while being chased by a company of NVA.

I pulled the cyclic trigger to the first click for the intercom. "When we put them down, cut the ropes. We have another extraction to make."

I pulled the trigger further. "Hootch, cover One-Two, then head for the other team. I'll meet you there."

I was handing out assignments like I had been doing this all my life. I never thought about being the junior AC on the scene.

As soon as the three LRPs on the end of the ropes had their feet on the ground at Birmingham, Burnell cut the ropes and said simply, "Go."

I didn't respond. I just lowered the nose and headed for the next pickup. 348 was soon beating the air at 115 knots.

"Credit Two-Four, Kingsman One-Eight, on the way. Estimate Lima Zulu in zero three mikes."

"We'll be . . . pant . . . there."

I could see the LZ. The guns were closing.

"Two-Four, One-Eight, throw smoke."

There was no response, but in about ten seconds I saw two separate smokes rising from the jungle. One purple, one green.

I called one. "I got goofy grape."

"Negative. Mine is looney lime."

"Roger lime. Break. Hootch, waste the grape."

Hootchmaid was on the numbers again. Rockets started impacting in the purple smoke as fast as I released the mike trigger. I had already begun the slowdown for the approach in the LZ. The green smoke had only been ten meters out. As I cleared the trees, I called. "Two-Four, you have ten seconds to have your ass on this bird, or I'm outta here." It was a lie, but I did not want to wait in another hot LZ.

The response was tiger stripe uniforms breaking out of the tree line. Doc Brubaker was the last on board. He was standing on the skid. The door gunner pulling him in by the ruck sack as I pulled pitch. On climb out, I could see the guns working over the hillside where the purple smoke had come from. Served the little bastards right, trying to sucker me into their LZ. Pearce called and said he had picked up the three I had dropped at Birmingham. He fell in behind, and we headed for Acid pad. As soon as I had shut the engine down, I jumped down from my seat and started looking for the holes I knew had to be there this time around. Amazingly, there were none. We ate LRP rations during the debriefing. I sat there, feeling pretty good about my first test as an AC under fire. I had not screwed up. I didn't want Captain Senita to be able to throw my words back at me. *Opera Non Verba.*

On return to the Castle, I got all the paperwork finished and headed for the club. I wanted a drink. I was also looking forward to letting everyone know that I still had my cherry and hadn't gotten anyone killed. In flight school, the grade slips were white for passing flights and pink for failures. In Vietnam, the failures were marked with black plastic bags.

THE TEENYBOPPER

It was the ninth of September when he arrived. I didn't get to meet the new guy till I returned from Phuoc Vinh. By then, I had been in country for almost six months and was considered one of the "old" guys. Many of the original Kingsmen had DEROSed; a lot of the peter pilots who I had arrived with were being considered for AC; my mustache was now substantial enough that I wasn't constantly being ribbed about it.

WO1 Kenneth D. Roach looked every bit of sixteen years old. This was a crime which he would pay dearly for. It was bad enough to be an FNG, but to be a FNG that didn't look old enough to graduate from high school was unforgivable. It did not take long for him to be dubbed "Teenybopper." (I think I may have been the perpetrator of that moniker.) A good nickname was important to being a Kingsmen, it meant acceptance. While "Teenybopper" was not intended to be the most flattering nickname, the Teenybopper was quickly accepted, particularly among the LRP pilots. Ken had the right attitude, he took the ribbing well, and was anxious to learn from the guys who had been there a while.

Once I made AC, Ken became like a puppy, followed me around, asking me to take him on LRP missions. The policy in the Kingsmen was that you had to have three months in country to be eligible to volunteer for LRP or FOB missions. Ken and I hit it off well from the beginning. It got to the point that, when I walked into the tent without Ken, Dave Poley would say, "Hey, man, where's your puppy?"

At least once every time we flew, I made a point of telling the Teenybopper that I hated his guts. What made me so mad was that Ken was a natural pilot. He had the smoothest most natural control touch of anyone I had ever seen. I don't think to this day I have ever seen another pilot who flew as if he had been created by God for the purpose of flying a helicopter. Control touch was important because the fewer the movements on the controls of a helicopter the more efficient the rotor system becomes. There are lots of technical reasons for this, but simply put, if one shakes the stick around one "dumps" lift. This was extremely important when we were routinely flying our Hueys way over the intended weight limit of 9,500 pounds. It was also important to the LRPs. When making a McGuire rig extraction, the team is suspended 120 feet below the helicopter. Any movement of the cyclic produces a pendular action like that of a grandfather clock. A six-inch movement of the helicopter could mean a six-foot swing for the team at the end of the rope. That could make for an exciting ride at an amusement park. But, for a team being extracted, at best, through a two-foot hole in the jungle, it would mean a lot of cuts and bruises. Now, most of us had developed that fine and delicate touch on the controls. For me, it was something that required concentration, hard work, and reaching to the depths of my soul. The Teenybopper was born with it; I hated his guts.

It didn't take long for him to wear us down. By the end of the month, The Dave and I couldn't stand his begging any longer. We requested that operations make an exception to policy and let Ken fly LRPs. Besides, after flying a few CAs and log missions with him, it was obvious that his ability to handle the pressure and precision was not in question. He learned fast and was ready. When I made AC, there were no more regular LRP peter pilots. Some guys would fly the missions once in a while, but only the truly deranged insisted that they be included constantly. Ken was definitely LRP pilot material. He was a good pilot and not smart enough to recognize the danger and say, "No!"

This did not mean that Ken was off the hook for looking sixteen. During my entire time in the Kingsmen, every time he came into the club while I was behind the bar, I always carded him. All the officers in the unit met the army's age limit (18) to drink; you had to be eighteen before you could enlist to go to flight school. Teenybopper's enlistment was delayed till his eighteenth birthday so he could attend flight school. While most of the rest of us were college drop-outs and at least twenty by the time we arrived in Vietnam, Ken managed to hit country at nineteen. I later learned that he had tried to enlist for a Special

Forces A team before he tried flight school. He was afraid the war would end before he could graduate from high school, and he would not get to play. The SF's loss would be the gain of the LRPs.

Once Ken started bugging me about flying LRPs, I decided that he had better have an idea about what it was like. To simulate McGuire extractions when we flew log missions, I made him make vertical takeoffs to about a hundred feet with a load on the aircraft. Every time the cyclic stick moved enough for me to see it, I reached over and smacked him on the flight helmet.

The problem with Ken was that, many times, I would have to pretend to see the cyclic move, just so I could smack him because he made me so mad by not moving it. I got the Teenybopper started on LRPs just the way Dave Poley had gotten me started.

Sometime during the month, FSB Rakkasson installed its neoprene helipad. The pads measured one hundred feet square. The neoprene pads made it possible to quickly install a helipad on any level surface, and they kept down the dust and debris that would normally be blown around by the helicopters' rotor wash. The pads were light gray and could be joined together for a large area. The division headquarters pad at Eagle was made up of six or eight of the pads. The landing area on FSB Rakkasson was on a ridgeline and was not near big enough for one pad. Consequently, the front side of the ridge was covered with about thirty feet of neoprene. With yellow paint, the artillerymen had painted HO CHI MINH SUCKS in large letters on the light gray surface. It could be seen for miles into the flatlands.

THE RUFF PUFF INCIDENT

The status of an aircraft commander was never really something that was open to debate. When it came to the operation of the aircraft, the only one who got to overrule the AC was God!

This rule would be severely tested during the Ruff Puff incident. Ruff Puffs were what we called the Regional Forces/ Popular Forces, also known as RFs/PFs. These were a local militia that was ill equipped, ill armed, and ill trained. Aside from this (and being poorly motivated), they were some pretty fierce warriors. The opinions varied from believing that they did not know which end of the weapon the bullet came out of, to their knowing quite well at night when they became VC.

One fine day, some genius at division headquarters came up with a new concept. Aircraft of the 101st Airborne would work with these indigenous forces on a single-ship basis. That part of the reasoning was sound, since in many cases the enemy was probably able to figure out where our troopers were going by the huge number of helicopters in the area. Battalion-size operations in the paddies frequently yielded no contact in areas where VC were known to operate. The plan was that a single Huey, operating as though on a log mission, could insert Ruff Puffs into unsecure villages without scaring Chuck off. Now that was probably true. It was also true that it was an excellent way get your ass shot off.

This line of thought may sound a little strange coming from someone who had already proven himself dumb enough to fly such missions as LRP and FOB. However, there were many flaws in this plan; the foremost being that on special operations missions when Charles decided to get feisty, he got a large and instant dose of 2.75 FFARs, 40 mike mike, and miniguns from your gun cover, which was only a prelude to the arty and tac air that was on call to handle any of his temper tantrums. The Ranger and Special Forces missions were conducted in areas that were clear of friendly troops, and clearance to fire was already in place. These were, in fact, free-fire zones. The Ruff Puff assaults were to be conducted into villages of suspected enemy activity and without *any* fire support on call.

The next flaw was that since Marvin the ARVN usually managed to avoid being inserted into any area that contained enemy, what made anyone think that the Ruff Puffs were prepared to attack a village occupied by Charlie? Unless, of course, the plan was for the Ruff Puffs to set up the helicopter so Chuck could blow it away as it took off after the Ruff Puffs were dropped off.

After careful consideration of the new policy, the general consensus of the Kingsmen could be summed up briefly, *bullshit*!

Since there was only the 101st Aviation Battalion to support the entire division, we were spread pretty thin most of the time. One of the methods employed for us to fly resupply missions to the units of the 101st was to assign an aircraft to support from two to four battalions in the same day. A block time, one to four hours, was assigned to each battalion to be supported. Then a short period between battalions to allow time to fly to the next unit, and a block of time for that unit, and so on till the end of the day.

* * *

21 September (179 days to go). I was flying in support of the 2d Brigade. I had been an AC for a whole five days. Ken Teenybopper Roach was the pete on one of the multiple-unit support missions. The mission started by supporting a 2d Brigade battalion in the Phu Vang area. The mission brief said I was to fly two hours for that unit then fly two hours in support of a 1st Brigade battalion located in the hills southwest of Hue. Then on to another battalion in 1st Brigade, and so on. Since this was the only 2d Brigade unit, that part of the mission must have been a last-minute add-on. Normally, to prevent bouncing a crew all around the division AO and to save wear and tear on aircraft and crews, a crew worked for one brigade.

We arrived at the log pad and found out that this was also to be a Ruff Puff mission, which put everyone in a cheerful mood. A captain came to the aircraft and showed us on the map the village where the RF/PFs were to be dropped off. The mission would involve six sorties of about ten minutes each. The Ruff Puffs would come from the village where the log pad was located, so there would only be an unsecured LZ on the drop-off. The battalion had about an hour's worth of log, and wanted us to fly that first; by then they would have the Ruff Puffs rounded up and ready to go.

The log mission was uneventful, but not well planned. That was not unusual. Frequently, loads were not ready on time, so we were given two half-loads to take to one location. Many times a unit would not have its backlog ready to go when its log showed up. This would require an extra sortie to go back to pick these items up. Often, the mission would be complete, and someone would come out to the bird and say, "Take these two soldiers out to Bravo Company." We'd say, "But we just flew out there three times with half-loads." The response would be something like, "Sorry 'bout that." Whenever we got the chance to shut down at one of the pads, which was not often, we would try to educate the guys who ran them, which helped until he DEROSed, and we would start all over again. A little planning and having everything ready to go before the aircraft showed up would make things a lot easier on everyone and make the blade time go further toward logging the entire division.

When the log mission was over, it was time to haul Ruff Puffs. The area just east of Highway 1 around Hue was one of rice paddies and tree-lined villages. While not near as dense as the jungles in the mountains, the lush vegetation was more than thick enough to hide small armies. This area extended about halfway to the coast, a distance of three to four miles. Many of these villages had some permanent buildings of concrete and stucco. With their tree-lined pathways, a lot of the villages were scenic enough to belie the ugliness of the war that went on in and around them. The village receiving that day's attention was one. The LZ we were to use sat on the northwest corner of the ville. It was surrounded by bamboo shoots and low trees. The LZ itself was sandy, covered with grass, and large enough to accommodate a normal approach. The wind was not a factor that day, so we would land from the north and depart to the north because the trees had a gap facing north, and that was the direction for the return flight to the log pad.

The captain from the battalion headquarters announced that he would ride along with us to show us where he wanted the Ruff Puffs inserted and to help get them out in the LZ. Like Marvin, the Puffs many times needed encouragement to get out. As we got close to the village, the captain who had a headset, asked the door gunner for his wire so he could talk to me. The gunner complied. We made the insertion and took off. The captain still had the gunner's wire. I told him that I would need to be able to talk to the gunner, which would mean he would have to have the wire back. The captain gave the wire back to the door gunner. We picked up the second load and headed back to the LZ. Once again, the captain insisted on taking the wire when we got on final. On takeoff I explained, "The door gunner has to assist in clearing the aircraft during landing, and I have to be able to direct his fire if the LZ goes hot."

He said, "We have been in the LZ twice, and it is not hot, and I can direct fire if necessary."

When the crew was all plugged in again, I said, "This jerk don't know shit about dinks; he don't know that the more 'friendly' dinks you put in an LZ, the more likely it is to go hot."

The rest of the sorties went the same way. He had to have the wire so he could run his mouth and leave me trying to clear the left side of the LZ both front and rear on each landing. After the third trip in, I had made up my mind that there was to be an unsat mission report at the end of today's flight. the tension rose with each sortie. We were essentially unarmed on the most critical part of the flight, and on the side most likely to receive fire, the village side. The gunners in the back were not allowed to fire on a target without the AC's clearance. This made sure of the target, and covered the gunner's ass—if there was a screwup, he had been told by the AC to fire. Sometimes there was something going on that would come over the radio that would preclude engaging a target. With no wire in the back, the door gunner would not be aware of it and might accidently fire up friendlies. We inserted the rest of the Puffs without incident and without commo. When the asshole had the wire, the rest of us just shut up and said nothing.

When we got back to the log pad, the captain got out. The NCO running the pad asked if we had time to take a passenger to LZ Sally to the brigade pad. I said, "Time will get tight, but I think we can fit it in." It took about ten minutes for them to get their act together and get the passenger out to the aircraft. We made the run to the brigade pad at LZ Sally and dropped off the passenger. On the way back we made what we called a "courtesy landing" at the battalion log pad. We did this in case the supported unit had anything going in the direction of our next mission. Even if we were done for the day, we would always ask if there was someone or something they wanted hauled in the direction we were going. On occasion, it would mean an extra sortie that was out of the way, but we preferred not to fly anywhere empty. Many times, it would mean that some lucky grunt would get flown to the rear for R & R or DEROS rather than have to ride in the back of a truck. It always felt good to make those types of runs.

As we landed on the large penaprime pad, I could see a major standing on the edge of the pad. At that point, we were about ten minutes over our time to support the unit. The major looked up and made a cutting motion across his throat with his open hand. This was the accepted signal to shut down the aircraft. Since we were allowed fifteen minutes to fly to the next mission, I knew we were going to be late. I pretended not to notice his signal by looking down like I was tuning radios or performing some other cockpit chore. He strode across the pad and stood on the skid of the aircraft. He yelled over the noise of the aircraft, "Shut this thing down, boy!"

I yelled back, "Sir, we are going to be late for our next mission if I shut down."

He countered with, "Shut this fuckin' thing down now, *punk!*"

It would have been a simple matter to just roll the throttle back up to operating RPM and proceed with the takeoff. This guy would of had to make a decision, to hang tight standing on the skid, or step off and get to live; he had no right to tell me, the aircraft commander, what to do with the aircraft. But I sensed in his attitude that now would be a good time to be a good little soldier. Something told me that compliance at this point would be the very thing that would help fix this son of a bitch in the end. I hollered, "Yes, sir!" and closed the throttle. As the rotor coasted to a stop, I left the peter pilot with the controls and hopped down from the aircraft. I strode over to him, presenting my best military bearing, and saluted. He stood with one of those GI little green note books in his hand, one of the ones that say Memorandum in gold script on the cover. He said, "What's your name, punk?"

I said, "WO1 William T. Grant, sir!"

He started writing so I continued with my service number, "W3159977, call sign Kingsmen One-Eight, aircraft tail number 16348, sir!" By now, I was still at attention but leaning slightly forward so I could be sure that he was getting all this down.

"OK, punk! what's all this bullshit about my captain not being able to use the commo in the aircraft?"

"Sir! I need to be able to communicate with the crew at all times, especially during takeoff and landing."

"What the hell for?"

"Well, sir, going into these unsecure areas, I need to be able to direct the crew's fire if we come under fire."

"My captain can direct fire."

"This guy is a bigger dickhead than the captain," I thought.

"Besides, sir, the crew chief and gunner have to clear the tail during landing . . ."

"My captain is an infantry officer, he has been in country for six months and knows every rock and tree in I Corps, he can clear the tail."

"Excuse me, sir, but these crew members are specially trained to perform their jobs."

"Are you trying to tell me that, that punk, can do something better than my captain?" He pointed to the door gunner and said, "C'mere, boy!"

I was pretty sure by then that I had the guy down for the count on the afteraction report. All I had to do was keep my cool, and hope Spec Four Maynard would keep his mouth shut. That might be a problem. He was normally on the fringe of insubordination. He had, in fact, managed to circumvent anything resembling good manners with the captain. He really didn't do anything wrong, he just wasn't the smiling host.

Specialist Maynard came bounding over, snapped to attention, saluted, and barked, "Yes, sir!" I was shocked. I could only hope that he would continue to behave himself. Maybe he caught on to the way I had reacted and knew that I was letting this guy run with the hook. The army had taught me, do what you're told, then squawk about it later.

Major Nutcase said to him, "How long have you been in combat, boy?"

The gunner said with pride, "I've been in combat thirteen months and twenty-seven days, sir!" The statement let Nutcase know that he had extended his tour. As he said it, he adjusted his flight glove so the major could see the scar on his wrist where the AK round had gone through.

The major said, "How long have you been in the infantry, boy?"

"Sir, I have been with the Kingsmen the entire time; I extended to stay with the Kingsmen!"

"Boy, until you've been in the infantry you haven't been in combat!" I almost lost it at that point. How did this shithead think he got in and out of combat, and who brought the ammo under fire so he could fight back in combat? At that moment, I wanted to rip out his lungs and eat his liver.

Then he told us how we had better straighten out and how we were nothing more than taxicabs for the infantry and so on. Then he told us, "Remember, when you work for this battalion, things are different!"

That was for sure.

As I strapped back in the seat, Teenybopper started the aircraft. I was so pissed that I could have breathed in the engine intake and the engine would have fired up. As Ken finished the run-up, I turned the radios on, and before they had a chance to warm up, I had the mike button mashed down. I snatched the aircraft into the air, climbing at max power.

"Kingsmen Operations, this is Kingsmen One-Eight."

Ken said, "Hey W. T., you know we won't get them till we at least clear the trees."

"Shut up, Ken. Kingsmen Operations, this is Kingsman One-Eight.—I don't give a shit, Ken, they better answer." I knew that it was important for me to squeal on this major before he squealed on me. The rule of thumb in these matters was that whoever squawked first was right. It didn't make much sense, but it was part of the game. Besides, if I didn't start griping about this right away, I would explode.

"Kingsmen Operations, this is Kingsman One-Eight.

"Kingsmen Operations, this is Kingsman One-Eight."

Now I wasn't even giving them time to answer between calls. I looked over at Ken, and he was giving me a funny look. I realized I was out of control. I was taking it out on the bird and Ken. I calmed myself down and said, "You have the controls. Take us to the next log pad."

"I have the controls," he acknowledged.

"Kingsmen Operations, this is Kingsmen One-Eight."

"One-Eight, this is Operations. What is the problem?" I guess they heard some of the early calls, and we didn't hear their response 'cause I was already calling again.

"Operations, this is One-Eight. When I get in tonight, have a typewriter, a typist and plenty of paper ready. I have a big-time unsat mission report to complete."

"One-Eight, Ops, can you give us a rundown?" They, too, knew the importance of being first to tattle.

"Ops, One-Eight, it's a long story, but this major on the 2d Brigade support mission was calling us names, and ordered me to shut down the aircraft after I told him it would make us late for the next mission. There was also a captain who was interfering with crew communication."

"Roger, One-Eight. We'll make note of that and be ready for the rest when you come in."

We went to work for a battalion of the 1st Brigade to the south and west of Nui Khe mountain; the mission was much of what we were accustomed to doing. We hauled Cs and personnel to various firebases and LZs within the AO. Occasionally we flew some replacements out to the field. One would feel pity when a cherry was loaded on board all by himself with a load of Cs. There he'd sit, with his new green fatigues and his confused look. You could always tell by the eyes. It wasn't that the cherries all had the same look, it was the guys who have been there a while that had "*the*" look. The look that said these eyes have seen things that I'll never tell you. If you had more than one stop with a load, the NCO running the log pad would step up on the skid toe and say something like, "Don't let the cherry get out till you get to Bravo Company." Somehow it seemed unfair that those guys should go directly to the woods as replacements. It would have been a much easier transition for them to come into a unit while it was on standdown in the rear.

After that mission, we flew a second for another battalion of the 1st Brigade. It was midafternoon when I got a call on the unit push.

"Kingsmen One-Eight, this is Kingsmen Two-Nine." It was Rod Heim.

I shot a puzzled look at Roach and answered, "Two-Nine, this is One-Eight go ahead." Normally, we did not use FM for communications between aircraft; calls from another Kingsmen came over the UHF, since that was what we used for flight following. FM was used to communicate with ground units, as that was all they had. When we flew log missions, we used that radio to talk to the supported units. A battalion had five different frequencies, one for the battalion net, and one for each of the four companies. An aircraft would change from the battalion net at the log pad, to each company freq as it approached the LZ of the unit. So just to find an aircraft by calling on those frequencies, would be a job.

"One-Eight, this is Two-Nine. Ops says to go back to the Castle."

"Two-Nine, One-Eight. But I haven't finished my mission here."

"They sent me to relieve you on station."

That never happened unless you got shot down. Even then, if you weren't hurt, they would probably just bring out another bird.

"Two-Nine, One-Eight, did they say what was up?"

"Nope. They just told me to *didi* out of here and finish your mission. You must be special or something."

I had a good idea what it was. I was up to my ass in water boo shit for the incident that morning. I said, "Roger, Two-Nine. I'll see you later."

I told Teenybopper and the rest of the crew that we had better keep our chicken plates on when we got back. "I think we might be receiving some friendly fire." We dropped off our passenger at the brigade log pad and called Eagle Tower for reposition to the Castle.

As we landed, I called operations and told them we were down at the Castle. They told me to come straight to operations when the aircraft was tied down. As I climbed the hill to operations, I was scared. I knew that we had done nothing wrong, but this was the army. Here I was a brand new AC, and I just had a run-in with a major. Right or wrong, the army would probably decide in his favor; he was a lifer, and I was just a snot-nosed kid.

Rick Haines was waiting for me in operations. He said that the clerk and the typewriter were waiting for me in the back, and to go and get started.

"Hey, Rick, how come I was pulled off the mission to do this?"

He said, "The guy you had the run-in with is trying to make a big deal out of it. He's been whining to everybody since you left there."

It took about two hours to get it all down the way I wanted it. The unsat mission report was about two-and-a-half typewritten pages when it was done. Usually we were satisfied with just a comment or two on the mission sheet. But this guy had been a wild man. I made sure that every "punk" and "boy" that came out of his mouth was included. The report ended, "We were left with the golden parting words, 'Remember when you work for this battalion, things are different!' " Then my signature block and signature. There was more sarcasm in it than that one line, but I felt it was appropriate.

The next day when I came back from my mission and called down at the Castle, operations called and said, "One-Eight, let the peter pilot shut the aircraft down, and get up here right away. The battalion commander wants to see you." I figured that I must have been right yesterday. I was on my way to have my head handed to me. As I approached the operations tent, I saw the battalion commander's jeep sitting outside. *Holy shit, he must be really pissed, he came himself to get a chunk of me.* As I stepped inside, Rick looked at me across the counter. He turned his eyes down after giving me a wry smile. He said, "The BC's driver is here to drive you over to battalion."

As I rode over to the battalion TOC, I remembered that I had left my hat in the aircraft. Here I sat in the battalion commander's jeep, flight helmet in my lap, chicken plate still on, and no hat. *Oh well! One more thing to add to the ass chewing.*

The 101st Aviation Battalion TOC sat in the low ground about a quarter mile from the division TOC. I guess that was to help the shit roll down hill. The TOC was made up of several GP medium tents connected together, supported by a wood frame, a popular style of architecture on Camp Eagle. I entered and looked around; the only one there was a specialist five class behind the counter. I said, "I'm here to see the battalion commander."

He said, "Are you Mr. Grant?" *Great, the whole world knew I was to be crucified.*

I looked down and realized that he couldn't see my name tag because of the chicken plate. I replied, "Yes."

He then said, "Sir, you don't have to see the battalion commander." *That's nice they have delegated shooting me to this guy.* "You just need to sign your unsat mission report again."

"What?"

"You just need to sign the report again, sir."

Things were looking up. Maybe it would be a good time to get cocky again. "What did you guys do? Pussy it all up?"

"No, sir. There was just one correction on the last page. So you have to sign it again." He handed me the last page. I guess he saw that I was not convinced, so he gave me the other two pages. "Here, sir, check it over. There is only the one correction." He broke into a big smile, as he must have realized what had been running through my mind and saw the relief on my face. He said, "To tell you the truth, sir, I kind of liked it." All the smartass remarks, every "punk" and "boy," were still there. They were either supporting me or hanging me out to dry. None of the staff was there to witness my signing, so I figured it must be the former. After carefully reading and rereading, I became convinced that there was only one change. The last line now read, "We were left with the parting words, 'Remember when you work for this battalion, things are different!' " I was amazed all they did was take out the word "golden." I signed, thankful they weren't rounding up volunteers for a firing squad, at least not yet.

The paperwork had gone forward, now all I could do was wait. I had the twenty-third off (177 days to go), or so I thought. I was stretched out on my bunk, listening to Simon and Garfunkel on the stereo. In spite of the heat, I was lost in the music and about half asleep. Then one of the operations clerks came to get me. He said that Mr. Haines wanted me in operations, that I had a mission to fly.

I pulled the tent flap back in ops and said to Rick, "Damn it, Rick, I'm supposed to be off today not on standby. How's anybody supposed to get any rest?"

"I'm sorry, W. T., but this is a special mission, and you have to be the one to fly it. It's a pickup at Sally, fly to the group pad at Eagle, wait and return to a field site. Less than an hour's flight time, a short wait, and you'll be finished. Then you can come back here and relax."

I rounded up the rest of the crew, preflighted, took off, and headed for LZ Sally. We landed on the 2d Brigade TOC pad and rolled the throttle back to flight idle. I noted that we were actually a couple of minutes early for our pickup. I looked over and saw Major Nutcase coming out of the TOC, and he did not look happy. I reached up, lowered the sun visor on my flight helmet, and busied myself with the radios. He looked down all the way to the aircraft. He got in without saying a word. I looked over to the pete and held out my hand, palm up, meaning "you have it." He rolled the throttle up and took off. Other than required radio communication for arty clearance and talk to Eagle Tower, no one spoke on the way back to Eagle. We got our clearance to the Group pad and landed. The pete hovered off to one side and set down. Major Nutcase got out and headed for the TOC.

Analyzing the situation, I could have been sent on this mission so I would be handy when Colonel Crozier was ready to cut off my head. At this point, that seemed unlikely, or I would been summoned in with Major Nutcase so he would have the pleasure of watching. Plus, he looked as though he had just had a good ass-chewing when we picked him up. On the other hand, it would have been bad form in army etiquette for me, a junior officer, to be invited to Major Nutcase's ass-chewing. As the clock ticked off the minutes, I began to relax more and more. After twenty minutes passed, I knew that I was in the clear. Colonel Crozier had a reputation: conversations were short and sweet when you were not in trouble; when he chewed you out, it was thorough. As the fifteen-minute scheduled wait turned to thirty, I felt almost sorry for Nutcase. As the clock passed forty-five minutes, he reappeared at the entrance to the TOC. He was pale. We cranked up and flew him back to the log pad where it had all started.

By the time I returned to the Castle, I felt as if a great weight had lifted from my shoulders. When I went into operations, Rick had something that made things even better. He showed me a new 101st Aviation Battalion policy: previous policy on single-ship insertions had been revoked, and except for emergencies, no aircraft would go into unsecure areas without gun cover. Emergencies were to be determined by the aircraft commander.

That was really good news and a major victory for airmobile operations. It meant that the higher-ups were beginning to pay some attention to what we had to say.

My fellow Kingsmen saw to it that I was not thirsty that night. Over the next couple of weeks, no one saw Major Nutcase, and that battalion was now running one of the most ef-

ficient log pads in the division: Reporting crews were presented
with maps that had the sites to be logged marked on them; sorties were preplanned to eliminate wasted trips; if only a half
load was to go to one company, the cargo for two companies,
sorted and marked for two destinations, was loaded. The new
procedures meant that more time was left for things like hauling
cold beer or hot meals to the grunts.

I never thought to ask Rick who selected me for the flight,
but it seemed to me it might have been Teddy Crozier's idea. It
would fit well with his reputation. Major Nutcase was not seen
or heard from again.

Tuesday, 24 September (176 days to go). My assigned aircraft
was in for maintenance so I was assigned to fly 650, a new aircraft with about twenty-five hours on it. A new helicopter is
much like a new car. Everything has that brand-new feel and
look to it. Even the smell is different. Much like a new car, a
new aircraft can have things that are very wrong with it. As I
flew that day, I noticed a binding sensation in the cyclic stick.
It did not occur constantly, but only in a certain position, and
only once in a while. When I noticed it, I gave the controls to
Ken Roach and asked if he could feel it. He could not. At the
end of the day, I wrote up that the controls wound bind occasionally in forward flight. The bird came out of maintenance the
next day, signed off "checked and found okay."

With 348 still down, I was given the same aircraft again on
the twenty-fifth. Once again, I noticed the binding problem.
Once again, I wrote it up. Jim Weaver, one of our maintenance
officers, had told me that if it occurred again to be more specific
in the write-up, that would help them locate the problem. This
time I wrote, "Cyclic binds in the right front quadrant at eighty
knots, twenty-two pounds of torque and a twenty-degree angle
of bank." The Huey spent the next two days having its flight
controls disassembled and put back together. Still, maintenance
found nothing.

I was given the bird again on the twenty-eighth. Jim Weaver
told me that there was nothing wrong that they could find and
that the problem was probably just stiffness from being so new.
It happened again. This time, I was pissed. In the write-up I
gave them every instrument reading, including the outside air
temperature and readings from the voltmeter, oil pressures, and
temperatures. I even put down some radio frequencies. Maintenance failed to see the humor. They just told everybody I was

nuts and that there was nothing wrong with 650. I told operations not to give me that aircraft again, 'cause I would not fly
it. I also told them that if anyone asked, I'd tell them why I refused to fly the aircraft. Operations made me promise that I
would not just go around telling everyone, because they already
knew that I was nuts.

That night I wrote to Jackie, reminding her that there were
only sixty-nine days till R & R. I had put in for it back in July.
I wanted to wait till December for two reasons. The first was
that the more senior you were, the more likely you were to get
the allocation that you wanted. The second being if I held out
through three-quarters of my tour, it would be easier to get
through the last couple of months. I also told her a friend of
ours from flight school had been reported missing in action for
two months. I realized, as I wrote, how callous that I had become. The news of his loss had not bothered me till I wrote
home about it. Writing to Jackie about it associated the news
with life back in the World and made it real.

During August, I had begun painting things. I started with my
helmet. On the visor cover I had painted the words "Happiness
is Getting Short." The words were surrounded with a ring of
pastel colored flowers. Nobody was too upset with that or the
gothic "WT" on the back of the helmet. I did get some ribbing
about not having been in country long enough to know what
short was. What did cause an uproar was when I painted a large
bright red cherry on the back of the helmet under the WT. Some
thought that I was defying the gods of war; some just thought
that I was daring every gook in the universe to blow my ass
away. Nobody liked the cherry, except me. I kept it.

They would ask, "What are you going to do if it gets
busted?"

"I'll just paint it splattered all over the back of the helmet
with cherry juice dripping from my initials."

None of my fellow Kingsmen wanted me to push the issue.
If I could stay cherry, they might be able to make it home.

I painted nicknames and cartoon characters. I painted a
Snoopy on Meacham's aircraft, which he called The Dog. That
was in defiance of a 101st prohibition on nose art. Some fine
work had been there prior to the ban. There were aircraft named
Hell Bringer, Society's Child. The Hustler was decorated with
crossed pool cues, five aces, and a pair of dice on the doors. Ta-
ter was painted on the nose of the maintenance bird, but most

of the names were on the doors, because the Kingsman logo (a black spade with a lance, a dragon, and a knight's helmet) was on the nose. The banner read *Opera Non Verba*; Actions Not Words. The nose of 348 had a plain black spade that we kept highly waxed. On Gene Gillenwater's Jefferson Airplane, we got around the ban by painting the name and a broken-down bi-plane on the ammo boxes.

One night Rod Heim came into my hootch and said, "You son of a bitch."

"What did I do Rod?"

"As long as we been friends, you go paintin' everybody else's helmet around here but mine."

"Well, Rod, you didn't ask."

"Here, I'm asking." He tossed his helmet at me and turned to leave.

"Wait, Rod. What do you want on it?"

"I don't know, just paint somethin' cool on it." He kept walking as he shot that back over his shoulder.

I thought for a while and started to work. I painted a block of ice with "29" on it for his callsign. Above it, in ice-block letters, the word "Somethin' " and below, in the same frozen letters, "Cool." When I gave it back to him, he was pissed. He thought it only meant that I had played smartass with his own words. The next day when he flew with it, he came back and apologized. Every grunt who saw it thought it was great, some because they knew he must be "somethin' cool," some just because even a picture of ice was a welcome sight. It was probably the best looking helmet I did over there.

Sunday, 29 September (171 days to go). The mission for the day was FOB. I would find on that day that the scope of the operations inside Laos were much broader than I had imagined.

Rick Haines was the flight lead that day. About four miles out he had our slicks form up in a V-of-three formation. We started a descent, so that at about two miles out we were on the deck at a hundred knots. The Huey is incredibly loud and can be heard from a long way off, but when flown on the deck, some of the sound is lost in the trees, making it sound farther away. At a hundred knots, you are eating ground up about a mile and a half per minute, so even when you are expected, it is possible to arrive with a surprise. We held the low altitude till we were over the middle of the triangular compound, careful to avoid the large antenna that stuck up in the middle of it. Directly over the compound, the flight initiated a cyclic climb with birds two and three breaking, at forty knots, to their respective sides of the V. It was a turn with both cyclic and pedal that reversed your path and took the aircraft from a nose-up climb to a nose-down dive. Lead would hold his climb till he went through twenty knots, and then he would follow. The flight would then fall into a trail formation and land on the dirt strip. The maneuver was called a return to target, and has since been prohibited in the UH-1 helicopter; those with a less gentle touch on the controls had a tendency to snap off the rotor system.

The Special Forces guys would never admit to being surprised or impressed by these maneuvers, but as we dove back toward the compound, we could see that we had the attention of everyone on the ground. We shut the aircraft down, went inside the compound for the now familiar briefings. When the curtain was closed across the door and the guard posted, Major Sincere pulled the curtain back from the map on the wall. This time he only pulled the map a short distance past the border. He began his briefing.

"Gentlemen, today's mission is to fly resupply and reinforcements to a company operating a fire support base approximately twenty-one nautical miles southwest of Khe Sanh."

My mind was racing, "Fire support base? Company-size element? Resupply?" Silly old me. I thought the mission here was recon, just like with the LRPs. Just when you had things figured out in this war they changed the rules.

He continued. "You will be flying out with rations and ammunition for their 81mm mortars. They also have some slightly wounded that will be coming out. These personnel will be replaced. Friendly situation: The nearest friendlies are the Marines at Fire Support Base Vandergrift. Fire support will be provided by Delta 101st Aviation Battalion. There will be no air force or artillery on this one, gentlemen. We estimate there will be about four sorties. The LZ is located here." He pointed to where we would landing on the map. "The LZ is located about five kilometers from the unit. The resupply will be carried to the unit to maintain security."

I was surprised that he gave us that much information. The last part was probably just to let us know that this was not as stupid as it sounded. I took a closer look at the map on the way out of the briefing room. The LZ was on a horseshoe-shaped ridge that overlooked a valley that was five miles wide and about twenty-five miles long. Along the valley floor ran two high-speed trails, major highways in that neighborhood. Now I understood what this was about. The roads were part of the complex known as the Ho Chi Minh trail. The trails branched off to the south through Laos and southeast toward the A Shau Valley. From the ridgeline, the company commanded a view of the entire valley and both trails. They could just sit back and drop mortars on anyone coming down the trail. It was far more direct approach to supply interdiction than most of the rest of the operations we were conducting.

We started in early afternoon. The flight took off from Mai Loc and headed west. The route took us west toward Khe Sanh. We would cross the border just north of Co Roc. The route had become so routine I had begun to wonder if maybe there was some secret agreement with the bad guys. After crossing into Laos, we turned to the south and crossed a ridgeline, and the terrain opened up into a large valley. On our left was the horseshoe-shaped area in which the unit we were supporting was operating. The view of the valley was spectacular. I smiled at the thought of the gooks coming down the trail one night with a large convoy of rockets headed for Saigon. Then, without warning, mortars begin walking up and down their column. I liked it.

The turnaround time for each sortie was about forty-five minutes, so with refueling time it took all afternoon to complete the mission. Each lift was cold, and there was no sign of the enemy, but something about landing in Laos kept the pucker factor high. As we departed the LZ for the last time to head home, I was drained. That may have had something to do with the upcoming events. The sun was setting as the flight of five—three slicks and two gunships—headed back to Mai Loc, the day's work complete. We had refueled at Vandergrift on the way over, so we all had plenty of fuel. The setting sun had painted the haze in the sky pink rosé. We were in a loose trail formation at about seven thousand feet, the two gunships in the lead. I was the last slick, and all four of us had been admiring the beautiful sunset. As I looked back to the flight, the strangest thing happened. The first Charlie-model disappeared. The second gunship just disappeared right behind. I was amazed and confused. The first slick had begun to dissolve before I realized what was happening. We were punching into a cloud bank. At a hundred knots, knowing what was happening and being able to do anything about it were two different things. In an instant, I was surrounded by a world of white.

I transitioned to flying by reference to the instruments. I immediately began wishing that I had spent more time practicing. The whole flight initiated the proper IFR breakup. It was only a couple of minutes till I realized the instruments said that we were in a left turn. My senses told me that we were in a right turn. I responded by turning further left. I realized that I had vertigo. Without visual references, the inner ear tends to tell lies about the motions that your body is experiencing. The practiced instrument pilot learns to overcome those sensations and believe his instruments. The inexperienced instrument pilot falls prey to vertigo. I announced, "I have vertigo, you have the controls."

Lieutenant Picarella replied from the other seat, "Roger, I have the controls."

I felt better, I had recognized the problem and had taken the correct action to fix it. A few minutes later, I saw the instruments indicating a right turn. I said, "We are in right turn."

He replied, "Roger," and turned further to the right.

He also was suffering from the lack of practice. I took the controls back, even though I didn't feel quite ready to try again. I frantically fought my senses for control of the aircraft. I carefully analyzed the situation. I had vertigo. The peter pilot had vertigo. There was only logical thing to do. Panic. I lost it. I started calling everyone for help. R. L. Smith responded. He didn't concern himself with proper radio procedure. "W. T., this here's Hootchmaid. Y'all got to calm down and fly instruments."

His slow Texas drawl had the desired effect. I began to realize that I was the only one that could do anything about my predicament. If flying instruments was my problem, the answer was to get back visual flight conditions. Panic was still in charge here, but Hootchmaid had me thinking again, and that was a start. I slowed to fifty knots and pulled fifty pounds of torque. I started to climb; 348 was riding a rocket. I didn't realize it, but I was now flying instruments with the purpose of escaping having to fly instruments. We broke out into the night sky at 10,300 feet. I had no idea where I was, but at least I was able to fly visually again. The others had all headed east and began to find holes in the clouds to get back down again.

I spotted a hole in the clouds. There was a fire on the ground, the area looked to me like FSB Vandergrift. I started a tight spiral descent, but something did not feel right about this sucker hole. The clouds were closing in around us. I began to climb out again. Later, the Sugar Bear told me the hole was also full of muzzle flashes. It sunk in finally that I could hear the Special Forces camp at Mai Loc doing long counts over their powerful FM transmitter so that the aircraft could FM-home back. Hootchmaid continued to talk to me. I centered the homing needle and rolled the nose over to one hundred and fifteen knots. I was back in control. As we flew the course back to Mai Loc, the clouds beneath us began to thin out. We could see the ground again. I started my descent, warning all the crew to watch for the glow of the position lights in the trees so we would not go too low. Finally, we broke out beneath the clouds. The flight back to Mai Loc took forty minutes. We later plotted our heading and airspeed and discovered the sucker hole had been in North Vietnam. The uneasy feeling I had about it had probably saved our lives.

I landed the bird on the airstrip at Mai Loc. The rotor system coasted slowly to a stop. I felt deeply ashamed of the way I had panicked. I jumped down from my seat and kissed the ground as I whispered thanks to the Lord for saving my stupid ass again. The other crews were gathered in a circle over by the Charlie-models. When we started over to join them, I stopped my crew and said, "I apologize for almost killing us tonight; I know it is not enough, but it's all I've got to offer."

The gunner piped up with, "Shit, sir, we made it, didn't we?"

"Yeah, but that hole in the clouds was full of mountain."

"Sir, it was also full of bullets, but you had enough problems at the time, so I didn't bother to tell you."

We joined the others, and my hands shook as I lit up a Marlboro. I could only look at the grounds as I said, "I'm sorry for being such an asshole tonight."

Bill Turner smiled and said, "We're sorry that you're such an asshole all the time, Grant." He turned, went over to his bird and opened the heater compartment in the back. "I have some medicine right here for such situations." He pulled out a quart of Old Granddad and twisted off the cap. He took a swallow and handed me the bottle. I took a long pull, the bourbon burned all the still-raw nerve ends on the way down. It felt good. I passed the bottle to my left. It made three laps around the pilots and Major Sincere before it was gone. No one mentioned the flight home. I felt no effect, it just calmed me back down to normal. I began to realize that I was not the only one who was scared that night. At the time, instrument flying was just not considered an important skill for army helicopter pilots, and nobody got much practice. I made a note to move it up on my list of priorities.

Wild Bill Meacham returned from Phuoc Vinh on the thirtieth. What better reason for a party? But, flying FOB, I managed to miss the celebration. Johnny Quick from the LRP company had come to party and say good-bye. He was headed south the next day to go home. As the evening wore on, Johnny was feeling no pain from all the booze and enjoying the notoriety of being an enlisted LRP in our club. He began to brag a little. Bringing LRPs to the Kingsmen club had become a more regular occurrence, and pilots who did not fly LRPs were always properly revolted by the things they did to provide entertainment. Those of us who did fly LRPs enjoyed the fact that the more the others were revolted, the more it enhanced our own image as LRP pilots.

Quick began to tell of how he had been a survival instructor at Fort Bragg before coming to Vietnam. Eventually he got around to describing the "chicken to go." The responses he received were immediate.

"Bullshit."

"Ain't no fuckin' way."

"There is a limit to how much of this bullshit I'm going to believe."

Johnny, not about to be intimidated, said, "Get me a chicken, and I'll do it right here!"

Whether he wanted to do the chicken or not we will never know. If he did not want to do it, he probably felt fairly confident that they would not be able to produce a live chicken on the spot. Several aviators went scurrying out of the club to find a chicken for Quick to eat.

Things calmed down again when some of the great hunters returned, chickenless; there just were no live chickens to be had on Camp Eagle. After a while, one of the aviators came back with a large toad. He walked in the club and over to John and said, "Will this do?"

Johnny responded immediately, "No problem." By then Johnny was pretty drunk. He grabbed the wiggling toad by the hind legs and held it high in the air for dramatic effect. The club fell silent. In a civilian club, drums would have rolled and the house lights would have dimmed, leaving the Amazing Johnny Quick in a pale spotlight. Johnny tilted his head back, opened his mouth, and bit into the live toad. Blood and toad juice ran from the corners of his mouth. Certain Kingsmen with less than cast iron stomachs decided it was time for some fresh air. Johnny Quick continued his toad munching. He had a little help from his friends, Sir James Thompson took a leg so Johnny did not have to eat alone. Quick washed his snack down with copious amounts of alcohol.

The party was still going strong about an hour later when Rod Heim encountered the company medic, who said, "Sir, come with me, that LRP is really sick."

Johnny Quick was on the ground, holding his stomach and shaking all over. Rod knelt next to him and said, "John, what's wrong? What can I do?"

In a pained and weak voice Quick said, "It was bad toad; get me to the hospital, quick."

Johnny, a biology major in college, gave Rod the technical name for the toad and told Rod that he would need an injection to counter the poison. He knew the medicine he needed and the required dosage. Rod was worried because Johnny looked very bad and was convulsing. He and the medic lifted Quick and carried him to Rod's aircraft. Rod had no helmet, no chicken plate, and no crew, but he set the sick LRP on the floor in the back of the aircraft and left the medic with him while he went and untied the rotor. With the blades untied, he strapped himself in the seat and cranked the aircraft. Unable to call the tower, Rod came to a hover and did a 180-degree pedal turn and headed for Two Two Surg in Phu Bai.

Night missions were rare enough that cranking a Huey attracted attention, especially when the only aircraft flying that night were the FOB aircraft, and they would be returning and shutting down, not cranking. By the time Rod executed his pedal turn, everyone who'd been in the club was standing on the side of the hill, wondering what was going on.

Rod arrived at the hospital pad, shut down the aircraft, and ran into the emergency room to get help. A doctor and two orderlies went back out with him to the bird. Rod explained to the doctor, on the way back to the aircraft, all the things that Quick had told him. When he mispronounced the medication, the doctor corrected him so Rod knew that he had gotten the message across. They loaded Quick on the gurney. He was pale and was still shaking. He managed enough strength to repeat his message to the doctor. Rod could hear him say, ". . . and whatever you do, don't pump my stomach; I've had a lot to drink."

The doctor responded, "Sure, son."

Rod followed them inside till he and our medic were stopped at the emergency room door. The last thing he heard as the door closed was the doctor ordering a stomach pump. After they pumped Johnny's stomach, they set him aside to sober up.

Johnny Quick died. The official cause of death was heart failure induced by alcohol and toad poisoning. My finding was "killed by doctor."

Another friend was gone. It was a senseless death, but I had begun to wonder if any of the others made more sense. At least Johnny Quick had been having fun when he gave up his life.

The next morning, Rod was on the carpet for flying an unauthorized medevac, flying while intoxicated, *stealing* a helicopter, and failing to call the tower prior to takeoff. I could not believe it—Rod had tried to save a life, and instead of hunting down the doctor who would not listen, the Idiots in Charge were shitting on Rod.

Rod was let off with an ass-chewing, but a new policy forbid us to fly medevacs. Medevacs were the job of Dustoff, and they had become the only ones allowed to do that job. What saved Rod was that he had had the medic with him on the flight.

Somebody must have been smoking dope when that policy was enacted; there were not enough medevacs in all of I Corps to haul the wounded that division birds carried on a busy day. And there was the time factor. If a unit was a twenty-minute flight from Phu Bai, even if Dustoff took off as the call came in, it would take forty minutes to get a wounded soldier to the hospital. With delays for relaying requests, miscommunications, etc., it could take over an hour to get to the hospital. There were a lot of pissed-off Kingsmen over the policy. It was not that we did not have confidence in the outstanding job done by Dustoff—they went unarmed into hot LZs and saved many thousands of lives; but asking them to do it all was unfair. We were particularly concerned that there were times when speed was all that counted. If a slick happened to be on the scene when the wound occurred, there was just no way Dustoff could beat our time to the hospital. The CO's argument was that the medevacs had a medic on board. We responded that the unit medic almost always accompanied seriously wounded from the field to the hospital. It was apparent that it would not be long till this new rule would be tested with one of our necks on the line.

CHAPTER 8
OCTOBER 1968

Tuesday, 1 October (169 days to go). Once again I found myself flying the FOB mission. The briefing had become routine—the room was sealed, and we were reminded that the mission was classified. We were not to tell anyone that we had been flying into Laos, not even our crew.

It was always hard to suppress the snickers each time we heard that one. Could the people we were working for possibly have believed that the two enlisted men sitting in the back were that stupid? The crew knew their way around the countryside as well as the pilots. Some of them were even so sophisticated that they were aware that the sun rose in the east and set in the west. You would even find enlisted men who cheated by looking at the radio magnetic indicator on the dash. As many times as I told the instrument to lie to the enlisted men, it refused. The compass just seemed to not understand that insignificant enlisted swine should not be allowed to know any secrets. Not even if knowing such things might insure their survival if we were to be shot down.

The terrain itself was also a good indication. A short flight to the east left one with the "big water" under the aircraft. To the west of that, the first land after the beach was covered with rice paddies. Just to the west of the paddies, the rolling hills could be found. Beyond those, the foothills and the mountains. The plateau region around Khe Sanh gave way to more mountains just on the other side of the border. Farther west, the mountains gave way to gently rolling hills all the way to the western border of Laos.

The briefing always ended with what I called the "Mr. Phelps warning." Major Sincere would say, "Remember, if you are shot down and captured, the Secretary will disavow all knowledge of your existence."

I always wanted to ask, "Whose secretary?" But I didn't; Maj. Clyde Sincere was the type of officer who left you with the feeling that he would not bring you up on charges for disobedience. He would simply take you by the head and screw you into the ground.

If we went down in Laos, our story was supposed to be that we got lost and wandered around the sky until we ended up wherever it was that we ended up. To that end, we carried only the maps that we normally carried in country. Navigation was the job of the air force FAC who led us to our LZs and PZs. The mission that day was to pick up a team that had been inserted some time before. We were only told where to pick them up; we were given no background mission information. This kind of treatment made FOB unlike LRPs. Supporting F Company, we were given every piece of information available. On FOBs, the lack of information gave the missions a sense of mystery, but left us feeling as though we were not fully a part of the operation. The teams generally consisted of two or three Special Forces NCOs with about fifteen "Yards" (Montagnard tribesmen).

The flight fired up: three gunships, known as a heavy fire team, and three slicks. The team was fifteen men. We would not need the three VNAF H-34s that sat on the dirt runway at Mai Loc with our aircraft. The Vietnamese pilots of the Kingbees, as they were called, did a fine job, and we all respected them. They worked hard to make us understand that we could rely on them just as well as we relied on Kingsmen pilots. They took great pride in showing us that they were not going to screw up when the chips were down. Some of them had flown the same AO for years. Their tours had no DEROS date.

I was flying Chalk Five that day. We always let the guns lead on FOB so we would not run away from them during the long climb to ten thousand feet. The altitude kept us above the 23mm and 14.7mm machine-gun antiaircraft fire. As we got to operating RPM, I keyed the intercom and said, "May I have your attention please. This is your warrant speaking. Welcome aboard international flight 348. I would like to take this opportunity to tell you that we will be flying at an altitude of ten thousand feet today and that we will definitely not be crossing any borders into any other countries on this flight. Please fasten your seat belts and place your machine guns in the upright and stowed position. Thank you for flying Green Weenie Airlines."

The PZ was about fifty nautical miles from Mai Loc. It would take about forty-five minutes to fly out there, including time to climb to ten thousand feet for the border crossing. We would stop at Vandergrift to top off the fuel tanks. The Marine base was only about ten minutes west of Mai Loc, but that would leave us a total of twenty minutes' more fuel on board at the end of the mission. On some of the deeper missions, we returned to Vandergrift with the twenty-minute fuel advisory light on.

On the west side of the border, with the Teenybopper on the controls, I decided to relax with a Marlboro. It was tough to get the ol' Zippo lit at ten grand, but mine always came through. As I put the lighter back in the pocket of my chicken plate, I noticed the black cloud below the chin bubble. When I looked out again, I noticed that there was a row of black clouds that started under the FAC and continued the length of the flight. As we flew along, the clouds seemed to be following us. It was 23mm antiaircraft fire, and it followed the flight because it was radar guided. Flak! Holy shit!

I leaned out the window and yelled, "Hey, you stupid bastards. You got the wrong fuckin' war. I ain't Robert Ryan, and this ain't no fuckin' B-17."

I put the cigarette back in my mouth and smiled over at Roach, and he just shook his head. With the stuff going off five hundred feet below us, it was laughable because it couldn't reach us. It wouldn't have been funny if it had been 37s. The air force guys always seemed to manage to keep us away from the 37mm locations.

The pickup was uneventful. The team was dirty and ragged; fatigue showed heavily in their eyes. They must have been out for an extended period. They loaded aboard the aircraft quickly, and we headed back to Mai Loc.

I had the second off. I went by operations to ask Rick Haines, "When do I go back on LRPs?"

"Not for a while."

"Why?"

"They decided that you need a rest. You've been flying LRPs too much."

"Who is they?"

"I don't know. I've just been told not to schedule you on LRP missions."

While I had the day off, Dave Poley had flown 348 on the FOB missions, bringing her back violated; she had taken a hit in the vertical fin just below the tail numbers. A .30-caliber machine-gun bullet had entered just below the numbers and punctured eleven structural panels on its way to the top of the fin, just missing the ninety-degree gear box as it exited. Had it hit the ninety, he might have had a tough time getting the bird back on the ground in one piece again. It was only 348's third hit, but it would take maintenance a while to have her back up again. I told The Dave that I would never speak to him again. "Never" lasted about two days.

All reports of enemy fire were plotted, especially accurate fire. Dave's explanation to operations was a classic. Since FOB was classified and information was on a need-to-know basis, Poley was not going to give out much information.

"Mister Poley, where were you when you got hit?"

"In the aircraft."

"Where was the aircraft?"

"In the air."

"Where in the air?"

"About three thousand feet."

"Where were you located?"

"In the aircraft."

"Where were you located in the aircraft?"

"The left seat."

"Damn it, Poley, what were the grid coordinates?"

"I can't tell ya."

The operations officer began to get flustered. "Look, Poley, we are on the same side here. I need to have this information plotted at division. I know the nature of the mission; we send out people to fly it several times a month. Now, where were you when you took the hit?"

"Can't tell ya. It's classified."

They continued to play "Who's on First" for about twenty minutes. Poley was immovable. The ops officer's blood pressure must have been up about thirty points by the time The Dave was through with him. Everybody in the Kingsmen thought it was funny, except the operations officer. It still wasn't enough for me to forgive Dave for having holed 348.

3 October (167 days to go). I was assigned to fly log missions. How could they just pull me off LRPs to give me a rest and then send me out to fly log missions? I'd get a lot more flight time on log missions. I stomped my way to the aircraft to fly. I was fuming, and I had to think of way to get even. I flew sortie after sortie, then something occurred to me. It wasn't much, but it would have to do for my retaliation. We never filed flight plans; each sortie was reported over the radio to operations. Operations kept a log. The call would report the point of departure, the number of people on board, and the destination. The whole procedure was called flight following. I started making my calls in a whisper the way the LRPs did.

I whispered, "Kingsmen Operations, Kingsmen One-Eight."

There was a pause. "One-Eight, Operations. Go ahead."

Again I whispered, "Operations, One-Eight is resting from Eagle, enroute to Sally with eight souls on board." That told them I had four crew and four passengers. It made it easier when searching wreckage to know how many bodies you were looking for. I continued to make all the calls at a whisper to tell operations where I was "resting." After some time, I noticed that the operations clerk on the radio was whispering as well. It finally occurred to him that he been caught up in the whispering.

"One-Eight, Operations. Why are we whispering?"

"Operations, One-Eight. Cause Charlie is listening," I said, alluding to the security posters that were all over Vietnam that warned that everyone should be careful what they said because of who might be listening.

4 October (166 days to go). I logged 10.1 hours of flight time on a log mission. I continued with whispered calls. It was a very long and hard day. Sugar Bear and the gunner got a workout as we resupplied companies in the mountains. Many of the LZs were hover-downs where they had to talk us down through the trees. It was late afternoon when one of the units, on a ridgeline south of FSB Zon came in contact. They quickly expended much of their remaining ammo and started screaming for more. The LZ was one of the better that we had seen that day, still it required that we hover straight down among hundred-foot trees. The ground was littered with fallen trees so we couldn't really land. The best we could do was put one skid down on a log to hold the aircraft still while we unloaded. Arty was going into the west face of the ridge intermittently, forcing us to arrive up the east slope and sneak in and out the same way.

We had just dropped the last load of ammo and were departing when the radio came to life. "Kingsmen One-Eight, this is Top Notch Two-Six. Come back; we have wounded."

I thought, "Shit! Here it is, up against the new policy already."

"Top Notch, this is One-Eight. No can do, GI. Ya gotta call Dustoff. They don't want us doing medevacs anymore." It tore at my guts just hearing myself say it.

"Kingsmen, this is Two-Six Mike." It was the medic. "We got serious wounded; there's not time to get Dustoff."

"They've been tellin' us we can't do it."

It looked like it was going to be my neck that tested the new policy. I looked over at the peter pilot and shrugged as I turned around and headed back.

I could hear the strain in his voice as he came back. One of the wounded must have been a close friend. "Please, sir, I can't help these guys no more, they need a hospital."

He didn't know that I had already turned around; if I hadn't, I would have then. "I'm on the way."

As I put the skid back on the log again, weapons opened up on the perimeter. Charlie was back for another visit. I listened carefully as they loaded the wounded on board. Amongst the popping sound of the M-16s and the deeper voice of the M-60s, I could occasionally hear the sharp crack of an AK-47. The grunts were not just putting down suppressive fire. One look in the back told me the medic hadn't just been stroking me to get me to come back. There were three of them. The first had head and stomach wounds. The second was hit in the shoulder, and one leg was missing a large piece from the thigh. The shoulder wound was large enough that it appeared that he would lose the arm. Several large field dressings were unable to cover the wound or contain the bleeding. As the last one was loaded, the medic crawled in next to him. The medic held an IV in one hand, and the other hand was at the patient's chest. When I looked again I could see that the hand was actually in the chest. The medic was desperately trying to hold a plastic bag in a sucking chest wound.

Sugar Bear said, "We're up, sir."

I pulled pitch, and as soon as we reached the treetops, I kicked right pedal and spun the bird 180 degrees. I lowered the nose and dove the aircraft down the hillside to get airspeed quickly. The airspeed indicator quickly read 115 knots. I leveled off and made a beeline for the hospital in Phu Bai, allowing the speed to creep closer to the red line at 124 knots. I glanced over my shoulder at the medic, who was squatting just behind the radio pedestal. He looked up at me with tears filling his eyes and yelled over the aircraft noise.

"Sir, I'm losin' him. The only help left is speed."

I checked the airspeed again and let it creep up to 130 knots. In flight school, they preached that "retreating blade stall" would be encountered just after exceeding the airspeed red line. (Retreating blade stall occurs when the forward airspeed is so great that the relative wind speed nearly equals air flow over the retreating blade. The retreating blade then stalls, and the advancing blade is still developing lift. This causes the helicopter to pitch up and roll to the stalled side. The retreating blade is the one moving aft, the advancing blade is the one moving forward. During forward flight, there is always a disparity in the lift developed, due to the difference in velocity through the air.) I looked back and again saw the terror in the medic's eyes—135 knots; 348 was flying smooth as glass. She was behaving like a thoroughbred racehorse exhilarated at being let run—140 knots. No vibrations, no nose pitching up, I let her run a little more—145 knots. Everything was still holding together. I was wound so tight that if someone had touched me, I would have shattered like crystal—147 knots. I was just too scared to try and let her go any faster. There was a great deal of bleeding going on in the back of the aircraft, small specks of blood were starting to dot the windshield. The wind in the back was kicking it all over. The flight to Phu Bai took only a little over eleven minutes. On touchdown at Two Two Surg, we were swamped with doctors, nurses, and medics. As they loaded the guy on the stretcher, the unit medic leaned up between the seats and gave me a big smile, a thumbs-up, and yelled, "Thanks, sir." His buddy had made it that far. If he didn't make it, it wouldn't be because somebody had not given it his best shot.

I stood at the operations counter, filling out my after-mission report. How many sorties? How many pax? How many tons of cargo? Contact with the enemy? Where? Remarks? That was where I had to stop and think. I could report the medevac myself, and the shit would hit the fan right away, or I could forget to put it down and hope for the best. The grunts would report it through their channels. Would the two marry up somewhere? Ah, hell! The good little officer tattles on himself first, at least that's what they taught us. I guess that was so they can have you shot before sundown instead of at sunrise. I scribbled out a brief summary of the medevac staring that it was not feasible to wait for Dustoff and that the unit medic was onboard with the patients. I handed the paper across the counter to Rick Haines. He looked it over to see if he would have any questions. He got to the bottom and raised his eyebrows at me. He shook his head and mumbled, "Some people just don't know when to quit."

I laughed and left operations. I stepped outside, It had gotten dark. The air was cooler, and it felt good. I stepped to one side to be out the way of the traffic coming and going from ops. I just wanted to be alone for a minute or two. I felt drained of all energy. It was as if I was in one of those grade-B science-fiction movies. The ones where the aliens come down and suck out your very being and leave their victims walking zombies. I set my flight helmet on the ground and leaned against the sign outside operations. I was still wearing my chicken plate. I reached in the pocket of the vest and pulled out a cigarette. I took a deep drag, and it felt good. The smoke purged the smell of blood from my nose. I thought about going to the hootch and heating up some Cs for dinner. I had been quite hungry when the call came for the emergency ammo resupply, but somehow the hunger had passed. When it was finished, I stepped on the cigarette and headed for the club. A drink would sit good right now.

I set my flight helmet on the hat shelf as I entered the club. As I walked to the bar, Surfer Lou Pulver called out, "Hey W. T.! Still got it?"

"Still got the cherry; not sure about my ass," I mumbled.

Lou was well aware of how numb your butt could get sitting on those Huey seats for a long day's flying.

Sir James was tending bar that night. "Hey, W. T., when'd you pick up the measles?"

Carl Hienze was sitting on a stool at the bar. "It appears zat da clothes hass caught da measles as vell."

I asked, "What the hell are you talking about, Carl?"

He pointed at my right sleeve. I looked down, and it was speckled with blood. Jim said that my face was spotted as well. He handed me a wet bar towel to wipe my face. I had to relate the whole story. I stayed at the club until the images faded.

I won! On the fifth, I started my longest stint of flying without a break, fifty-one days without a day off. Many of those days, I flew missions for LRPs or Special Forces. The last thirty-five of them would be spent working from the Acid pad. Many would count my marathon session as a company record.

I was flying Poley's wing on the fifth. During a VR, Scott

AH-1G "Cobra" helicopter of 2/17 Cavalry in November 1968. This one is equipped with a minigun and 40-mm grenade launcher in the chin turret, two minigun pods, and thirty-eight rockets on the wings. Cobras provided much of the devastating firepower required to save the LRP team surrounded by the NVA on 20 November 1968. The Cobra remains the only army aircraft that is not officially named in honor of a Native American tribe. Photo courtesy of Darol Walker.

"Hootchmaid" Smith's Charlie-model Huey gunship hovering in May 1968. The eagle-eyed may note the siren mounted on the left rocket pod. Since the "Hog" is hovering, Hootchmaid must have shot up his ammo to lighten it up. Photo courtesy of Darol Walker.

An OH-6A "Loach" of the 2/17 Cavalry, November 1968. These little birds often served as the C & C ship for LRP operations. The minigun and Eklund's adjusting artillery from on board gave the Loach a nasty bite. Photo courtesy of Darol Walker.

Ladder training in July 1968. Photo courtesy of Darol Walker.

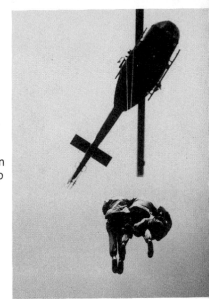

McGuire rig training in February 1968. Photo courtesy of Darol Walker.

A LRP team loaded and ready to go in May 1968. Photo courtesy of Darol Walker.

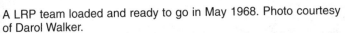

The aftermath of the Horace Pearce/Ken Eklund crash, October 1968. Photo courtesy of Darol Walker.

Dave Greenlee and "Sir" James Thompson had a bad day: shot down, July 1968—but no fatalities. Photo courtesy of Jim Thompson.

(From left to right) "Deeds Not Words"—17th Assault Helicopter Company patch (later that of B Company, 101st Aviation Battalion); "Wings of the Eagle" crest worn then by members of the 101st Aviation Battalion (now the crest of the 101st Aviation Regiment); pocket patch for Forward Operations Base I, Mai Loc (part of Command and Control North, "CCN").

OPERA NON VERBA

The Kingsmen's calling card, front and rear.

INTRODUCING "THE KINGSMEN" U.S. ARMY
17th Assault Helicopter Company

SPECIALTIES:	SIDE LINES:
Combat Assaults (Day & Night)	Worlds Greatest Pilot
	International Playboy
LRRP, Ins. & EXTR	War Monger
Emergency Ammo Resupply	Renowned Booze Hound
Flareship & Phyops	Social Lion
Emergency Medivacs	Ladies Man
VC, Extermination	
People Sniffer & Defoliation	

PROVIDING: Death and Destruction 24-Hrs. a Day. If You Care Enough To Send The Very Best, Send **KINGSMEN**

The "Castle," home sweet home?

A Huey's-eye view of a fire support base (FSB) in the 101st, 1968. Writing visible in the upper left-hand corner of the windshield is a tally of flight time, passengers, and cargo.

CW2 Surfer Lou Pulver as
short-timer. Photo courtesy of
Jim Thompson.

Carl Heinze (left) and Jim
Thompson. Photo courtesy of
Jim Thompson.

Rod Heim with his "Somthin
Cool" helmet.

The author chilling out
between flights with his
"cherry" flight helmet.

"Wild Bill" Meacham, Da Nang, August 1968.

"Sir James" Thompson eating LR[ ] steak on the Acid Pad in February 1969.

(From left) the author, Bill Meacham, and Jim Thompson, survivors celebrating New Year's Eve, 1970, in Ozark, Alabama. Photos B and C courtesy Jim Thompson.

Wilson, Poley's crew chief, spotted about twenty NVA along a trail in the vicinity of Fire Support Base Brick. Dave had inserted Ray Zoschak's team in the area on the third. Zo had Barry Golden, Ken Munoz, Mike Reiff, and Gary Linderer out with him. Due to the teams' being rearranged, they had gone in one man short. The team had been trail watching and had not had any activity. The NVA Wilson had seen appeared to be heading in the direction of the team. F Company's commander, Captain Eklund, decided to extend the three-day mission and resupply the team with food, dry socks, and more radio batteries. Normally, the risk of compromising the team with resupply would not have been taken, but its batteries wouldn't last more than another day. The team would have gladly gone hungry rather than blow the mission by compromising its location with a resupply. These were men who wouldn't allow a little thing like hunger to keep them from doing damage to the enemy. We flew out as a flight of two, but I stayed well clear as Poley went in for the drop-off; a single Huey wouldn't attract as much attention from Chuck. Dave had trouble finding the team, but finally managed to drop the resupply.

After having established a new patrol base on the sixth, Zoschak's team began reporting many gooks using the trail. They were not carrying rucks, which indicated a base near by, and many moved as though they had a purpose in mind. Some of the hardest times flying long-range patrols was having a team in close proximity of the bad guys with no actual contact. Once the stuff hit the fan, we had something to accomplish, but reported movement just left us on standby, with nerves on edge. When I'd get nervous, I would start thinking about what it must be like for a team, hiding in the bushes, just feet from the enemy, wondering if the pilots will be dumb enough to come get them this time. That particular neighborhood was really turning bad and would get worse.

LOSER

Monday, 7 October (164 days to go). A quiet but significant day of flying LRPs. We flew a few VRs with no contact. Zo's team continued to report beaucoup movement. After spending the rest of the afternoon on standby for the teams in the field, I was tired and anxious to get back to the Castle, have dinner, and get some sleep. Sergeant First Class Burnell came down to the pad as we were getting ready to go and asked if we could wait a few minutes to take someone back with us. I was disappointed to have to fly another sortie, but I wasn't about to turn down anything that Uncle Burnie asked of me. I walked over to Poley's aircraft and told him to go ahead and return to the Castle. I would fly the passenger and follow up later. I returned to Burnell and asked, "This guy going to Phu Bai to catch a flight?"

"No, he's gong with you."

"I don't understand."

"He's assigned to the Kingsmen, sir."

Burnell went on to explain that this guy was a Canadian citizen who joined the American Army to fight in Vietnam.

"Hasn't he got it backwards?" I asked.

Burnell laughed and told me that the man had been with a recon platoon down south and had been injured in a jeep accident. While he was in the hospital, the army had offered to send him home and discharge him. Since he wasn't an American and not really obligated to serve in the army, they would release him from his enlistment. He had declined and asked to be assigned to a long-range patrol unit. Since he was jump qualified, they sent him to the 101st. But a week of training taught him that six-man patrols deep into Indian country were not his cup of tea. There was no room on recon teams for anyone who had doubts. When he was asked where he wanted to go, he said he wanted to be a door gunner. The kid just kept volunteering for things that would get him shot at. While we helped the guy load his belongings on the Huey, he looked up toward the engine and asked, "If you fly these things over ten thousand feet do you have to adjust the carburetors?"

The entire crew had all we could do to keep from rolling on the ground laughing, while I explained that turbine engines did not have carburetors. This one was going to be fun to have around.

Gossip travels very quickly in a military unit. To this day I believe that the carburetor story spread throughout the Kingsmen while we were still hovering into the revetment. That evening, Captain Senita had a pilots' meeting for the platoon. Several problems were discussed and resolved. And as the last order of business Senita made an announcement.

"We have a new gunner in the platoon."

Snickers traveled through all the pilots.

"Now settle down . . . Who wants him?"

Guffaws that time. Everyone looked at one another, waiting

to see which fool would take the new gunner. Finally, I slowly raised my hand.

"I'll take him, sir."

"You got him, Grant."

More laughter.

"I would like to know why you volunteered to take the carburetor kid, though?"

"Well, sir, the way I see it, I'm the last one to be made an AC here, and I have no assigned gunner. So, I figure that you're going to give him to me anyway."

Not much time passed before it was apparent that this guy would not just peacefully blend into the crew of 348. Where Juan Sablan was quiet and made you wonder about him, this guy was bubbling and left no doubts. The name Carburetor Kid went away quickly; his nickname became Loser. He was the type of guy that things happened to. To inspect the tail rotor we would stand on the stinger, a metal pipe that stuck out of the end of the tail boom to prevent the tail rotor's striking the ground in tail-low attitudes during landing. Scraping it on the ground was cause for the offending pilot to buy the crew chief a case of beer. Many times, on wet mornings, someone would slip and fall off a wet stinger. Most fell left or right. Not Loser. He always fell straddling the stinger. Most often at the expense of the family jewels. Nobody in the unit fell off the top of the Huey more than Loser did. But he was a fast learner. Within a week, he had learned so much from Sugar Bear that he could conduct a twenty-five-hour inspection on a Huey by himself. A couple trips out over the ocean for gunnery training proved that Loser was a natural door gunner. We would toss out ammo boxes and let the gunners go to town on them. Loser showed quickly that the knowledge of the machine gun he had picked up as an infantryman was coupled with an inborn instinct for leading targets to account for the speed of the bird.

In spite of all misfortunes on the ground, Loser proved a valuable asset under fire. His energy complimented the laid-back Sugar Bear. While, alone, neither of them rated as the best in the platoon, as a team, I was blessed with one of the very best crews.

The next morning at crank time, Poley repositioned to the Acid pad, and I took 348 out over the ocean to start training my new gunner. If a hot extraction came up, we would meet them en route. There was no time to leisurely train crews up to mission standards. A gunner with a warm body had best get familiar with his 60 in a hurry. After the first session, I had no doubts that Loser could manage to cover the aircraft during a hot mission.

We landed at the Acid pad and shut down. When the rotor had stopped, Sugar Bear gave Loser a lesson in tying down the rotor system. Each rotor blade has a tab at the end with a quarter-inch hole in it. To prevent the rotor's flopping around when the engine wasn't running, a metal rod with a hook shape is inserted in the hole. The tie-down has two nylon straps that hang from the rod. At the end of the straps are two leather bags filled with lead shot. Then the tie-down straps are wrapped around the tail boom and the stinger and the weights hang and hold the straps in place. Sugar Bear showed Loser how to hook the blade and toss the weights over the tail boom and wrap them around the stinger. Bear then untied the blade to let Loser try it. He hooked the blade and tossed the weights over the tail boom. The weights promptly swung around under the boom and hit him in the nuts. It was to become a routine sight for anyone flying on 348.

One time, while we were flying a combat assault, we landed on a road that ran between rice paddies to pick up troops. The road was built up about three feet above the water level in the paddies. We were there to move a company of infantry from the lowlands, just south of FSB Anzio, back into the mountains. The radio informed us that there was a delay of about ten minutes in the LZ prep. I rolled the throttle back to flight idle while we waited. As soon as the engine RPM decreased, Loser piped up from the gunner's well. "Sir, do I have time to take a piss?"

"Yeah, go ahead."

"Thanks, sir. Stepping right." That told us he was getting out of the aircraft on the right side. After several minutes, I began to wonder why he hadn't checked back in. I told the peter pilot to look out on that side and see what he was doing. When he complied, he burst out laughing.

"W. T., you gotta unbuckle and see this for yourself."

I unfastened my seat belt and shoulder harness and leaned over the radio pedestal. When he came into view, he was waist-deep in the rice paddy and was being dragged out of the mud by two grunts. As he was freed, I sat back and quickly buckled in, trying to keep a straight face when a wet and muddy gunner reported, "Back with you on the right, sir."

Nobody said anything. We were too busy trying to suppress our laughter.

8 October (162 days to go). Zoschak's team came out without contact. Poley made the extraction, with me flying chase.

That night, Karl Heinz and Sir James Thompson were tending bar in the club. There were several of us that took turns running the bar. One of the new lieutenants came up and said to Jim in a snotty tone, "Gimme a beer."

Jim looked over at Karl, "He wants a beer," Jim said, with his eyebrows raised.

"He vants a beer, jah?"

"Jah, he vants a beer!"

Karl opened the fridge and took out a Budweiser. "Iss diss da beer he vants?"

"Jah, das iss da beer he vants," Jim said as Karl vigorously shook the can. Karl then tossed the can to Jim.

"Here iss your beer, Herr Lieutenant." Jim slapped the beer down and pulled the zip top at the same time. Beer sprayed everywhere. When the can finished spewing, there were only a few drops left in the can. The lieutenant calmly drank what was left and politely said, "May I have another beer? . . . Please?"

On the ninth, I was woken up by the CQ early for an emergency ammo resupply. I was scheduled to be off that day. For missions like that, rather than interfere with a scheduled mission, they grabbed someone who had the day off. I went off and flew the mission. The situation was cold by the time I got there. I hauled the ammo and returned to the Castle. When I got back to the hootch, Lieutenant Dipstick was sitting in my lawn chair, waiting to chew me out for not making my bed before I left! I'd been dragged out of bed to fly and the asshole wanted to ream me out for not making my bed. On top of that, he was violating the rules by sitting in my lawn chair. We should have let The Dave shoot him.

Friday, 11 October (159 days to go). It had been raining heavily on and off. There was a thick overcast hanging along the mountaintops. The weather was dreary and damp. Standby was uncomfortable, so when Gordon "Snuffy" Smith's team reported movement, it was almost a welcome relief. We sat around the radio in the TOC waiting for something to happen. It didn't take long; the team was in contact and on the run. So were the flight crews. On the way to the vicinity of Leech Island, we knew that the pickup would have to be by McGuire rigs. There was no place to land along the ridgeline. The team had outdistanced the pursuing enemy, and the extraction was accomplished with only a minimum of getting shot at. When the guns placed a few rockets on the ridge, the bad guys lost interest in the team. The worst part of the operation was the flight back to Eagle. The cool temperatures and the wind took a terrible toll on the wet LRPs hanging below the Hueys. Hypothermia was not far off by the time the soggy LRPs set foot back on the Acid pad. But the shivering smiles on the faces of Snuffy Smith and Sandman Saenz told me that they would rather have the chills than have been left where they were.

Sunday, 13 October (157 days to go). The changing weather patterns had made themselves more evident. The monsoons were coming. Honest John Burford's team had been in the field since the ninth. It had rained almost every day, and the ceiling was rising and falling. The cloud levels varied from fifty feet to three thousand. Often, the changes came on fast. When the rains came down, they came down harder than I had ever seen before, even in the thunderstorms in Texas and Alabama. It was dangerous flying weather. The radio replay had lost contact with Burford on the afternoon of the twelfth, and the team was due to be extracted on Sunday morning. We tried to get to the planned PZ. The pickup point was on the same ridgeline as Nui Khe, on the western side above the Khe Dai River valley. The ridge remained covered in clouds for the entire day. We circled for as long as the weather allowed, attempting to make contact with the team. There was no response. Eklund repeatedly made calls in the blind, telling the team to move to the alternate pickup point. Finally the weather closed in, and we had to return to Camp Eagle.

When I got back to my hootch, a letter from Jackie was waiting for me. But instead of being the usual bright spot in my day, the letter only made my mood worse. She wrote that her boss had been hitting on her. She also told me the guy that we had known in high school had been around again, just "to see how she was doing." It was just what I needed to put me in a really ugly frame of mind.

That night, I sat alone in the corner of the club, listening to the rain pounding on the roof. I sat with my chair tilted against the wall and my right foot propped on the chair next to me. My right forearm was draped across the right knee, and in its hand was the familiar red and white can with blue lettering. The can was about half full. Two matching empty cans stood guard on the table in front of me. I was worried about my LRP friends. A cloud was hanging over me, darker than the ones that poured rain down on the roof. I had been nursing the last beer for about forty minutes. I would swirl the can around and take a small sip from the spinning beer. The arm would then return to its perch on my knee. The left hand slid another Marlboro from the battered pack that kept the empty cans company on the table. The ashtray was filling up. I'd been chain-smoking as I sat there contemplating lost friends and wondering if John Burford was about to join the list. Up till then, I had not been directly involved when I had lost someone over there. I had inserted John's team, and I should be the one to extract them. The procedure was for them to move to the alternate LZ if they did not make the primary pickup. The alternate LZ was in the valley, near the river, so we'd have a better chance of getting to them. Assuming that the enemy wasn't the cause of the lost commo. If we didn't make contact the next day, we wouldn't even know where to look for them. I was depressed about not being able to do anything but wait. It must have showed because nobody bothered to even ask if my cherry had been busted.

Then Gene Gillenwater walked in. He pulled out a chair, turned it around, and sat on it backwards. "Well, W. T., drinking alone now, I see."

I looked around the table, surveying the obvious, and replied with a smirk, "Apparently so."

"I'm serious, Bill. I'm worried about you. You've been drinking an awful lot lately."

I took a drag on the cigarette, swirled the beer again and took a sip. "Ain't near enough. Ain't numb yet."

"Look, you dumb shit, I'm trying to tell you that I'm worried that you're becoming an alcoholic."

I tried one of Meacham's lines. "I'm not an alcoholic. Alcoholics go to meetings." I punctuated the remark with a big grin. At least Gene had made me forget about being depressed.

"Stop screwing around; I'm really worried about you."

I could see that Gene wouldn't be happy till I got as serious as he was. I put the foot down and turned to face him with my elbows on the table. "Gene, my mother died from booze. I fully understand your concern. There was a time when I swore that I'd never take a drink. I also once swore I'd never smoke. It seems that 'never' comes early in the Nam. Right now, I see drinking as a good way to unwind from what we do for a living. If you look around you, you'll see I'm not alone in that thought. I figure the odds of any of us having our bad habits cured by lead poisoning are pretty high. But I am not self-destructive, and I drink because I want to, not because I have to." I fired off on him pretty hard without really meaning to.

"All right, W. T., but if I catch you having a beer for breakfast, I'm gonna kick your ass."

"Then I'll make damn sure you don't catch me." I grinned at him.

Gene shook his head, got up, turned the chair around, and slid it under the table. He started to leave. I glugged down the rest of my beer and said, "Hey, wait up, I think I'm gonna hit the sack."

I crushed out my cigarette and retrieved my hat from the shelf in the corner. I caught up to Gene just outside the door. As we started to walk back to the hootch, I said, "Hey, thanks for caring . . . you asshole."

I slapped him across the back of his head with my hat, and took off running. He chased me all the way back to the tent.

Monday, 14 October (156 days to go). I woke up and saw that it was quite dark. I squinted at my watch and made out that it was just 0500. It would be another half hour till the CQ came by with the morning wake-up. I could hear the gentle pattering of rain on the canvas above me. Shit. The weather was still going to be bad. I sat up and began to dress as quietly as I could. I knew that I wasn't going to get any more sleep just then, but I didn't want to wake anyone else before they needed to be up. I shut off my fan. The breeze was cold in the damp morning air. I slid a T-shirt over my head and fumbled with lacing my boots in the dark. I left my fatigue shirt and hat sitting on my bunk and went out on the "back porch." The rain was a fine mist that came down steadily. I stepped out into it and looked up, trying to see how low the clouds were. It was still too dark to tell. My shirt and hair were quickly wet, it was coming down harder than it appeared. The cool water ran down my face as I walked over to operations.

Operations was already alive with activity. The bright lights hurt my eyes. With the help of two operations clerks, Rick Haines was busily preparing for the day's flying.

"What's the real deal, blood?"

Rick looked up at my wet hair and said with a nasal twang, "Where is your hat and shirt, Mr. Grant?"

"Fuck you, lifer pig! What's the weather like?"

"Same shit as yesterday only worse. Asshole."

"Well thanks a lot. Dipshit." I smiled as I turned to leave.

Rick got serious. "I heard you got a team outta radio contact."

"Yeah. Today's our last chance to get 'em out."

"Who is it?"

"Burford," I said over my shoulder as I stepped through the flap into the rain again.

I was sitting on my bed, finishing the last of the peaches from the ham-and-eggs C-ration meal, when Rod Heim came in the hootch. It was light enough by then to tell that the cloud layer was at about fifty feet. I pointed to my lawn chair and Rod sat down. He was flying my wing that day. I told him about the teams that were out and Burford's situation. I finished the peaches as I talked, and decided to eat the pound cake later. I finished a second container of milk. They actually had real milk at the mess hall that morning. I had gone by to get that and some coffee to have with the Cs.

"I plan to reposition to the Acid pad. When it warms up later in the morning, maybe the ceiling will lift some, and we can make an attempt to find Burford."

"Sounds like a plan. When do we do it?"

I looked down at my watch. It was just six. I could feel the bags under my eyes, and my shoulders felt heavy. "No point in rushing; we're not goin' anywhere for a while. Six-fifty crank, commo at five-five, we'll get down at the Acid pad on the hour."

"OOOOOOOOkay, fine." Rod stood and left.

I sat for a moment, sipped some more of the coffee and made a face, sticking out my tongue. Leaning over, I pulled up the side of the tent and dumped the coffee out. First Sergeant Walker had much better coffee in the LRP TOC. I stood, stretched, dropped the chicken-plate vest over my head, and fastened the Velcro straps around the front. I put a pack of cigarettes and my Zippo in the pouch in the front. As the lighter went in, I checked for my notebook, reassuring myself that it was where it belonged. I put on my hat and grabbed my flight helmet. Staring at the .38 hanging in my wall locker, I made a mental note to clean and oil it soon, in case someone checked.

I closed the locker, put the lock in place, and set out for operations. Just another day at the war.

As I sat, strapped in the aircraft, I checked my watch for the fourth time. I had been ready to for the last ten minutes. At 0650, I slapped the battery to the "on" position and pulled the starter trigger. As the engine sprang to life, I could see the rotor starting to turn on Heim's bird in the 2d Platoon area. When the Huey whined its way to operating RPM, I checked the instruments. Everything was in the green, so I pulled the mike trigger on the top front of the cyclic. "Kingsmen Two-Nine, One-Eight. Commo check on Victor."

"Lima Charlie. How me?"

I double clicked the mike trigger and reached down and changed the radio transmitter selector to the number two position.

"Two-Nine, One-Eight, Uniform."

"Lima Charlie. Me?"

I double clicked again and moved the selector to "1." I pulled the trigger again, this time waiting for a second to allow the FM radio to cycle up.

"How Fox Mike?"

"Same same, GI. How me?"

"Lima Charlie. Going tower."

The Teenybopper was in the right seat, and when I looked over, he was already turning the VHF radio to 126.3. Next I heard him say, "You're up three." That meant he had also moved the selector back to the number three position.

"Eagle Tower, Kingsmen One-Eight."

"Kingsmen One-Eight, this is Eagle Tower. Go ahead."

"One-Eight is a flight of two. Castle for reposition to Acid pad."

"Kingsmen One-Eight, Eagle Tower. Eagle is IFR at this time, reposition will be at pilot's discretion."

Translation: The weather is too shitty to fly; if you screw up and crash it's your fault, not mine.

He continued, "Current weather is ceiling less than one hundred feet. Visibility one-half mile with light rain. Winds are light and variable. Altimeter is two niner eight three. There is no other reported traffic." The last part meant, You're the only one stupid enough to be flying in this weather.

The two Hueys did a high hover just outside the perimeter around the west side of the encampment till we reached the LRP area and landed on the Acid pad. By the time the rotors came to a stop, it was pouring again. I called Rod on the Fox Mike and offered to make the hike up the hill alone.

"No way, man. You're not gettin' all that coffee to yourself."

I said to my crew, "I know the coffee here is good, but I don't know if it's good enough to swim upstream for." I jerked my head toward the hill we had to climb to get to the TOC. They all figured that they could wait for coffee till the rain let up some.

Heim and I both looked like drowned rats when we stepped into the TOC. One look at Captain Eklund and First Sergeant Walker told me what I wanted to know. The relay team still hadn't made contact. I tapped the coffee pot. The hot liquid filled the cup as Eklund asked, "What's the weather supposed to do?"

"More of the same, I guess. I figure the ceiling may raise a little as the day warms up."

"It's not going to break?"

"You see my face turning blue, sir?"

As he walked away, he mumbled, "Don't need it; can't use it in my business." A line he used often, and was often quoted by those around him.

About 1030, the sky started to brighten almost imperceptibly. It was still drizzling on and off. Rod and I stood at the top of the hill, looking at clouds that had lifted to about two hundred feet. I turned to Rod and he nodded. I shrugged in response and we went to go find Eklund.

In less than ten minutes, we cranked, and I once again called for departure. "Eagle Tower, this Kingsmen One-Eight. Flight of two Acid pad for departure westbound."

"Roger One-Eight. Eagle is IFR, departure will be at pilot's discretion. Eagle weather is estimated two hundred feet, overcast, with one mile visibility. No other reported traffic. You are cleared for takeoff at pilot's discretion."

The plan was to take out the two slicks and try to make radio contact with the team. The gunships would remain at Eagle unless we needed them. We flew west till we intersected the Perfume River. Upon meeting the river, the flight turned south in search of Highway 547. Where the river met the road, it branched to the west and south. The road followed the western branch toward FSB Birmingham. About two miles east of Birmingham, the river was joined by a tributary from the south. It was about five klicks up that tributary that the alternate PZ was located. As we joined the road, Eklund began calling from the back of my aircraft.

"Linwood Teams One-Nine, this is Linwood Teams Six. Over."

Silence was the only response.

"Linwood Teams One-Nine, this is Linwood Teams Six. Over."

Silence.

It continued that way for over an hour. Two Hueys pounding the air between the junction of the rivers and the road. Eklund would call every few minutes.

"Linwood Teams One-Nine, this is Linwood Teams Six. Over."

In frustration I finally tried from the front.

"Linwood Teams One-Nine, this is Kingsmen One-Eight. Over."

Silence. I knew that only possibility of my success was that the selector Eklund was using in the back wasn't operating. We could tell by the tone of the transmission that Eklund's message was getting out, but I was desperate enough to try anything. The longer we flew, the harder it rained. Visibility was down to about a quarter of a mile again. The clouds had pushed us to under a hundred feet. I finally told Captain Eklund that we had less than an hour's fuel remaining.

"Well, W. T., have you got any suggestions?"

I hesitated a moment not liking the options. "Sir, the weather's coming down again. The way I see it, we only have two options. One is we pack it in and go home. The other is go hovering up that river and maybe get our ass shot off."

"You wanna go up the river?"

"No, sir! But, if we go back, we might as well write off the team, and you can get started writing six letters."

"Will you go up the river?"

"Yes, sir!"

"Let's do it."

"I'm gonna have Two-Nine wait at Birmingham. No point in having two sitting ducks out there."

Anticipating my next move, Roach said, "You're up two." He was getting better all the time. He was always thinking ahead. He was going make a fine AC when his turn came.

"Two-Nine, One-Eight, Uniform."

"Go."

"Two-Nine, go to Birmingham, set down, and wait at flight

idle. We are going to head up the river and see if we can get to the PZ or locate the team."

"Negative, One-Eight. That's crazy. You'll have no room to maneuver if you come under fire."

"Two-nine, it's that or write off the team."

"At least let me follow to cover your ass."

"There won't be room for both of us to maneuver once the valley narrows down." I knew that after about a klick or two, the steep walls left the river only about twenty yards wide in some places. The mountains rose steeply on both sides. There were a few spots where the ground was flat on one side or the other, extending a couple of hundred meters or so. Those would be the only spots we would be able to turn around to come out again unless we came to a hover.

"Two-Nine, roger. Out." The conversation was over. I could tell from his tone that Rod was pissed at me for keeping him out of it. I guess I would have been if the situation were reversed. He knew as well as I did that this was the only way.

I turned south, and Rod turned toward Birmingham. I keyed the mike. "If I ain't out in thirty minutes, come pick me up, will ya?"

"If you ain't out in thirty minutes, I'm going back to Eagle to get your stereo." I laughed. I knew he wouldn't be pissed for long.

The valley quickly narrowed down. The rain pounding on the windshields made it near impossible to see. Larry Patterson was my crew chief that day. I told him and Loser to lean out and keep an eye out in front so I didn't run into anything. They both leaned out the doors looking forward and giving me clearance information. I slowed the airspeed to less than forty knots. It felt as though we were flying into a tunnel. The clouds were just above us, the mountains on either side, and the river below. The vegetation was such a bright green from all the rain that it seemed to glow. The shine of the wet leaves added to the illusion of luminescence. This part of the AO was much greener than the areas in the western parts. The defoliation efforts had been concentrated in areas out towards the A Shau.

I could barely see where I was going. As the river banks moved closer, I came to the realization that one little gook with a good slingshot could eat our lunch. I tried to concentrate on the team. I had a friend out there in the jungle, and I was going on the premise that he and his team were still alive. If they were still alive, they would be heading for the spot on the map that was my destination. I slowed the helicopter even more. The slap of the rotor blades resounding off the surrounding hillsides seemed to be calling to every NVA within a hundred miles. *Wop* . . . *Wop* . . . *Wop* . . . Easy . . . *Wop* . . . Target . . . *Wop* . . . *Wop*.

I could feel my ass trying to suck up 147 pounds of armor seat, as I waited for the staccato sound of the Huey taking the hits that I knew would come at any moment. Eklund and Roach both were desperately following along on their maps. The reduced visibility and the low clouds made reading the terrain next to impossible. Finally Roach said, "I think we've gone too far."

Eklund agreed, "Yeah, he's right. We're about five hundred meters too far south."

I brought the bird to a hover and turned back. Eklund got on the radio again. "Linwood Teams One-Nine, this is Linwood Teams Six. Over."

Silence. The rain suddenly let up.

Roach announced, "Think that's the area over there." He pointed to the low ground on our right. Eklund agreed. We were almost by it. I stopped and turned again. Eklund began calling, still there was no response. I started moving toward where the LZ should be. The terrain began to look like what I saw during the overflights.

"Is this a good idea?" Eklund asked.

"No." My terse response.

"Then why are we doing it?"

" 'Cause we're stupid and like to shit in our pants."

"Well, maybe we can kill a few of them before they blow our ass out of the sky."

"At least we don't have far to fall."

That's when the tracer went by. *"Holy shit, they found us."* I was just about to key the mike and tell the gunners to cut loose when I saw the movement. Something made me hesitate. Then I made it out. The movement was a tiger stripe bush hat with a painted face under it. It was a LRP. "Hold your fire; it's the team."

We found a spot that we could almost set down. It was full of logs, and there was a dead snag of a tree sticking up at one end. The only way to get in the LZ was to put the tail boom between a bush and the dead tree. Only a couple of feet clearance was available for the tail rotor. The wind had started to gust, and with people climbing on the skids of the hovering Huey, it would be hard to control. I reminded Patterson and Loser to keep a careful eye on the tail rotor. While the main rotor was more than capable of chopping down sizable tree limbs in the right circumstances, just the slightest wrong touch could tear the tail rotor from its mount. That would send us spinning into the ground, and Heim would get my stereo. Eklund started to hang out the door, trying to help the crew clear the aircraft.

Loser announced, "We got 'em all sir you are clear up on the right."

"Clear up left," came from Patterson.

I started to lift out of the LZ. We had to go to our left because of the hill on the right. Just as we were almost clear of the trees, with the left antitorque pedal against the stop, the low RPM audio sounded. I did not need to look at the instrument panel to know that the engine had bled off. I reduced left pedal to ease the demand of power, at the same time jamming my thumb against the RPM increase switch. I forced the aircraft to come around to the left with the cyclic. As soon as the bird cleared the last tree, I lowered the collective to allow the RPM to build back up, and lowered the nose to gain airspeed. The Huey dropped toward the ground like a brick, but almost instantly had flying speed and leveled off. The airspeed had already hit sixty by the time we were back over the river. With the rain stopped for the moment and my adrenaline pumping me to get out of there, the flight back to Birmingham was much faster than the flight to the LZ.

I looked over my right shoulder and saw John Burford sitting in the right doorway. As the TL, he would have been the last to get on the aircraft. He gave me a big smile. The smile was laden with the relief he must have felt. For whatever reason, there had been no commo with the team. The weather was for shit. He had no reason to expect that we would show up at the PZ, other than that was the alternate pickup point. I looked back to the front, and it slowly dawned on me that when I had looked at John, there was something wrong with his face. I looked back, and he was still beaming at me. His right eye was bright red with blood. I thought he must have run into a branch in the jungle.

I keyed the mike on the UHF frequency. "Two-Nine, One-Eight. We are on the way out."

"It's about damn time, W. T."

I realized then it must have been harder on Rod sitting at Birmingham waiting than it was on me being scared to death. He had no way of knowing from minute to minute whether we were ever coming out again. "Two-Nine, we have the team, they are okay."

"Great, let's go home before the weather gets worse again."

He joined back on us as we made the turn eastbound. The guy in charge of the spigot must have heard Rod's words. It started raining as hard as it had earlier. The flight back tracked the route flown on the way out. We set down on the pad, and the LRPs were out and heading up the hill. There were too many questions in my head to wait. I told Roach to shut the aircraft down and jumped out and ran after Honest John.

"What the hell happened out there? We thought the gooks got you."

No one had actually wanted to say that before. Now that I knew it wasn't true, it came out easily.

"Both radios crapped out. Guess the rain got to them."

"What happened to your eye?"

"Got a leech in it. Is it bad?"

"Looks like shit."

"Thanks a lot, son."

I looked him in the eyes. I could feel the emotions welling up inside. He stared back at me. "I'm glad you made it back."

"I'm glad you came and got me."

We put our arms around each other in the clumsy kind of hug men give each other when they don't want to do that, but can't find another way to express their feelings.

In the debriefing, we got the whole story. Once the team had lost commo, they never even attempted to get to the primary LZ. They knew that the ridgeline would be socked in. They moved to the secondary LZ because we would look for them there the next day. When the leech got in John's eye, they tried everything they knew to persuade it to let go. They blew smoke on it. Kenn Miller tried to pry its hooks loose with his K-bar. He had been partially successful, but each time he got one or two of the hooks loose, the leech would reattach them while he worked on the others. The final persuasion was when they put bug juice in his eye. The insect repellent was not meant to be used in the eyes. The doctor later said that Kenn should become a surgeon because of the way he worked on the leech with that big knife without doing any damage to the eye.

THE DAVE GOES HOME?

The Dave was getting short. He was due to go home. He had applied for an extension to fly Cobras and was turned down. The primary reason was that they had no Cobras for him to fly yet. He finally applied for an extension to stay with the Kingsmen, and that was turned down. It seemed that the army wanted him to go home and was not going to consider any other option.

The day came for David Allen Poley to go south to Bien Hoa and out-process. I watched as he opened his wall locker and took out a small AWOL bag, putting in his shaving kit and a couple of changes of underwear. He smiled at me and said, "I'll be back."

I thought, Oh sure, you will.

I knew that no one in his right mind would not go home when he had the opportunity. I never thought of the fact that I never had considered The Dave to be in his right mind.

Poley went to Phu Bai and caught the C-130 south. When he got to Bien Hoa, he out-processed from the division and went to Tan Son Nhut Air Base. He waited with the others for his freedom bird to arrive. When it did, Dave Poley stood in line with the others to board. As Dave reached the gate he stepped aside and watched as the plane took off for the world. After it was gone, he hopped the C-130 back to Phu Bai and came back to Camp Eagle.

The entire U.S. Army went wild. There were, after all, those that extended, but it seemed that no one in the history of the 101st Airborne Division had ever refused to go home. He had to go to division headquarters to explain himself. The army wasn't satisfied until he had actually worked his way up to the chief of staff of the division. Only then was his extension approved.

Six-month extensions were not uncommon. Some extended because they had fallen in love with war. That happens to some in every war. Some extended because they knew how chickenshit Stateside duty could be, and nobody really messed with you in Nam. Besides, if you were there, they couldn't threaten to send you there. Some extended to have their active duty commitment shortened. Lifers extended because an eighteen-month tour might get you out of your next tour, saving six months of time being shot at. I think The Dave stayed just because nobody stayed without a reason, so The Dave did.

One day, I was walking around the LRP area while on standby, and I came upon Ray Zoschak sitting on the steps of his hootch. He had a sharpening stone and his K-bar. Time and again, he methodically drew the blade across the stone. It was a familiar sight, Ray spent many hours honing a razor edge on the knife.

I smiled at him. "Whacha doin', Ray?"

"Makin' a stiletto, sir."

It was his standard answer.

"Ray, you know, all you're doin' is wearing out that knife."

"Sir, I want it good and sharp in case I ever get to cut a throat with it."

"Yeah, but mine is just as sharp, and I don't spend my life sharpening it."

"But mine is sharp enough to shave with."

"So is mine."

"Bullshit, sir."

"Bullshit yourself, sergeant."

"Well we'll see about that."

He hopped up and disappeared into his hootch. In a moment, he came back with a wide grin and a can of shaving cream. It cost me a couple of nicks, but I made my point.

16 October (155 days to go). The weather broke. The sun was shining, and it was to be a quiet day at the Acid pad. There were a couple of VRs to do, and some of the LRPs were going to get a day off and a flight to Coca Beach. The only odd thing was that Ken Eklund sent Lt. O. D. Williams on the VRs and took the flight to the beach himself. I had drawn the recons, and Horace Pearce had drawn the beach flight. I didn't much mind; since I had become a LRP pilot, I wasn't about to lose a good day of hunting to something as menial as farting around at the beach.

The flight went smoothly. We checked out some future LZs and even spent some time trying to find a gook stupid enough to shoot at a lone Huey that had instant artillery on call. We were not successful in that endeavor. O. D. quickly became bored with the game and asked us to head back to the Acid pad. When we got on final, I noticed that Pearce's bird was still on the pad. Closer inspection revealed that the Huey was lying on its side, without rotor blades, almost upside down. I landed 348 as far from the wreckage as the pad would allow.

Apparently the aircraft had started to depart for the beach, but Pearce had been in the left seat and Eklund in the pilot's seat on the right. As the helicopter lifted to a hover, it suddenly rolled over on its side. (Something told me that there was going to be a problem for someone over that mess, especially with Eklund sitting in the pilot's seat.) At least everyone had gotten out without any serious injuries. The aircraft was 650, the same piece of shit I had been writing up for a month because of its binding controls.

Since there were no teams in the field at the time, we finished up early. It was a welcome respite to arrive at the Castle in mid-afternoon for a change. We had invited Specialist First Class Brubaker and Specialist First Class Burnell to come over to the club to show off that night.

The club was good and rowdy that night. Everyone was unwinding, glad not to have been part of the accident. We were all worried about Pearce, afraid that they were to going to stick him for allowing Eklund in a pilot's seat. I was just relieved that 650 had come apart close to the ground and not killed anyone. I was celebrating my vindication; I'd received a lot of funny looks from some of the other Kingsmen when I had refused to fly it anymore.

Burnell and Brubaker were demonstrating a cute little game they liked to play. The two sat on chairs close together. Then they put their forearms together so that the arms had the fists even with each other's elbow. This gave a good line of contact between the arms, so there were no air gaps. Then a lit cigarette was dropped so that it rested between the arms touching both. The first one to move was a Leg! The game didn't last long, since the only ones who would play were Burnell and Brubaker. They were disappointed. Normally at the NCO club they could get one or two takers; none of the Kingsmen were buying into that one.

That led Burnell to announce, "I am a human flamethrower."

Someone said, "A what?"

"A human flamethrower. I can spit flame the length of this club."

I knew better than to challenge Uncle Bernie when he started bragging. He always had a way of backing it up. It might be a cheap trick, but he would back up his bragging.

Ed Regan was the one to take the bait. "Bullshit."

It didn't take long for the bets to be placed, and Burnell to set up the conditions. I just sat at my table, out of the way. When Brubaker winked over at me, I knew that fish were being reeled in. Burnell asked for a can of lighter fluid, then had Regan stand near the front door as he himself moved to the bar. He had the lighter fluid in one hand and a Zippo in the other. He was stalling for the proper dramatic effect. He said to Ed, "Sir, please place your hat over your face so you don't get burned."

"Aw, bullshit, you can't spit fire this far. I doubt you can spit fire at all."

Ed flew LRP missions; he should have known Burnell better than that. Burnell insisted that Regan at least close his eyes to protect them. Reluctantly, Regan gave in. Burnell filled his mouth with lighter fluid, set the can on the bar, then turned, and breathed deeply through his nose. He lit the lighter then exhaled explosively. An enormous flame stretched from the lighter to Regan. The club fell silent. The flame had been a foot around and thirty feet long. It parted on both sides of Regan's head.

Ed opened his eyes and said, "See, I told you he couldn't do it!" Everyone burst out laughing 'cause Ed had no eyebrows, and his moustache was all singed.

Sometime during October, Col. Ted Crozier paid a personal visit to the Kingsmen club. The group commander's call sign was Wild Turkey. Rumor said that had something to do with a favored bourbon. I was behind the bar serving up everyone's favorite when someone hollered, *"Ten hut!"*

I strained to see who had come in. If one of our fellow Kingsmen was just screwing around, there would be hell to pay. The only one in the company that rated that kind of treatment was Major Addiss, and he never came in the club. A commanding voice bellowed, "Carry on, this is a social call."

By then I could see Colonel Crozier. As he headed toward the bar, the silence that embraced the club was as thick as molasses. We called him Teddy behind his back. He sat on a bar stool and asked, "Got any Wild Turkey?"

I smiled. "You bet, sir!"

"Then gimme a Bud and a shot, son."

A man after my own heart. "Comin' right up, sir."

As I set his order down in front of him, he leaned forward and in a quiet voice asked, "Is this a club or a morgue?"

Of course, he was aware that his presence was the cause of

the silence. I leaned forward, and in a conspiratorial voice said, "I can't understand it, sir. Only moments ago everyone was cussing and raising hell. Then, all of sudden, things got quiet. I've never seen anything like it."

He smiled. "I guess I'll just have to liven things up a bit. Does anyone sing around here?"

"Yes, sir, often and badly."

"Good. Do you know 'Blood Upon the Risers?' "

"Not all of it, sir."

"How about you, Roach?" He turned to Ken Roach who was sitting next to him.

"No, sir. I only know parts of it."

The club really got quiet when the colonel started singing to the tune of "The Battle Hymn of the Republic."

"You guys join in on the parts you know."

He was just a rookie trooper and he surely shook with fright
He checked all his equipment and made sure his pack was tight
He had to sit and listen to those awful engines roar
And he ain't gonna jump no more.

Ken Roach joined in on the first chorus.

Gory, gory, what a helluva way to die
Gory, gory, what a helluva way to die
Gory, gory, what a helluva way to die
And he ain't gonna jump no more.

Is everybody happy, cried the sergeant looking up
Our hero feebly answered yes and then they stood him up
He jumped into the icy blast, his static line unhooked
And he ain't gonna jump no more.

Some of the words started to come back to me from basic and flight school.

Gory, gory, what a helluva way to die
Gory, gory, what a helluva way to die
Gory, gory, what a helluva way to die
And he ain't gonna jump no more.

Sir James, who always was one for a good sing-along, came over and joined in.

He counted loud, he counted long, he waited for the shock
He felt the wind, he felt the clouds, he felt the awful drop
He jerked the cord, the chute spilled out
and wrapped around his legs
And he ain't gonna jump no more.

Gory, gory, what a helluva way to die
Gory, gory, what a helluva way to die
Gory, gory, what a helluva way to die
And he ain't gonna jump no more.

Slowly the natural fear of the group commander was being overcome, and more and more Kingsmen joined in the song. Karl Hienz, Ed Regan, and Lou Pulver became part of the choir.

His lines were twisted round his neck,
connectors cracked his dome
His risers tied themselves in knots around his skinny bones
His canopy became his shroud,
as he hurtled toward the ground
And he ain't gonna jump no more.

Gory, gory, what a helluva way to die
Gory, gory, what a helluva way to die
Gory, gory, what a helluva way to die
And he ain't gonna jump no more.

The club was always a good place to forget about the things we saw each day, and song was always an important part of that. Singing was common, and Colonel Crozier was not having a great deal of difficulty drawing those aviators in. No one even seemed to care that it was a paratroopers song.

The days he lived and laughed and loved
kept running through his mind
He thought about the girl back home, the one he'd left behind
He thought about the medics
and he wondered what they'd find
And he ain't gonna jump no more.

Gory, gory, what a helluva way to die
Gory, gory, what a helluva way to die

Gory, gory, what a helluva way to die
And he ain't gonna jump no more.

The ambulance was on the ground, and jeeps were running wild
The medics screamed and danced with glee,
rolled up their sleeves and smiled.
For it had been a week or more, since last a chute had failed
And he ain't gonna jump no more.

The plywood walls of the club were soon reverberating with the sounds of the song.

Gory, gory, what a helluva way to die
Gory, gory, what a helluva way to die
Gory, gory, what a helluva way to die
And he ain't gonna jump no more.

He hit the ground, the sound was splat,
the blood went spurting high
His comrades were heard to say, a helluva way to die
He lay there rolling round in the welter of his gore
And he ain't gonna jump no more.

Gory, gory, what a helluva way to die
Gory, gory, what a helluva way to die
Gory, gory, what a helluva way to die
And he ain't gonna jump no more.

Soon, so many guys were singing that you didn't even notice that many didn't know the words.

There was blood upon the risers,
there were brains upon the chute
Intestines were a'dangling from his paratrooper suit
They picked him up, still in his chute,
and poured him from his boots.
And he ain't gonna jump no more.

Gory, gory, what a helluva way to die
Gory, gory, what a helluva way to die
Gory, gory, what a helluva way to die
And he ain't gonna jump no more.

The chaplain brought his Bible when he came around
He said some words of comfort to that wet and sticky mound
Then they poured him in a bottle and sank him underground
And he ain't gonna jump no more.

Gory, gory, what a helluva way to die
Gory, gory, what a helluva way to die
Gory, gory, what a helluva way to die
And he ain't gonna jump no more.

Wild Turkey quickly turned that night into one of the more memorable sing-alongs of my tour. He was finally standing on a chair leading us in song when we got around to singing "Phu Bai Oh Phu Bai."

Phu Bai Oh Phu Bai
A helluva place
The organization a fucking disgrace
With captains and majors and light colonels too
Thumbs up their asses, with nothin' to do
They stand on the runway, they scream and they shout
About many things they know nothing about
For the good they are doing they might as well be
Shoveling shit in the South China Sea

Ring a ding a ding ding
Blow it out your ass
Better days are coming by and by
BULLSHIT!

On you'll wonder where the yellow went
When the Napalm hits the Orient
Nuke it, nuke it, nuke it
Yeah team!

As we got to the part about captains and majors, the door of the club opened, and Major Addiss walked in. Normally he never came into the club. He was probably planning to tell us that we should calm down and go to bed. But as his mouth opened to speak, no sound came out; he saw Colonel Crozier standing on his chair leading the song. The CO slowly shook his head, turned, and left, without saying a word.

* * *

Thursday, 17 October (153 days to go). I was assigned to fly with Lieutenant Dipstick. Dipstick was one of those Real Live Officers who had a hard time understanding why warrant officers were in charge in the aircraft. It wasn't that warrants were always in charge while flying, just when someone wanted the aircraft back in one piece.

Warrants were intended by the army to be the professional pilots. We were supposed to be more flight proficient than commissioned officers, and in most cases, we got more flight time. In Vietnam, there were guys like Meacham, who always wanted to be in the cockpit and were good aviators. Then there were guys like Dipstick, who were too busy accumulating additional duties so they could make general. Dipstick didn't spent a lot of time in the air. It showed.

I was the aircraft commander that day. Our first sortie was to FSB Anzio, to the south of Camp Eagle. Since Dipstick had almost three months in country, I thought it was time to see what he had learned and what he still needed to be taught.

I called Eagle Tower and got our takeoff clearance.

Then to Dipstick, "Harry, call and get us an arty clearance."

In order to keep helicopters and artillery rounds from meeting in midair, a pilot called a control center and was advised of arty missions being fired in that sector. The center also assisted the pilot in finding a safe route through the area, routing him around the fire or, sometimes, under the path of the rounds.

"What's the frequency?"

"You should know that by now. How do you expect to make AC if you don't even know the arty freqs?"

"Well, I forgot it."

That pissed me off. If he couldn't remember, he should have it written down somewhere. I took my memo book from the pocket on my chicken plate and threw it on the center pedestal. "The first three pages are frequencies. Page one is towers. Page two is medevac. Page three is arty."

I felt if I made him work at it a little he might remember the next time. I let the aircraft descend to low level over the highway, knowing that it should be a safe route. Unless of course, a fire mission was being fired onto Highway 1, which was very unlikely.

"I can't find it."

Nobody could be that stupid and live, he had to be an asshole on purpose. I was getting good and hot now.

"The fucking freq is 38.45, Lieutenant."

Going south, the controlling arty center was Anzio Control. If we were going west, it was Bastogne Control. Since we were going to FSB Anzio, I thought it was a pretty safe bet that we would want to talk Anzio Control. Of course he started up with—

"Bastogne Control. Bastogne Control. This is Kingsmen One-Eight."

Maybe he was brain dead. And he was using my call sign instead of the tail number of the aircraft. It was normal for the peter pilot to use the AC's call sign, but he was not supposed to be stupid when he did it.

"One-Eight, this is Anzio Control."

"Roger Bastogne Control. I would like . . . uh an artillery clearance from Eagle to uh . . . uh . . ."

I keyed the intercom, "Harry, I'll make the call."

We were almost there.

"One-Eight, you are on Anzio's push."

"Roger, Anzio. One-Eight is off Eagle, en route to Anzio along Highway 1. Over." My call was rapid-fire.

"Roger, One-Eight. You are clear, we have negative firing at Anzio at this time." His change in tone told me that he knew there was a different voice on the aircraft radio.

The flight continued much the same way. Everything I gave Dipstick to do he screwed up. Finally, I switched the selectors for mine and Dipstick's intercom boxes to private so the crew chief and gunner wouldn't hear me chew him out. Of course, Sugar Bear and Loser both switched to private when they saw me change the ones up front, but I had made the attempt.

Very calmly I said, "Harry, I want you to sit back in the seat and relax."

He did.

"Now take a deep breath and let it out." Again with a soft and soothing tone.

He complied.

"Now fold your arms."

He slowly folded his arms across his chest.

Then I screamed at him as loud as I could. "Now don't touch another fucking switch, button, or control in this fucking helicopter unless I specifically tell you to do so! Do you fucking understand me, Lieutenant?"

He slowly nodded. The rest of the day, over seven hours of flight time, I did all the flying, made all radio calls, tuned all the radios. Dipstick sat and did nothing. At the end of the day, I calmly filled out my aftermission report in operations, and as I handed it to Rick Haines, I gave him my best killer stare and said, "If you ever schedule me with that fucking moron again, I will shoot him and you both." I smiled and walked out of operations.

A short time later, Lieutenant Dipstick became my section leader. I suspected that flight was not going to be good for my next OER.

Saturday, 19 October (151 days to go). It was to be an easy day on the Acid pad. We had no teams out. All that was on the table for the day was some VRs. Captain Eklund assured us that he would stretch out the flying so that both aircraft would get some flight time and be kept busy late enough to keep us from being tapped for other missions. It was nice that we might actually be able to look forward to a fairly easy day.

Dave Poley flew the morning flights. That afternoon, with Ken Eklund on board, we headed off looking for trouble. I was flying 345, Larry Patterson's bird. Loser was along as gunner. We reconned some possible LZs, but for the most part, we were just looking for trouble. After the real work was done, we headed south to a no-fly, no-fire area that was rumored to be the location of the summer palace of the emperor of Vietnam many years ago. Some said that it was an old French resort area. Others suspected that it was a NVA R & R center or training base. Whatever it was, it symbolized the ludicrous nature of the war. A war where real estate in the middle of bad-guy land could be protected from attack. I have come to believe that there may have even been a POW camp there. To me, it seemed ridiculous that we couldn't put a team in there to find out what was going on. Eklund apparently felt the same way.

Anytime that we were in the area and had some time, he would press our recons as close as possible to the no-fly area, a flat-topped mountain that was surrounded by dense jungle. A river divided around the base of the mountain, making it almost an island. That time, we spent the better part of an hour sniffing around the base of the mountain. Each time we climbed the side of the mountain, I pressed a little closer to the lip of the flat top. I caught an occasional glimpse of old, vine-covered buildings. On each excursion over the lip, I extended the amount of time we were exposed, trying to get a better look. Finally I heard the distinctive beep warning of a 37mm radar-guided antiaircraft weapon. I broke left and down the side of the hill to break the lock. So much for fun and games. We flew low-level on the way back to Eagle, trying to find some bad guys. Halfway there, we found one. I was flying at about 110 knots right down on the trees. The AK sounded like it was in the cargo compartment, it was so close. He got off a full thirty-round magazine. My eyes swept the instrument panel, all indications were normal. The intercom came alive.

Patterson yelled, "Son of a bitch."

Loser simply said, "Shit."

I looked around, and Loser was hanging out of the aircraft trying to bend the gun mount so that he could bring fire under the tail boom on the gook that shot us. I glanced over my left shoulder, and Patterson was doing the same thing. Neither could manage to get a shot at the guy. No one was hit, and the instruments still said that the bird was okay. At the speed we were traveling, we were clear of the area in a flash.

Patterson said, "Sorry about that, Mr. Grant."

"That's okay, Larry. We can't get them all."

"No, sir. I mean about your famous cherry. I think it's gone this time, for sure."

"Can you see any holes?"

"No, sir, but I can't see how he could've missed. It sounded like he was in the aircraft with us."

That was true. I was surprised that I had not been able to smell cordite after the firing.

"How 'bout you, Loser? Can you see any damage?"

"No, sir, but I have faith in you, sir. I think you still got it."

Patterson was convinced that we had been hit. When we landed at the Acid pad, we all went over every inch of 345 trying to find some damage. We found none.

After we had parked in the revetment back at the Castle and finished the postflight inspection of the bird, Patterson once again started going over the skin of the aircraft. I went back to my hootch, shaking my head, convinced that Larry had gone nuts. A short while later, he came to the door.

"Mr. G., I'm really sorry, but I knew that we must have been hit, and I was right. I didn't want to be the one to jinx you, but I finally found the hits. Guess you should have stayed just flying 348, and this wouldn't have happened."

"Larry, there is no such thing as a jinx; 348 and I have both just been lucky. Besides, God looks out for drunks and dumb animals."

Patterson smiled. He was familiar with Meacham's theory, but was not about to tell an officer that he qualified on both counts. "Anyway, sir, come on up to the bird, and I'll show you."

As we walked, Larry kept apologizing as if it had been his fault. I could only laugh. Finally, I said, "Look, Larry, don't worry about this. Actually it takes a lot of pressure off me. I mean everybody around here keeps worrying about my damn cherry like I was something special." He just grinned at me as though he felt that I was just saying that to make him feel better.

When we got to the revetment, he led me to the front part of the tail boom. He ducked down and pointed to the first inspection plate on the bottom of the boom. Diagonally across the middle of the plate was a deep scratch. On close inspection, one could see where the nose of the bullet had creased the panel as it went by. He then led me to the inspection panel back under the synchronized elevators. It had a crease that was parallel to the first. The paint was scraped, and you could see the direction of travel of the bullet.

Larry said, "Sir, I wouldn't have even noticed them, except that I did a rivet check on the tail boom this morning."

"Oh well! Everybody takes hits around here. I was just seven months overdue."

The word spread around the company like wildfire. "Grant took hits. His cherry is busted."

Some didn't want to believe it. Some said that it didn't count because there were no actual holes in the aircraft. There was a great deal of arguing in the company area that afternoon and during supper. That night there was a pilots' meeting in the club. I was told that I was not to attend. The whole thing finally came down to a vote. The democratic process determined that I was still cherry. The official ruling was that the skin of the aircraft had to be penetrated in order for the cherry to be broken. I did not have to repaint my helmet.

While I was waiting for the meeting to be over, I penned a letter to Jackie. Someone had given her the idea that Vietnam was nothing but party time for us; I wrote:

> You told me about your day, let me tell you about the average day here.
> Right now the monsoons have started, and I'm up to my ass in water. Not too long ago, I woke up with six inches of water in my bed. I was so tired, I just turned over and went back to sleep.

When I put on dry clothes, they are soaked by the time I get to the aircraft. They stay that way all day long.

I've had one day off in the last twenty. The only reason I'm sitting here now is that I got an early release from to-day's mission.

By the way, I'm soaking wet. I have a cold, I've had it for the last two weeks, and I'll probably still have it when I get to Hawaii.

Yesterday, I got up at five-thirty to go fly. Took off at seven and flew combat assaults all day. That's when the weather was good enough. When it wasn't, we sat in the air-craft waiting to go. We got in around 1800, had chow, and waited for today's mission. When I got it, I got the crew and everything squared away about midnight.

I started to go to bed, but one of the crew chiefs came and asked me to run up his aircraft for a maintenance check. His AC was too drunk to do it.

I finally got to bed around twelve-thirty, I got to sleep around one-thirty when the outgoing artillery stopped. I got up to go fly at 0400 this morning. Need I go on . . .

I was angry that she would listen to what people at home said it was like in Nam. From her description, we had wall-to-wall round-eyed women everywhere. Still, I refrained from telling her about the hits.

STICKY FINGERS

Part of the reason that flying ARVNs was unpopular was that they had sticky fingers. If anything was left within the reach of the passengers, it was sure to disappear. One day, Jim Thompson was flying with Lieutenant O'Neill. They had picked up a load of ARVNs and were proceeding to the LZ. After a short time in the air, the gunner asked, "Mr. Thompson, have you lost a flashlight?"

"No. Why do you ask?"

"This gook back here just put a flashlight in his shirt."

O'Neill, who was on the controls, looked down next to his seat.

"It's my flashlight."

Sir James said to the gunner. "Get the El Tee's flashlight back, and make sure that Marvin understands that what he did was a no-no."

The gunner reached over the seat, tore open the guy's shirt and retrieved the flashlight. The gook just sat there, grinning at the gunner. The gunner hauled back and smashed the ARVN in the face with the big flashlight. The fellow got off the aircraft, still grinning like a fool, his nose and mouth bleeding.

I had a couple of similar experiences. The first was on another CA. We had been given some fresh oranges by an American infantry unit that we had been resupplying. Three oranges were still sitting on the pedestal. Out of the corner of my eye, I noticed a hand slowly working its way toward the oranges. I turned quickly, surprising him, and forcing the hand to retreat. I said to Loser and Sugar Bear, "Keep an eye on the dink with the steel pot and no helmet liner."

I turned back as if I had not noticed his attempt to purloin the oranges. I reached down to my knife and undid the strap. Slowly, I removed the knife from its sheath and set it in the seat next to my right leg. When the hand started back toward the oranges I grasped the knife by the blade. As the hand wrapped itself around one of the oranges I brought the knife up and smashed the end of the handle against the lip of the steel pot like I was ringing a bell. It must have had a similar effect; when I looked down at Marvin, the irises of his eyes were going back and forth like little bell clappers.

The second time was very much like the first, except this time the attempt was to steal my lighter. It had a similar conclusion.

Monday, 21 October (149 days to go). Ken Roach started his week in hell. He began the week with a short-shaft failure on Monday. The short shaft is the foot-long drive shaft that connects the Huey's turbine engine to the transmission. When the shaft fails, the transmission is no longer driven, and the engine goes wild. The helicopter goes down. If the pilot reacts properly, he enters autorotation, reduces the throttle to idle, and lands the aircraft. The pilot's reactions must come in seconds. Ken was on the controls and reacted flawlessly; the engine, the aircraft, and the crew were all saved.

A few days later, Ken had compressor stalls as he was flying. They are caused by a disruption of the airflow through the turbine engine and result in power fluctuation and loud popping sounds. The emergency procedure calls for a reduction in power and landing. With a fully loaded aircraft over unfriendly terrain, the solution is not always as simple as it reads in the book. The Teenybopper again performed without error.

The final insult came on Saturday, during a combat assault being conducted from Firebase Birmingham to an LZ out west. As the first lift was taking off from Birmingham, Ken was again on the controls of the aircraft and Jim Thompson was the AC. About the worst time to have an engine failure in a helicopter is at low altitude and low airspeed with a full load. The airspeed indicator had just gone through thirty knots when there was a loud bang from the back of the aircraft. The noise was followed by complete silence. A quiet Huey on the ground is not anything to get excited about. In the air, silence is the worst thing in the world. Ken Roach was textbook perfect for the third time. If he hadn't been, it could have been a disaster for crew and passengers alike.

Colonel Crozier was flying in the C & C aircraft for the lift, and heard that an aircraft had gone down on takeoff with a full load of troops. He was immediately concerned. It was bad enough to lose troops in combat, but losing them to an accident caused by an engine failure was unthinkable. He turned his aircraft back to the FSB to see how bad the situation was. As the C & C arrived overhead, Colonel Crozier saw that the rotor of the downed bird was still coasting to a stop. As the group commander peered down at the stricken aircraft, he could see no damage. He landed his aircraft and hurried toward the down Huey to find out who the pilot was. When he got to the left side of the aircraft, he asked one of the infantrymen where the pilot was.

" 'Round the other side, sir."

Wild Turkey headed around the front of the aircraft and saw only a lone infantryman.

"Trooper, where is the pilot?"

"He jus' went 'round the back, sir."

The colonel went around the tail boom back to the right side. Still he saw no pilot. Frustrated and starting to become annoyed, he again circled to the front of the helicopter. Finally, on the right side, he caught up with Roach and Thompson. He saw Ken's drooping moustache, and hair that extended down the back of his neck and touched his ears on the side. He immediately forgot his original mission and lit into the Teenybopper. He chewed up one side and down the other. In spite of his busy schedule, he made the shaking WO1 an appointment to come see him in his office the next morning at 0900. He also arranged for Jim to trim his handlebar moustache on the spot.

"When you arrive, Mr. Roach, you will have a proper haircut and shave. Do you read me, mister?"

"Loud and clear, sir!"

"Good, I'll see you in the morning then."

Crozier turned and walked away, leaving Ken Roach wondering which was worse, exploding engines or exploding colonels. The colonel saw the open engine cowling and looked in. The evidence of catastrophic engine failure was clear to see. The engine deck was riddled with holes from the shrapnel of a disintegrating turbine wheel. He looked back over his shoulder at the shaken pilot, gave him a thumbs-up, a smile and said, "Damn fine job putting this one down, son." He turned quickly and headed back to his own aircraft.

Nam had a way of making very valuable things that we took for granted back in the World. A man's lawn chair was something that no one violated—a stereo, a fan, and a fridge were among the things that we valued most. Three of the four were susceptible to destruction by arbitrary power surges from the generators. For the most part, refrigerators were shared items. My hootch shared an old Fridgidaire that had been hauled from Fort Riley by the original members of the unit. Most of the other hootches had small Sanyos that were shared by two or three guys. The refrigerators were the most important of all the possessions. If the fans didn't work, at least there would be a cold beer. The power surges were hell on the little Sanyos, but the big three-by in the club and the old Fridgidaire seemed to hold up pretty well. After each surge, it seemed that someone had to replace a Sanyo.

24 October (146 days to go). We had experienced a rash of blade strikes. I should say that Dave Poley had experienced a rash of blade strikes. During October, he tore up five sets of rotor blades. Usually such a record would be an indication of a pilot's not being up to combat flying, but we flew into too many places that were not ideal spots to land a helicopter. We took great pride in how well our crews handled LZs that were so tight that you couldn't see the sky once you were in them. Hitting trees was not the kind of thing that was good for the aircraft or your health. If an LZ was bad, we simply told the ground unit to blow another tree or two to make it bigger. But there was not that option with a LRP team on the run.

Just a few days before, The Dave had knocked a full foot and a half off the end of each of his rotor blades. He had some vibration, but was able to fly the bird home. Had the amount been even a couple of inches different, it is likely that the aircraft would have vibrated to pieces. There was talk around the company about changing Dave's call sign to "Woodchopper Six." Ken Eklund started making jokes to Major Fitch, the Kingsmen maintenance officer, about adding another set of blades to his tab. After Poley's latest strike, Fitch went to Eklund and told him that it had to stop. There was a shortage of blades, and we couldn't allow it to continue. It was apparent that he didn't realize Eklund had no control over the situation. Nor did he understand that we wouldn't hesitate to tear up an aircraft to get a team out that was in trouble.

Then one of the teams that I had inserted was compromised and on the run. When I got to the LZ, there were a few small trees in the way on the right side. I began to hover straight down and noticed the rotor was hitting the trees. The branches being chopped were smaller in diameter than a pencil. I thought nothing of it and continued down until we were low enough to make a ladder extraction. The team scrambled on board, and we headed back to Eagle. We had fired more rounds at Chuck than he had fired at us for a change.

The UH-1H was capable of doing some pretty fine tree chopping if it was done correctly. The blades of the Huey are constructed around a metal main spar. That D-shaped spar is the strength of the blade and is part of the leading edge. Behind the spar is a honeycomb of heavy-duty aluminum foil. The blade is covered by a metal skin. The whole mess is bonded together and makes a lightweight, strong, and efficient airfoil. It also works well as an axe if necessary. The rotating blade that weighs 124 pounds, powered by a fifteen-hundred horsepower engine, will, with ease, chop four-inch diameter trees with a single swoop. That is, of course, if the tree is struck with the hardened leading edge. However, small twigs are capable of ripping through the skin that covers the blade.

When I shut down on the Acid pad I noticed something unusual as the rotor slowed. A streak of silver went by with one of the blades. I was surprised that the small branches that I had cut would damage the blade. When the rotor stopped I found that the skin on the underside was cut from just behind the spar almost to the trailing edge. As I put a finger in the tear I became aware that I could touch the upper skin of the blade from the bottom. The cut was about two feet from the end of the blade. Had the piece separated we would have crashed. Major Fitch was not amused when Captain Eklund called and told him we had torn up another set of blades.

I have often thought that it must have been a helicopter pilot that invented the vegematic.

The heavy rains of the impending monsoons continued to plague us during the month. In order to combat the tent leaks, we had scrounged sheets of plastic from artillery units, whose howitzer rounds came wrapped in plastic sheets. We stretched the plastic between the wooden supports, and overlapped the sheets so that leaks ran down and out the side of the tent. The system worked well enough to keep our bunks and personal gear dry, but puddles were still left on the floors because the wet plywood flooring swelled and sealed the crevices between the sheets, preventing the water from draining.

One day, B. J. Hoyt walked into his hootch and found Mike Ware standing ankle-deep in a puddle, with an electric drill in his hand.

"What the fuck are you doing, Mike?"

"I'm gonna drill some holes so the water can drain."

"You're gonna electrocute yourself, dummy!"

"How will we let the water out then?"

"I'll show you."

B. J. pulled out his .38 and quickly pumped six holes in the floor. He then calmly holstered the weapon and walked away.

The night Loser got promoted to specialist four, he invited Ken Roach and me down to his tent to celebrate. The lower ranking enlisted men could only afford a small party for promotions, so it was an honor to be invited. When the Teenybopper and I arrived, Loser had a case of Budweiser and a bottle of Seagram's. He took his P-38 and cut the top out of a can of Bud, chugged down about a third of the beer, refilled the can with Seagram's, stirred it with his finger, and handed me my drink. He repeated the procedure, giving Teenybopper his very first boilermaker. Ken was reluctant at first, but by the time he finished his second, he found the drinks quite tasty. I had five or six and announced, "I'm sorry but I've got to fly in the morning. Thanks for inviting me, Loser, but I need to hit the sack."

Ken stayed. I went back to my hootch and got ready for bed. I'd just settled in and was drifting off to sleep when I heard a tapping sound on the doorframe of the tent.

"Who's there?"

"It's Loser, sir."

"What's the matter?"

"Mr. G, you gotta come and help me with Mr. Roach. I think he might be dead."

I stumbled out of bed and pulled on my pants and stuck my feet into my boots. When we got back to the crew chief's tent, we found Roach passed out, draped over the sandbag wall. Loser and I had to haul him to his hootch and put him to bed. Teenybopper left the boilermakers alone for a while after that night.

Tuesday, 29 October (141 days to go). I had been flying for twenty-five straight days, the last nine days on the LRP mission. I was very tired when I got back to my hootch, and I hadn't shaved for about three days. I tossed helmet and chicken plate on my bunk and sat down. I had a couple beers and a C-ration meal. Afterward, I was sitting cleaning my fingernails with the pearlhandled switchblade that I had bought at the gook shop outside the PX.

Lieutenant Dipstick came in, took one look at me, and started lecturing me about my appearance and eating in the hootch. While he conducted his tirade, another lieutenant, an FNG, came in with his duffel bag and sat down on it, waiting for someone to pay attention to him. His name was John Hightower. While Dipstick ranted, I sat there, opening and closing the switchblade over and over again. I could tell by the look in Hightower's eyes that he expected that at any moment that the wild looking warrant officer would stick the knife into the belly of Lieutenant Dipstick.

Finally, he came to the end of his lecture. "Well, Mr. Grant, what do you have to say for yourself?"

"What the fuck do you want to be when you grow up, Harry?" I gave him my best big smile.

He stormed out of the hootch ranting, "I'm telling Major Addiss, I'm telling Major Addiss . . ."

I looked over at Hightower. "How ya doin', L T? What can I do for you?"

He just kind of stared at me blankly. "I think you want the new-guy hootch," I said. "It's the fourth one down on the right. Can I help you with your stuff?" As I made the offer, I folded the switchblade and put it in my pocket.

"Uh . . . uh . . . no . . . uh . . . thanks." He stammered as he gathered up his stuff and left hurriedly.

First impressions last, and from that time on, John Hightower always thought I was nuts.

CHAPTER 9
NOVEMBER 1968

The enemy was definitely getting more active since the bombing halt. On the first and second of November, teams were shot out of LZs on Leech Island. We were running more operations, and more of them resulted in hot extractions.

Rocket attacks on Camp Eagle seemed to be on the rise. The 122mm rocket had an extremely low trajectory and a range of about twelve miles, and Chuck liked to fire them from places where he could disappear in a hurry. They never did much damage, but they were a nuisance. They were also extremely frustrating, since every time they hit us, the guns would scramble and find nothing.

Eagle was situated at the first of the rolling foothills as you traveled west from the beach. The elevation varied from zero to fifty feet. The hills were grassy, and trees were only found along the river banks. The lack of cover and concealment left the enemy with few good places to mount a rocket attack on Camp Eagle. The base of Nui Khe mountain was one of his favorites. Nui Khe was the last big mountain where the mountainous jungle met the rolling foothills. There Charlie could launch the rockets from only nine miles out. He could launch over the hills, in the direction of Eagle, and melt into the endless jungle again to get away. There wasn't a large area to search when he struck, but it was large enough that he could be well hidden by the time the gunships arrived.

3 November (138 days to go, 14 straight days on LRPs). Wild Bill Meacham and I were briefed for the next day's missions with the LRP company. The plan to counter the enemy's tactic was to insert a team on Nui Khe and another in the vicinity of Leech Island, farther to the south. When the rocket crews attacked, the teams would either spot for artillery or ambush the launch crews during their attack. The first team would be inserted on the abandoned firebase on the top of Nui Khe just after first light, the second about a half hour later. The Nui Khe team would consist of Zoschak as team leader, Linderer as ATL, Terry Clifton, Indian Walkabout, Dave Biedron, and Stinky Schwartz. The Leech Island team would be Snuffy Smith's, with Sandman Saenz as ATL. Bill would make the insertion on the mountain, I would get the second one.

The next morning, we landed at the Acid pad, and Zoschak's team was there ready to go. Meacham loaded them up and took off first, and we headed for Nui Khe. We had agreed that since the mountaintop was exposed, the usual false insertion pattern would not be as effective. But I told Bill that I would make the high-speed pass anyway, just to draw any fire if the LZ was hot.

On the top of the mountain were bunkers, sandbagged trenches, and fighting positions from the last time GIs had occupied the site. There was even a PSP helipad to land on, but Meacham elected to bypass it and land on the top of the command bunker instead. Zo later reported that the pad had been booby-trapped with a two-hundred-pound bomb. Sometimes a little voice would tell you not to do the obvious. It was either a combat sense that you developed or God's whisper in the ear of the drunks and dumb animals.

In under twenty minutes, we were back on the Acid pad to pick up the second team. The second took around forty minutes for the round trip. There were no problems with the insertion. Since we had burned about an hour and half of fuel, we stopped off at the hot fuel point when we returned to Eagle. After topping off the tanks, we landed at the LRP pad and shut down, leaving the aircraft with the customary shotgun load.

It was about 0730 hours when we arrived at the LRP operations, looking for a cup of coffee. We sat around for awhile BSing with Lieutenant Williams. About eight o'clock, I announced that I was going down to the pad and crash in the bird. When I got there, the crew chief was sacked out in the middle of the aircraft on the floor, the gunner was curled up in the transmission well, and Teenybopper was reading a book in the pilot's seat. I took my chicken plate out of the left seat and headed around to the shady right side of the aircraft. I propped up the chicken plate for a pillow where the jump doors had been removed, and stretched out along the edge of the aircraft floor.

Now that might not seem like the most comfortable bed in the world, but it worked well. I logged Zs anywhere or anytime; you never knew when the next opportunity would arise.

Somewhere, far away, there was a voice calling something to me; I couldn't quite make it out. It was hot, and I was sweating; the voice kept calling. My eyes finally dragged open. I was in the aircraft, I'd been asleep, I must have dreamed the voice. It called again, "Zo's team is hot!" I finally realized that Bill Meacham was yelling that we had to scramble. I leaped up and threw the vest of my chicken plate over my head and closed the Velcro straps around the front, then ran around to my side of the aircraft. As I went, I saw that the crew chief was just beginning to untie the blades. I knew then that it hadn't taken very long for me to wake up.

As I was climbing into the seat, I reached up, threw on the battery switch, and engaged the starter trigger. I heard the engine coming to life. A quick look around told me that Ken was getting strapped in. I looked back to the gauges to make sure the start was progressing normally. As the engine reached flight idle, the crew chief and gunner were closing the pilot doors. I noted that the transmission- and engine-oil pressures were up, and opened the throttle to operating RPM. Ken reached his hand over the center pedestal with a thumbs-up, indicating that the radio call had been made. I looked over to see that 121 had not started to get light yet, so I pointed to Ken to take the controls. He did, and I started strapping in and got my helmet on. As I did, I felt the aircraft getting light on the skids. I glanced over and saw that Meacham's bird was off the ground and headed toward the perimeter. Ken was on the ball and following him. I plugged my helmet in and heard Eagle tower saying, "Roger Kingsmen Two-Five, flight of two on the go."

I heard, "One-Eight, Two-Five on Uniform." Wild Bill was calling on the company frequency on the UHF radio.

I just said, "Go."

"Sitrep. Zo's team was mortared on the side of Nui Khe. I'm going to pull them out. Just hang loose and watch; no point in both of us going over the top."

I thought, "Shit, if they already have the LZ zeroed in, it won't take long for a Huey to attract attention in the LZ." I just said, "Roger, Two-Five. Can I have your watch?"

He replied, "If you can find it."

As we listened to the radio traffic between the C & C bird and the team on the ground, we heard that the team had called for arty. Captain Eklund told us stay clear and circle. We waited. When the artillery lifted, Eklund went down and dropped yellow smoke for the Cobras. The snakes gave Chuck something beside the team to think about for a while. The team was still in close contact on the ground. Three NVA died on the third pass. Linderer got at least two of them. All we could do about it was cheer from the sidelines. By the time the Cobras had finished, a pair of F-4s had arrived. They worked out in the valley where the mortars had come from. There were some secondary explosions. Mr. Charles was paying the price for screwing with this team. Wild Bill and I were going to miss the show from the F-4s. Snuffy's team was now in contact.

Since we had all of our firepower directed at the Nui Khe fight, it was decided to extract the Leech Island team first. Their contact had been light, but the team was compromised and would have to be extracted. Since the F-4s were still working over the valley by Nui Khe, we couldn't extract Zoschak's team yet anyway. Wild Bill fell back and let me take the lead since it was my extraction. By the time we arrived, the situation had gone cold. The team had come upon a trail watcher and had wasted him. But there had been some movement in the jungle so they knew well that they had been compromised. The cold extraction went off without a problem. We flew with a sense of urgency because we knew that it would be about an hour before we could get back to Zo's team. It was almost forty-minutes round trip. We would need to refuel again.

We headed back to Nui Khe, with Meacham in the lead. Things had been pretty quiet since the last run by the Cobras. But we knew that the LZ had been zeroed by the mortar crew. We had to hope that the secondaries from the tac air were the mortars.

Bill and I had a fast conference at the hot fuel point. He said, "I'm going to try to sneak in low from the northeast side. We'll attract as little attention as possible." He knew that the less time the NVA had to watch us, the less time they had to set up the mortars. I told him that while he went in, I would swing around the south side of the mountain at altitude and set up like I was going in to pick up the team. If all went well, while the NVA were waiting for me to land, Bill would be able to sneak in and out again.

Once again, the extraction went well. We landed back at the Acid pad to a large welcome from the LRP company. The celebration was still going on when Captain Eklund returned from division. He put a fast damper on the festivities with the announcement that division wanted the team reinserted in the same area. There was a large volume of protest, with which Eklund was in full agreement; it was insane go back to same area. But the arguments were useless; Eklund had no choice, and neither did the rest of us. Division wanted a team in there to hunt down the rocket crews, and that was the end of the discussion.

I briefly argued with Meacham about my taking Zo's team in, but he refused to let me.

"No way, this is my mission," he said.

Everyone started to prepare for the insertion. Schwartz was suffering the effects of the heat, so Ray Zoschak got the CO to replace him with Saenz instead. Gary Linderer said later that he thought that Zo had picked Saenz because Saenz was an experienced soldier but new to the unit, and Zo thought the team wasn't coming back, so he did not want to pick someone he knew. The team members all went to the ammo bunker to replace the ammo they had expended earlier and to get a little something extra, since they knew the area was hot. Normally there wasn't time to think about the LZ being hot beforehand. This time, we knew the mission was stupid. It seemed that no one at division cared that they were sending this team into a meat grinder.

It was around 1930 when we cranked the aircraft for the flight back to Nui Khe. We were to insert the team into the valley where the mortars had been earlier in the day. The area had been clobbered by artillery and tac air and might be softened up a bit. We planned to swing out toward Firebase Birmingham, drop down low, turn back east, then south toward Nui Khe. The valley we were going into ran north from the base of the mountain, and opened up near Highway 547, which ran east and west. The ridge that formed the east wall of the valley dropped down to a low saddle against Nui Khe mountain. We would exit the valley there, after inserting the team just north of the saddle. That route would give the least exposure to enemy observation. Hopefully, it would seem like an aerial recon, not an insertion.

The cold insertion occurred just after dark. Not a shot was fired. Back at the Acid pad, Wild Bill and I climbed out of our aircraft as the rotors coasted to a stop. We met halfway between the aircraft, peeling off our flight gloves as we walked. Bill's face was set hard, the eyes showed "the look." His head tilted slightly down. He wasn't happy; I must have provided a mirror image to him. As we met, he looked up slightly, and as our eyes met, I said, "As soon as it gets fully dark."

He replied, "Fuckin' A."

Without another word, we started the climb up the hill to LRP TOC to wait for the call we knew would come soon.

Dark fell with a thud that night, we didn't want to see it. I guess that's why it came hard. Night was normally a good time for the LRPs; night was a friend. It meant they could disappear. It meant that Chuck could walk within inches in the dense jungle, and a LRP could just lay dog and not be seen. A LRP pilot knew that the darkness meant his team would be all right till morning, and he could lay his head down in a bed and rest easy until just before dawn.

Not that night. We all knew that from the time of the insertion—me, Meacham, Zo, his team, Eklund, and Chuck. Yes, Chuck; he knew that the helicopters didn't fly as much at night. He knew the team wouldn't be far from where it had been inserted. But most of all, he knew how strong his forces were and that he had the upper hand. We drank coffee in the LRP operations, and I watched the door. I watched the night turn into an inkwell. It seemed that it went from light to dark in an instant, like a switch had been turned off.

The first sound on the radio was just the breaking of squelch. I heard a *shhhhoooooottt* sound, then silence. We all jumped at the noise, expecting the worst. There was about fifteen endless seconds of silence. Then the first call came through. The whispered voice was more high pitched than usual. "Windy Guard Six, this is Windy Guard One-Six. Over."

Lieutenant Williams responded quickly. "One-Six, this is Five. Go."

"This is One-Six. We are in deep shit." You didn't have know the man at the other end of the radio to know that Ray Zoschak was scared.

"There must be a million fucking gooks out here. They're blowing whistles and bugles and banging sticks together. We need extraction now!" It was well known that Zoschak didn't like to call for extractions. He always hung on to the mission as long as possible. If he was demanding extraction, it was a bad situation. I think Zo was still talking on the radio, but all I remember hearing was the thump and screech of the screen door spring protesting as Wild Bill hit it at a dead run. I heard it well because I was right on his heels. Williams probably told us to go extract the team, but we'd already stumbled halfway down the hill. Eklund jumped into the radio conversation from the C & C OH-6, as he was on his way back from division to the Acid pad. I can remember yelling, "Go, go, go!" to our crews as we ran. In the blackness, we couldn't see the blades getting untied. We just assumed everyone was doing his job. I hit my seat, and the practiced hand found the battery switch, and 348 came alive. I saw the fire-warning light and caution panel illuminated, so I hit the trigger, and the familiar popping sound was my reward. I looked over at Ken. He was strapped in and putting on his helmet. As soon as I released the trigger, he turned on the radios and waited for 121 to make the call that we were on the go from the Acid pad. As I rolled the throttle to 6600 RPM, 121 lifted to a hover, and the nose dropped. Wild Bill was on the go. The corner of my eye caught Teenybopper's thumb pointed up. The radio calls had been made. I pulled pitch. As I did, I added extra left pedal to turn us to follow 121. The instant the bird started to respond, I moved the cyclic forward to let the nose drop to an acceleration attitude. The aircraft picked up and pivoted around the front portion of the left skid. This wasn't a takeoff that would've made my instructor happy in flight school, but it got us in the air and headed toward one hundred knots in the shortest possible time. We followed the small valley that ran between the LRP company area and the Cav area. I watched the airspeed build as we flew east; we hit one hundred knots just as Wild Bill broke hard left over the 2/17 Cav area. I followed him, holding a hundred knots to let the aircraft climb. Now going southwest, we quickly left the lights of Camp Eagle behind. Damn, it was dark out there. It was never comforting to head west at night, the blackness seemed like a wall of velvet.

"Windy Guard One-Six, this is Kingsmen Two-Five over," Meacham called.

"Kingsmen Two-Five, this Windy Guard One-Six. Go ahead," Zo whispered.

"This is Two-Five. Hang on partner; we're on our way."

"Roger. There are boo coo dinks out here. We can hear them on both ridgelines."

"This is Two-Five. Are you in contact?"

"This is One-Six. No, but we can hear them all around us, and there's a bunch of them."

"Kingsmen Two-Five, this is Windy Guard Six." It was Eklund.

"This is Two-Five. Go ahead, Six."

"I am over the area now, the LOH was just about to drop me off when we picked up the first call."

"This is Two-Five, I'm halfway there; be on site in zero five mikes."

"This is Windy Guard Six. Where are the Snakes?"

"Guard Six, this is Saber Two-Three. We are right behind the slicks, about to pass them on the right side."

We knew now that the NVA were closing in on the team from at least three sides. They probably had lost some buddies that afternoon and would love to take it out on some LRPs. A favorite tactic for the LRPs at night was to hit, break contact, and beat feet for a while, then just melt into the jungle and disappear. The skill with which they executed this saved us from many dangerous night extractions. But it was becoming apparent that night that the only way out for the team was straight up. Well, that was our specialty. The fluttering of fear began in my stomach. I was afraid for the team, I was afraid for Bill. I wasn't going in, so I wasn't afraid for me. We swung out toward Birmingham again.

Meacham called, "One-Eight, this is Two-Five. We'll fly it just like this afternoon. We'll go in low; you follow up and take it if anything goes wrong."

"Rog."

I knew then that Meacham was also worried about this one. He never considered that anything might go wrong on a mission, and it was established procedure for the wingman to take the extraction if something went wrong. As we turned toward Nui Khe, I made the turn just a little wider than Bill's to get the proper separation. That's when he called, "One-Eight, Two-Five, my attitude indicator just went tits up. I'm pulling up; it's your extraction."

Now it was me going in, but there wasn't time to get scared. We were only about sixty seconds out.

"Guard Six, this is One-Eight, I'm going as low as I can get. I won't be able to see the strobe till I'm on top of it, so vector me if I need it."

"This is Six. Roger, One-Eight."

I told Teenybopper, "Ken, put the position lights up bright. I know they can see us better then, but we can use them to see when we get close to the trees."

I kept a slow descent going and was watching out the side for the trees to be illuminated by the position lights. Once we saw them, we knew we were five or six feet off the trees. Ken saw the trees first, and I told him to keep giving me clearance information.

As I flew, he said, "Come up a little." Then, "Go down a little."

Then I spotted the strobe light. It was blinding up close. I called, "Kill the light." It went off almost instantly. They didn't want the light pinpointing the team. When we were on short final to the LZ, Meacham called, "W. T., the whole mountainside just opened up on you, must be two hundred muzzle flashes out there."

I keyed the mike. "Thanks, asshole. I really need that piece of information right now."

The response was a soft chuckle over the radio.

This was going to be a ladder extraction; there was a large boulder in the LZ that would keep us from landing. I tried to keep the right skid on the boulder to help stabilize my hover. Through the noise of the aircraft, I could hear the sound of M-16s firing. To my left, in the glow of the aircraft position lights, I could see the team backing out of the tree line, emptying magazines into the jungle as they came. I felt the aircraft's center of gravity shift to the left as the first LRP started up the ladder. Now I could hear the deeper crack of AK fire. One LRP was on the ladder, I could see two steadying it and three providing cover fire, all six accounted for. I announced, "Clear to fire," to the crew chief and gunner. The Loser announced he was looking at a wall of rock on the right side so I said, "Don't kill the rock." The Sugar Bear responded with 60 fire. I thought, "Take that assholes, we bite back."

The aircraft was shaking with LRPs scrambling up the ladder. It seemed like we'd been in the LZ for about two and half days. I looked over my right shoulder, two in, Clifton and Walkabout. Saenz was just getting to the door on the ladder. Biedron was close behind. Linderer and Zo were still shooting up the woods. I got pissed and yelled out the window. "Will you assholes get the fuck in the aircraft and let us get out of here? You don't have to kill all the gooks yourselves." Of course no one could hear me over the aircraft noise and gunfire, but I wanted to get the team and my crew out of there alive, and we were running out of time. The crew chief announced, "Five in and one on the ladder still shooting up the jungle."

I thought Screw this, and pulled pitch, we're getting out of this motherfucker. After he felt the aircraft rising, Ray Zoschak hooked himself to the ladder with a carabiner for the ride home.

As we rose from the LZ, Ken called out the engine torque to me.

"Forty.

"Forty-five." Both 60s and six LRPs continued to pour rounds into the jungle below. The Huey continued to rise vertically.

"Forty-seven.

"Forty-nine.

"Fifty, hold it there." Fifty pounds was the torque limit for the aircraft. I held that power setting, and when we cleared the trees, dumped the nose over to grab airspeed as fast as we could. We were approaching the low saddle on the ridge to our left. We had about thirty knots, the enemy was on the ridge, but through that saddle was the shortest way out of the valley. It was also the lowest obstruction. That path would let me gain airspeed sooner. So I took it. As the saddle passed under us, I pushed the cyclic forward, letting 348's nose down, and watched the airspeed race to 115 before I backed off again and let the bird climb. At that time, the crew chief called us clear of the enemy fire. When it hit 120, I reduced the power and let the aircraft start to cruise. I now could begin to breathe again. It seemed that it was forever that we were in the LZ. It probably took more like only ten or eleven seconds for all the team to scurry up the ladder. I looked down and saw that my hand was shaking on the cyclic, definitely uncool. I tried to appear as calm as possible when I looked over at the Teenybopper and said, "You have the controls, take us home." Of course, since it was dark he probably wasn't able to see all that cool I'd worked so hard on. I quietly thanked God for saving my ass again. I thought, "Settle down, asshole, you're out, no need to be scared now." When you tell scared to stay put, it only listens so long, then when you relax, out come the shakes. I reached in the pocket of my chicken plate and pulled out a pack of Marlboros; smoking always looked cool. It worked for the Marlboro Man. As I lit up, I hoped that no one could see the lighter shaking. I tried to smoke a least half the cigarette in one drag. It never occurred to me that everyone else was scared shitless too. I looked in the back and smiled. Clifton and Biedron weakly smiled back with painted faces. I threw the rest of the pack of cigarettes in the back. It disappeared in a hurry. Soon there were several red-orange glows just above the floor of the helicopter.

As we came back to the Acid pad, Ken stopped the aircraft at about a six-foot hover to let Zo unhook and climb off the ladder. Once again, the pad was crowded with LRPs waiting to celebrate the return of the team. We shut down for a postflight inspection to see how many hits we'd taken. When I'd finished, I asked Ken how many he'd had found, and he confirmed what I already knew. Unbelievably, I still had my cherry. I called over to Wild Bill, "Hey, you old turkey, I still got it."

He knew what I meant, and yelled back, "I'm clean, too."

Eklund had taken several in the C & C bird.

I was anxious to get my aircraft back to the Castle; a drink was now rapidly becoming a necessity. There were great plans to get the aircraft put away, turn in the aftermission paperwork, and go back to the Ranger Lounge for some serious unwinding. As I left operations, I looked over at the Kingsmen club only a few yards away. I looked over at Bill and could see he was thinking the same thing I was. A little fortification for the trip back to the Acid pad. A couple of drinks and the absence of adrenaline in the system made the call of the bunk stronger than the call of the celebration. There would be other parties. Sleep was more important right now.

THE HUE BRIDGE

The Hue Bridge spanned the Perfume River at the southeast corner of the city. The bridge was about a half mile outside the citadel. It just sat there like an enticing temptress to every aviator in I Corps. Those who flew out of Camp Eagle found it especially tempting. It just sat there every day, screaming, "Fly under me." This bridge had a mystical call, much like the sirens of the sea that have called many a sailor to his death. The devil bridge called to one of the Comancheros one day. It was a call he couldn't resist. The impact was at about ninety knots. The mast hit the bottom edge of the bridge just above the swash plate. All four crew members were killed.

I myself had heard the enchanting call of the bridge, it came as a whisper. It was a soft and gentle call, but it contained all the demand of an angry drill sergeant. I once went so far as to hover over the river, right up to the bridge to check the clearance. My crew had even encouraged me, their confidence in my skill was flattering. However, I decided that the river was too high and passed on the opportunity.

It was inevitable that the temptress should one day call to another Kingsman, and inevitable that the poor Kingsman would in a weak moment be unable to resist. He sized up the situation just as I had by hovering next to the bridge. Then with the professionalism the Kingsmen were noted for, he hovered through. Having established the proper clearance, he made the next pass at ninety knots. Once again, he cleared the obstacle. He was so proud of himself that he made a second pass at ninety knots, and once again was successful.

The next day, this highly skilled aircraft commander was sent for by the group commander. He was to present himself in front of Col. Ted Crozier's desk by 0930 hours. It seemed that Colonel Crozier had been standing on the Hue Bridge at the time of that extraordinary demonstration of airmanship. The young WO1 walked into the group commander's office and reported with the crispest salute he knew how to present. Colonel Crozier said, "Son, I was standing on the bridge that you flew under. You would've been all right, except that you had to be an asshole and fly under it three times. The first time, I recognized the aircraft as a division aircraft. The second time, I recognized the Kingsmen diamonds. The third time is when you really fucked up, because I got the tail number."

The colonel then yanked his aircraft-commander orders and told him to take the message back to the unit that "showboating" risks would not be tolerated. We all knew what the AC did was dumb, but we were proud of him anyway.

One night in the club, things were going along in their usual wild state. Some of the new guys were sitting around with Wild Bill and Rod Heim. One of them started bragging about all the things he was going to do in Vietnam. He went on in great detail for a while. Suddenly, Rod leaped up on the table and pointed down at him and said, "Don't tell me what you're going to do, show me."

Bill Meacham burst out laughing. It was only a few months ago that Bill had said those very same words to a bragging new guy named Rod Heim.

Tuesday, 5 November (134 days to go, 16 days in a row on LRPs). We landed on the Acid pad that morning and reported to the TOC for our daily briefing. Ken Eklund informed us that we would have an unanticipated mission that day. There would be an Arc Light in thirty minutes, just to the north of Leech Island, and division headquarters had requested a BDA (bomb damage assessment) as soon as possible. We would insert a team to check out the area. It would be prepared for a three-day mission.

Ken asked, "Who's doing the insertion?"

Dave Poley grinned at me.

I looked back at Eklund and said, "I guess I'm going to do it. 'No Balls' over there can't handle it."

"The team is getting packed up right now," Ken said. "We'll go in as soon as possible after the strike. Maybe the gooks will still have their heads down. We won't do a flyover, the B-52s should leave plenty of places to land."

As we were heading down the hill to the aircraft, we could feel the shake of the ground as the bombs were falling, some nine miles away. By the time the team arrived and we got airborne, the strike was ten minutes old. When we arrived in the area, the dust had settled, but it was easy enough to tell by the devastated jungle where the strike had been. I made my approach along a river. As we arrived in the bombed section, it was as though you could feel death in the air. After the mission was over, the team said that they had the same feeling on the ground. As we got on short final to the LZ I'd picked, I looked to the left, and I saw a five-hundred-pound-bomb crater next to the river. There were many craters next to the river, all filled with water. This one was unusual because the water was red. I had a mental image of some poor bastard running to get away from the bombing and a five-hundred-pounder landing right on his head. The LZ was cold, and the team inserted quickly. As we departed west, I saw a two-foot-thick slab of concrete that had been turned up out of the earth during the bombing. That had been my closest look, and it had left me with a strange empty feeling inside.

On the sixth, the BDA team called in that they had some movement in the area. Eklund jumped in the back of my Huey, and we headed out. Ken had his usual armament, his M-16 and a case of white phosphorus grenades. We got out to the area and established an orbit, well clear, so as not to give away the team's position. The team was located on the south side of a stream. Eklund called as we got on station. "Windy Guard Two-Four, this is Windy Guard Six. We are on station with one slick to provide assistance as needed."

"Six, this is Two-four. We are pinned down at the bottom of the hill by two or three snipers at grid Yankee Delta 8134 0162. We are unable to raise arty from here. Can you get us fire support? Over."

Eklund made the call for arty. There was none available. Our gunships were off with Poley on a recon out near the A Shau

Valley. The team wasn't in a position to be able to move to the nearest PZ.

Ken asked, "Can we get in there and give them some 60 cover so they can move to a PZ?"

It wasn't a smart thing to do with no gun cover, we would be sitting ducks for the snipers. However, an attempt at a McGuire extraction under those circumstances would be even worse. I told Loser that I'd put the gooks on his side and started to move in. In short order, we were hovering between the gooks and the team with Loser hosing down the bad guys with his M-60. I thought, Maybe it wasn't such a bad idea after all.

Then Loser's gun stopped firing. "It's jammed, sir!"

It was not a problem. I calmly kicked in right pedal and spun the aircraft 180 degrees, putting the target on Juan's side of the Huey. Sugar Bear promptly showed the bad guys that his bite was just as bad as Loser's. We had the same height advantage on the gooks that they previously had on the team. Our days as gunship were to be shortlived. Juan's gun soon quit firing as well. I turned the aircraft again hoping that Loser had his weapon cleared.

"Loser, if you have to, use your 16." I glanced back over my shoulder as I said the words. Once again, Loser was flawless under fire. He was already half outside of the aircraft with his rifle, popping rounds off at the NVA. It just then that two dinks had enough and broke cover, beating feet down the trail.

Eklund yelled, "Go after them!"

I was already sucked into this one. Like a Loach pilot with a pair of Cobras on tap, I began to hover down the trail after the retreating NVA. I flew partially sideways so that both Eklund and Loser could get a clear shot. Eklund was kneeling in the door pitching willy pete grenades at the enemy. He called Loser off. Here we were doing stupid shit chasing these guys down a trail, and he wanted to see if he could get them with his fast ball. They disappeared into the tree line at the same time as the last willy pete. A pair of maybes.

We backed off while the team humped the last five hundred meters to the LZ. Poley called, "One-Eight, this is One-Nine."

"Go ahead One-Nine."

"Whatcha been doin'? Ya ain't been havin' fun without me, have ya?"

"Naw, we just been hangin' around playin' Loach and checking out Six's pitching talents."

"Roger that. We'll be on station in zero three mikes to cover your extraction."

As 348 settled in the LZ, I again admired the damage done by Arc Light to the whole area. The LZ was a good size, but was littered with the broken remains of the trees that had once thickly covered the terrain. The team was having a great deal of trouble negotiating the debris to get to the aircraft. We were spending far too long in the LZ, and we started taking some small-arms fire. That was when Poley found it necessary to complain, "One-Eight, this is One-Nine, will you hurry up in there? The mess hall has steaks tonight, and I want to get there before they burn them."

"Just give us a minute, and I'll be gone like a mutha."

When I got back to the Castle, my orders for R & R were waiting. I couldn't wait to write Jackie and tell her. Christmas in Hawaii. It was like a dream. I spent the next month and a half waiting for Santa to arrive. I also wrote that it had been thirty-five days since I'd had a day off.

Ray Zoschak was due to go home on his extention leave after a routine intelligence-gathering mission. They hadn't made significant contact, but each day they reported just enough information to keep the mission going. In fact, they were following a company of NVA infantry, noting its movements. By the fifth day of the mission, the team had the enemy's routine down pat. They even had figured where the gooks would NDP that night. The enemy had made the mistake of using the same location the two previous nights. Ray's team made sure that they arrived at the NDP early. The NVA must have been pretty sure of themselves; they had not chosen a good position. The terrain was bowl shaped, providing the LRPs with good fields of fire from above. They set out their daisy-chained claymores and waited. When the last AK-47 was at stack arms and the last rice bowl was placed in someone's lap, the LRPs blew the claymores.

It was about 1600 hours when the radio came alive in the LRP TOC.

"Linwood Teams Three, this is Team One-Three. We are in heavy contact with a company-size force. Request immediate extraction. Over."

Four pilots made the familiar scramble out the door and down the hill. We would get the coordinates en route. The sight of four pilots running and stumbling toward the aircraft set the crew chiefs and gunners in action without a word being spoken.

In less than a minute, rotors had been untied, and ignitors were ticking deep inside the turbines of the two Hueys. Soon we were on a balls-to-the-wall run to the rescue.

About halfway out, the call came over the Fox Mike. "Kingsmen Two-Five, this is Team One-Three. Save the birds."

"One-Three, Two-five. Say again?"

"Save the birds." Ray knew well that we called on our helicopters to deliver everything they could give on the way to a hot extraction. Time was of the essence. Thirty seconds in a firefight could mean the difference between survival and extinction.

"I thought you were in contact?"

"We were."

"What happened?"

"They died."

"All of them?"

"Yes, sir."

The count was 155. The team had set it up perfectly, the claymores, the prearranged artillery and rifle fire. The NVA never had a chance. Only one of them was able to even get to his rifle to try and return fire. It took a couple of hours to get a reaction force in and count all the weapons and gather all the equipment, but the effort was well worth it. Missions like that one made it easy to understand why Charlie hated the LRPs so much. The same reasons that I took such great pride in working with them.

Later that night in the debriefing, a lieutenant colonel on the division staff asked Zoschak, "Sergeant, do you expect me to believe that you went out there with six men and killed 155, not VC, but trained NVA infantry?"

Zoschak didn't say a word, he simply stood and picked up his weapon and ruck. His team automatically stood with him. He looked over at Meacham and me and asked, "Captain Meacham, Mr. Grant, would you please come with me?"

Before we could respond, the lieutenant colonel asked. "Sergeant, where do you think you're going?"

Ray turned back to him and said, "Sir, I'm going back out there to get you 310 fucking ears, sir!"

The deputy commanding general glared at the lieutenant colonel and said, "Sergeant, that won't be necessary. We are going to credit your kills."

Ray Zoschak wasn't one to brag about his accomplishments. If he said something, it was merely a statement of fact, and he expected to be taken at his word. He was offended that he should be doubted, and would have asked us to reinsert his team in the dark at 2300 hours to bring back the required proof of his word.

10 November (129 days to go, 21st day in a row on LRPs). Four solid days after the mission of the fourth, the entire area around Nui Khe was pounded with Arc Lights and artillery. Chuck just couldn't seem to get it in his head that there was a big price to pay for screwing around with the guys who wore tiger stripes. That afternoon, we inserted Phil Myers's team on the front side of Nui Khe. Supposedly they were on rocket watch. I think the real reason was to see if the B-52s and arty had left any bugs or birds alive in the area. We also inserted a team in the mountains to the south of FSB Roy.

That night, there was a going-away party for First Sergeant Walker of F Company. There was real food and plenty of beer. How could we resist? John Sours and Frank Souza had just returned from Recondo school; it would also be a welcome-back party. I was looking forward to having a beer with John and Frank again. Normally, for parties at the LRPs, we would walk, knowing that it was unlikely that we'd be able to drive on the way back. But this time we'd have to be better behaved since we had teams out. Poley parked the jeep facing back toward the road, ready to haul ass back to the Castle if a team came in contact. John and Frank got blitzed, along with Linderer, Clifton, Schwartz, Miller, and Larry Chambers. They were just starting to be fun to watch when The Dave and I had to leave. The next day was another LRP day for us.

About halfway through the next morning, Phil Myers discovered life on the planet Nui Khe. The planet was still inhabited by little people. As we sat in TOC, monitoring the situation on the radio, the team down south came in contact. Eklund looked over at us and said, "Let's go. Grant, you go out to Nui Khe and support Myers's team. I'll take Poley and the guns and extract the team down by Roy."

We departed Eagle as a flight of two, and split up. I headed west, and Poley south. I could see the guns a half mile to the south and Poley falling in behind. It felt strange to be departing from the normal procedure. Especially since it was me that was heading out, single ship. I glanced over at Barry Schreiber, and I could see he wasn't all that happy about the situation either. We set up an orbit well to the east of the team's location and contacted Myers. They'd started moving toward an extraction LZ but had been pinned down by fire from two or three snipers.

They were also reporting a lot of movement in the area. Phil whispered into the radio that he couldn't raise arty support from where he was and wanted to know if we could get him a fire mission. I told him that shouldn't be a problem and that we'd extract him after the other team. I let Barry continue his orbits as I called Bastogne Control.

"Bastogne Control, this is Kingsmen One-Eight. I need fire support for the east side of Nui Khe mountain. Over."

"Roger Kingsmen One-Eight, this Bastogne Control. Stand by one. Over." The radio procedure was always more formal when dealing with artillery because there was no room for misunderstanding.

"Kingsmen One-Eight, your fire support will be on two five seven point eight five, call sign New Jersey. Over."

"Roger, two five seven point eight five, New Jersey. Over."

It never occurred to me that he had just given me a UHF frequency or the significance of the call sign. I automatically dialed it in the radio and called. "New Jersey, New Jersey, this is Kingsmen One-Eight. Fire mission. Over."

It was the tone of the UHF radio as he responded that made me suddenly aware I had just contacted a battleship and not a battery of army artillery. "Roger, Kingsmen. This is New Jersey. Send your mission. Over."

My mind was racing. Myers had given me good coordinates for the target, but he assumed the biggest thing he would get would be 155mm artillery. I was now aware that each shot would be 2000 pounds of high explosives. "Kingsmen One-Eight, this is New Jersey. I say again, send your mission. Over."

"New Jersey, this will be danger close mission, I say again, a danger close mission. Grid Yankee Delta 7590 0512, request HE, penetrating ten meters, target is personnel. Will adjust. Over."

Now it was his turn to be worried. "Kingsmen, this is New Jersey. How close are your friendlies?"

"Stand by, New Jersey."

Back to Myers. "Normal Credit Two-Eight, Kingsmen One-Eight. I have your arty on the line, they want details on the danger close."

"Roger we are five zero Whiskey off the target. Over."

"Hang tight, it's coming most ricky tick."

I switched back to UHF. "New Jersey, Kingsmen One-Eight. Friendlies are five zero meters Whiskey."

There was a short pause while he digested that information.

"Kingsmen, I have you on radar orbiting five zero zero zero southeast of the target and clear of the GT line to the south. Penetrating will not be necessary. Shot. Over."

"Shot out," I replied. I quickly turned the selector to one and said to the team, "Heads down, it's on the way, and it's big."

I barely switched back when the New Jersey called. "Splash. Over," letting me know there were five seconds till impact.

I said, "Spla—sh. Over," pausing in the middle as a vibration passed through the aircraft as the sixteen-inch round, weighing as much as a Volkswagen, passed by us. It impacted on the face of Nui Khe and looked like it took out an entire grid square. The whisper came over the Fox Mike radio. "What the fuck was that?"

"I told you it was big."

"Well, move it three zero zero closer and do it again."

"Roger that." Then back to the UHF radio.

"New Jersey, are you sure I'm far enough clear of the GT line?"

I could almost feel the smile on his face as he said, "Yes, sir, you are well clear."

"Roger. Left three zero zero. Over."

"Left three zero zero." A short pause then, "Shot. Over."

The second round was on the way. "Shot out.

"Splash. Over."

This time I was more prepared for the passing Volkswagen. "Splash out."

The center of impact seemed to be right where I wanted it. I was astounded at the amount of damage one round could do. It seemed like another grid square had been blown up. The Fox Mike came alive with Phil's whispered voice. "Kingsman One-Eight, this Normal Credit Two-Eight. That did the job. Over."

I did not even respond to Phil. I called the New Jersey. "New Jersey, One-Eight, thank you. That did the job."

"Kingsman, this is New Jersey. Don't you want a fire for effect?"

"Uh, I . . . uh don't think so. I'm afraid you would knock the whole mountain down. Besides, I think you have already blown the entire NVA Army back to Hanoi."

"Roger, glad we could help."

I couldn't bear to tell him that he was shooting those big guns at a couple of snipers.

"Credit Two-Eight, this is One-Eight. What's your situation? Over."

"Everything is quiet down here. What the hell was that you sent in here?"

"Sixteen-inch naval gunfire."

"Our ears will never be the same."

I continued to circle well clear of the team. I wanted to be sure that all was truly well and that it would stay that way. It was not long before Poley called me on his way back to Eagle with the other team. I reported to him the situation and that all was now cold, for the time being. He said that Eklund would like me to stick with the team for the rest of my fuel load. A short time later, he called from the LRP TOC and told me to return to Eagle and top off before coming back to the Acid pad.

The team was briefed that division wanted it to continue the rocket watch if there was no contact before dark. They spent the night on rocket watch again. Charlie wanted no more of those sixteen-inch guns. Eagle was not rocketed that night.

Later, in the Ranger Lounge, we gave Ray Zoschak a big send-off on his extension leave. A strong drunk front moved over Camp Eagle and became stationary over the LRP company area. There were several Kingsmen there, and an argument ensued about who was the craziest, the LRPs or the pilots who flew them. A number of points of view were expressed by both sides. Dave Poley said, "The LRPs are really crazy because they want to go out there in small groups to try to find Chuck and they stay out in the woods in the dark."

Waving his arms in the air, Zo stepped forward. "No. No. No. The pilots are the most crazy, and I can prove it."

He was wearing tigers and held up the front of his shirt for emphasis, "See, I go out there, and if Chuck comes along, I go, 'Pssst, hey, Chuck, I'm a tree.' " He held out his arms like drooping branches and stood on his toes. "But," he continued, "when you guys come out there, there ain't no way in hell you can convince Chuck that fucking thing is a hummingbird." He shrugged his shoulders and walked away, indicating there wasn't room for further discussion.

BRIG. GEN. ALLEN M. BURDETT

General Burdett became the deputy division commander during November. He was a real aviator, not a general who had been given the twenty-five-hour "Q"(qualification) course. We then had two generals who understood aviation, and both took a personal interest in the LRP company. It certainly made a difference to know that at the very top there was concerned leadership.

General Burdett made sure that he flew often enough to stay proficient. He liked to show up unannounced at operations early in the morning. The first time he did it, he gave everyone quite a shock. He strolled into flight operations without his aide and told Rick Haines he wanted to fly.

"Yes, sir. No problem, the C & C aircraft is ..."

"No, no, Mr. ... uh Haines. You don't understand, I want to fly in the lift."

"Flight lead then, General?"

"I'd prefer to be somewhere in the middle of the flight if you don't mind."

"Would Chalk Three be all right, sir?"

"That would be fine."

A short while later, a hung over WO1 stumbled out to his aircraft to find someone already finishing up the preflight. Surfer Lou started to protest.

"Hey, what the hell ..."

Then he noticed the stars on the collar. General Burdett smiled and said, "I'm your peter pilot today."

The general was known to be sharp enough on the aircraft to point out mistakes in the log book to the crew chief. He did, however, have the class to always pose the correction as a question. He managed not to make you feel stupid when he corrected. I don't think I would have liked to be the one he corrected for the same mistake a second time.

Lou gave the general a mission briefing, and the general gave him some background on why the lift was being flown. They strapped in and went through the checklist, and as they got to the point of starting the engine, General Burdett stopped Lou.

"Son, before we go any further, I want to make sure you understand something." He pulled his collar up so Lou could clearly see the star there.

"Right now I am the deputy division commander of the 101st Airborne Division. I want you to remember that as soon as we pull the starter trigger, you are the ranking man in this aircraft. If I screw up, I expect you to chew my ass just as you would any other peter pilot."

The young aircraft commanders were always impressed with his flying ability, and he never needed that ass-chewing. It was apparent that he understood the airmobile concept and that the warrant officers were meant to be the aviation professionals in the army.

12 November (127 days to go, 23d day in row on LRPs). That afternoon, Team Two-Eight heard enemy movement all around them. We scrambled with the guns and headed to Nui Khe. While we were en route, Myers said that he thought the gooks were monitoring the radio frequency. We would have to pull the team. There could be little doubt about the team having been compromised this time.

Smoke grenades were frequently used in Nam to locate the LZ and indicate wind direction. When smoke was popped, the pilot identified the color, and the ground unit confirmed the color. This was to prevent Chuck from popping smoke to lure a helicopter into *his* LZ and then blow it away. Most pilots liked to say cool things, identifying purple smoke as goofy grape or green as looney lime. Ground units liked to preempt us by saying the cool stuff first. Then again, sometimes they just screwed up and said things like, "Yellow smoke out." Each mission brief for LRP operations addressed "wrong color smoke." In the event that a team suspected Charlie was monitoring the radio, it would be preplanned for the team to give away the color of smoke they were throwing. The giveaway would be a lie. The color was briefed so that whatever color the team announced, we knew what color they would actually use.

When the aircraft approached the mountain, radio contact was established normally. Then Myers said, "Popping yellow smoke."

I acknowledged and waited for the expected green smoke. As the green smoke rose from the trees, a column of yellow rose from a location a couple of hundred meters down the mountain. The next transmission on the radio came in the familiar Texas drawl of R. L. Smith. "Rollin' in hot on yellow smoke."

I would have given almost anything to see the look on Charlie's face as he squatted by his radio with the pin from the yellow smoke grenade dangling from his index finger.

Late that afternoon, as evening began to creep over the dense jungle, Snuffy Smith's team went hot. They were working the area around Leech Island. It was just getting dark as the flight broke ground. It would be full dark by the time we reached the team at the LZ, a sandbar in a river. While we were on the way, they called and said that the gooks had caught up with them again. As the RTO spoke, I cold hear sporadic rifle fire over the radio. I told him that it would be dark, and we would need a strobe to mark the LZ. I knew that they wouldn't be enthusiastic about standing in the open with a strobe, but there'd be no other way to identify the LZ. I would wait till the last possible moment to call for the light.

I located the silver slice that was the river and started to follow it. When I knew I was getting close, I called for the strobe. I had timed it just right; I had barely enough time to slow down for the landing. On short final, I could see that there wasn't enough room to set down on the sandbar.

"Kick out the ladders!"

"Yes, sir," was the instant response from the back.

In the light of the strobe, I could see that it was Snuffy who was standing on the sandbar, under fire, holding the strobe. I hovered as low as possible. When the blades began to trim the vegetation, I held the aircraft as still as I could. The distinctive crack of AK-47s sounded.

Sugar Bear said, "Sir, the ladder isn't long enough."

"Shit."

"Never mind—they're climbing up the team leader."

Each team member climbed up Snuffy's back until he reached the ladder, and then they hauled themselves up to the aircraft. The last two hung from the ladder and hauled Snuffy up by the rucksack. All the weight on the one side tried to force us into the trees. As soon as the crew reported everyone on the ladder, I pulled pitch and hauled ass out of there.

BLACK WEDNESDAY

18 November (121 days to go, 29th day in a row on LRPs). Captain Eklund told us we would be briefed that day for two heavy insertions the next. Two twelve-man teams in the same general area meant that "heavy" was short for heavy shit. We would be inserting in the Roung Roung Valley, twenty-three klicks to the south-southwest of Eagle. The Roung Roung, while never receiving the notoriety that the A Shau did, was always rife with enemy soldiers. Beaucoup bigtime bad-guy land for sure, GI.

Burnell would lead one team. The primary mission was to observe enemy movements. The secondary mission was to locate and destroy an enemy radio transmitter that had been operating in the vicinity of his insertion LZ. Contreros would lead the second team. The mission was twofold for the second team. Part one was recon. The second was "hunter/killer;" they were to locate and, possibly, ambush NVA units operating in the area. This type of operation served two purposes: it gave Charlie some of his own medicine, on his own turf, "hit 'n' git." The next was that bodies yielded valuable intelligence. Intel had indicated that the 5th NVA Regiment was in the area. The outside hope was that the team could get to and kill or capture the infamous Colonel Mot, the commander. Another NVA regiment was also reported in the area. Both teams were to try and confirm the presence of the 5th and to confirm the presence of and identify the other regiment. Later, some would claim that the ambush and hunt for Colonel Mot were inventions of the team leader.

Meacham asked Eklund, "Is it fair to use a whole twenty-four LRPs against only two regiments of NVA?"

The comment drew nervous laughs from all present. We all knew damn well that things had been heating up for the last couple of months, and this was likely to be a hot mission. Ken Eklund raised an eyebrow and said, "Shut up, Meacham." He wasn't being nasty to Bill; it was just the best answer he had for the question.

We went about the business of preparing the missions. Since they were heavy teams, both birds would be used to insert and extract. That meant we would both go on the overflights and VRs of the area. We also had other teams out, some of which were scheduled for extraction that day. It was going to be a long day. Before it was over, Barry Schreiber and I had logged 9.7 hours of flight time.

On the nineteenth, we lounged around the LRP compound all day. The insertions would be in the late afternoon. There was time to catch some Zs on the floor of a Huey, and BS with the LRPs who were going out on the mission. They were packing heavy for this trip because of the heavy concentration of bad guys, and because they would be far enough out to slow our response time if they got in trouble. Burnell's team would go in at 1530 and would consist of Lieutenant Williams as junior RTO, Snuffy Smith, Boom-Boom Evans, "Tiger" Ken Miller, and Jim "Stinky" Schwartz on the first aircraft. Honest John Burford as ATL, Joe Don Looney as senior RTO, Doc Proctor as medic, John Meszaros, Don Harris, and Larry Chambers on my aircraft.

Contreros's team would go at 1630 and would consist of Al Contreros as TL, Jim Venable as ATL, John Sours, Billy Walkabout, Terry Clifton, Mike Reiff, Art Heringhausen, Gary

Linderer, Frank Souza, Riley Cox, Steve Czepurny, and Jim Bacon as the RTO. One of the concerns was that the second team had only one LZ in its recon zone. So the contingency plan was for them to break contact and E & E into Burnell's RZ (recon zone), a dangerous procedure due to the possibility of being mistaken for enemy by the other team. LRPs were not used to having friendlies in their area.

As we headed out, the sun was already casting long shadows. We saw the ridgeline where we were going to insert teams, on both sides, from a long way out. The mountains had that hazy purple look mountains get in the late afternoon, but the beauty of the scenery went unnoticed by the soldiers on their way to meet the NVA.

For Burnell's insertion, the plan was to proceed along the east side of Nui Khe and FSB Brick. We would pass by the Roung Roung and then turn west and insert on the back side of the ridge. The drop-off went off like clockwork, and we headed back to Eagle for the second team. We took off at 1630, on schedule, and arrived at the LZ with the proper separation for the insertion. This time, we went west first and turned south just before FSB Birmingham. When we reached the Roung Roung, we turned east and flew to the LZ. Even though the LZs were close together, our flight paths kept us well clear of the one we were not working. Bill had Contreros on board and went first. I swung wide and set up on final approach about four hundred meters behind him. When Bill came to a hover over the LZ, nobody exited the bird. This was unusual since on insertion the quicker the LRPs were rid of us the better they liked it. Just as I was about to key the mike and ask what was going on, Meacham broke the airway, "Linwood Teams Six, this is Kingsmen Two-Five. Up close, this LZ is not an LZ but a ravine filled with elephant grass."

That wasn't really a surprise to anyone, since we made a point of not paying too much attention to our LZs before the actual insertion. The theory was that if we didn't look interested, Chuck wouldn't think we were interested. It seemed to be effective, since the regular infantry paid a lot of attention to their LZs and had trouble finding the bad guys. The LRPs never seemed to have any trouble locating some. One of the reasons we always picked alternate LZs was that sometimes one would turn up bad. The problem with elephant grass was that, even up close, it was hard to tell if it was five feet tall or twenty feet tall.

Just as Eklund called the abort, LRPs began dropping from

Bill's bird. Contreros had ordered his team to jump. I had slowed to allow Bill more time in the LZ. As he started his climb out, I lowered the nose to continue my approach. We were committed; if one man goes in, the whole team goes in.

The LZ was small, and we could get no lower than four feet above the elephant grass. Even then, we were modifying the scenery with our forty-eight-foot weed-eater. The team crawled out on the skids and hung by their hands to drop into the LZ. All the moving around in the back of the aircraft made it hard to hover, but it turned out to be a wise move on the part of the team. The grass proved to be about twelve feet tall. From the floor of the aircraft, it would have been a twenty-foot fall.

We headed back toward Birmingham and circled well clear of the AO as we had done after Burnell's insertion. We were waiting for the all-clear call from the team after they lay dog to make sure the area was cold and they had not been observed being inserted. At the time, we didn't know that John Sours had been injured by the jump when he landed on a log. Souza had tried to get him to call us back to take him to Eagle, but John wanted to stay with the team. He told everyone his ankles were just twisted a little and would be all right. By the next morning, it was obvious that his ankles were broken. The airborne soldier: two broken ankles, a jungle full of bad guys, and he wants to go for a five-day walk with his friends. No wonder that Charlie didn't want to engage the unit of the "horse" or the "chicken." (During a Special Forces mission, we had captured an NVA officer who had written orders not to engage units of the horse or the chicken, meaning the First Cav or the 101st. They referred to the eagle in the 101st patch as a chicken, since there are no eagles in Vietnam.)

Later on, the team reported that as they were scouting around the area, they had heard a single shot. It was probably a signal that the bad guys knew that they were no longer alone. I thought sure that it would mean another damned night extraction.

The twentieth dawned a bright sunny day; it wasn't too hot, and there was a pleasant little breeze blowing. It was about as nice a day as one could have in a war zone. I guess that's why, somewhere, some lifer decided that it would be a good day to fuck things up. I would like to think that it was the same asshole that made all of the bad decisions that day.

I was brushing my teeth when Wild Bill came by. I smiled. "Good morning, you old turkey."

The look on his face said he was not in the mood for my warrant officer act. I said, "What's up?"

"We've been pulled off the LRP mission to do CAs."

I said through toothpaste, but fairly calmly, "That's pretty fuckin' stupid. We know where all the teams are."

"Yeah."

"Who they puttin' on?" I mumbled while still scrubbing.

"No one."

"What the hell did you just say?"

He eyes looked sad. "I said they're not puttin' anyone on."

Could we have lost all the teams last night so fast that they didn't even wake us up? I asked, "What happened?"

He said, "Nothin', they're jus' pullin' us to fly CAs. They promise that, if we're needed, they'll break us off for the LRPs."

I exploded. "Are they fuckin' crazy? They're gonna just send us off on some goat screw and leave all those teams hangin'? If anything happens to any of those LRPs, I'm gonna fuckin' frag everybody."

He said, "Calm down, junior, it's not that bad yet. I agree with you, but there's nothing we can do right now. I tried, and they wouldn't listen."

I knew then it was useless to get worked up about it. He explained that they wanted max effort for some lifts out west of Veghel. We already knew that activity had stepped up, and we suspected that Nguyen was planning another big offensive for Tet '69.

When the CO briefed us for the mission, the overview made it seem as though the entire division was on the move. I crossed the gully and climbed the hill to my revetment. Barry was the peter pilot again that day. He knew I was pissed, so he didn't say much as we walked and did our preflight. First flight of the day, we always made sure we did a good preflight. There was no telling when we'd get to check the bird again. That day would turn out to be a real test of the Huey's reliability. After I briefed the crew chief and gunner, they wanted to know if they should strip out the ladders and McGuire rigs. I told them no, as far as I was concerned if we got the call that the LRPs needed us, we'd be ready. I was going to have them throw out any grunts at the nearest firebase on the way to pick up the LRPs. We were just about ready for the scheduled 0700 pitch pull when Captain Muhlethaler came by to say we were on a hold. Barry asked him, "Why?"

Captain Muhlethaler said, "Damned if I know. The usual hurry up and wait."

We sat around and waited, and waited, which drove me crazy. Not only were we being kept in the dark on what was going on with our teams, but no one was telling us what was going on with this mission. It was getting harder to tolerate ordinary missions after being so close to what was going on with LRPs. About 0830, Wild Bill came by and told us that L T Williams had sent word over that John Sours had been medevacked. Not only that, but the team had reported that just after the medevac departed there'd been two shots fired. Mr. Charles must have thought the team had been extracted and was sounding the all clear. I was relieved to hear that, maybe we could get the CA over with without losing a LRP team.

Finally, the word came to crank.

We flew out to FSB Veghel and found the grunts there ready to go. I realized they had probably been sitting there since first light, waiting for us to show up, thinking that we were at fault for the delay. All the while, we were sitting at Eagle thinking they were at fault. The CA went off like everybody knew what they were doing. In a half hour, we had moved the entire company. The PZ loaded almost as fast as the LZ off-loaded. It was about 0930 when we headed back to Eagle in two flights of five. Normally the flight was organized by platoon integrity; in this case, Wild Bill and I had been put in the same flight as the last two birds, to facilitate an easy break off if we were called to our primary mission. Instead of the infantry freq, we monitored the long-range-patrol frequency on the FM.

At 0945, the radio came alive on FM.

The usual whisper called, "Linwood Teams Six, this is Linwood Teams Two-Three."

The whisper came again, "Linwood Teams Six, this is Linwood Teams Two-Three. Over."

There was a short pause and then, "Linwood Teams Two-Three, this is Six. Go ahead."

"Six, this is Two-Three. We have sprung an ambush."

My mind went into high gear, and the adrenaline hit my veins immediately. I thought, They're hot!

Contreros continued, "We wasted nine and a probable; we are searching the bodies now."

Eklund asked, "Are you still in contact?"

Contreros came back, "Two-Three. Negative!"

"This is Six. Standby, I'll get back to you."

The flight landed at Eagle in the hot fuel area. We had to wait for the first flight to clear the fueling points so we could take our turn. The place was busier than usual. The rest of the company was off working scheduled CAs and resupply missions. Operations had called us on the way in and told us to go to Firebase Birmingham for the next lift. I looked over at Barry in disgust. He just nodded; there was no need to say anything.

Refueled, we took off and headed west toward Birmingham. It was starting to get hot now, and as we lined up along Highway 547 for the penaprime runway at Birmingham, I could feel the sweat build up along the leather band inside my flight helmet. At about a half mile from touchdown, I noticed that the next company was at the pad and ready to go. It would be another fast lift. When we landed, I felt the touch of the red clay dust that rose in the rotor wash. It came in my window and stuck to the sweat running down my face. Barry was at the controls, still I did not bother to wipe the grit from my face. It only would be replaced with more on takeoff.

The grunts walked slowly to the aircraft in the heat, heads down and weapons pointed at the ground. The heat had gotten their attention and had slowed my temper as well. These troopers must've not been waiting as long as the last batch or were not as anxious to get where they were going. They were in no hurry. We kept the aircraft running, and only the AC of Lead and Chalk Two from each flight got out for the briefing. The rest of us would just follow along. If the first two got waxed, we would abort anyway. Once the first flight was in, the rest would be able to see where to go and continue the lift. Just like the LRPs, once troops were on the ground, it didn't matter how hot things got. We would finish the job. It was about 1030 when we took off with the first sortie. These troops were being inserted in an LZ just to the north of Highway 547, about a thousand meters northwest of the company we had put in earlier, about a twenty-klick move, fifteen minutes round-trip flight time. With load and unload time figured in, about twenty minutes per sortie. The ACL would be eight, so we could move the company in two lifts with the ten aircraft. Forty minutes to bang this one out.

We had just dropped the first load at the LZ and were returning to the PZ for the next lift when, at 1035, the Fox Mike started to get busy again.

"Linwood Teams Two-Three, this is Linwood Teams Six."

It occurred to me that Eklund had sure taken his time getting back to the team.

"Six, this is Two-Three. Go ahead," came the whisper.

"Two-Three, this is Six, tell more about what you have out there."

Contreros whispered, "They were from some kind of medical unit. Four were nurses, we think; two were females, and one was an officer."

Eklund asked, "This is Six. What about the officer?"

Contreros said, "Some kind of staff officer; we got a whole bag full of documents, maps, and stuff."

"Two-Three, this is Six. Okay, here's the deal. A reaction force is going to be sent out to develop the situation. You'll be extracted and reinserted in the other AO. Your extraction bird will be bringing more ammo, frags, and claymores for you to re-arm with."

I looked over at Barry and he was smiling, just like me. We felt we'd just been let in on a secret that only the crews of 121 and 348 knew. We now knew what our next mission was going to be before anyone else in the flight. Who else but the ready reaction force would be supplying the LRP team in the Roung Roung with a reaction force. Maybe someone higher up did know his ass from his elbow after all.

At 1130, we were just leaving the LZ after dropping the final load when we heard Eklund on the radio telling the team that not only were they not getting a reaction force, but they weren't getting extraction either. Well, that would certainly even up the odds some, now the whole two regiments were looking for just one team. The one that had been compromised. Eklund told the team that all of the division's helicopters were committed. It was true we were committed, but we were supposed to be committed to the LRPs. He had managed to get a LOH and told them that he would be out there as soon as he could. It took all the discipline I could muster at that point to keep from breaking formation and turning south to the Roung Roung Valley.

Then I heard on the internal UHF, "Kingsmen Six, this is Kingsmen Two-Five, on Uniform." It was Meacham.

Six responded, "Go, Two-Five."

Bill said, "Boss, we got a LRP team in trouble. You gotta get us outta here and back to the team."

"Roger, Two-Five. I'll do what I can."

It was another fifteen minutes until we got back to hot gas at Eagle. That would be an hour and forty-five minutes on the fuel load. We might as well top off while we waited. As we were landing at Camp Eagle, I could hear Eklund talking to the team from the LOH. When we were on short final, the Old Man called on our internal UHF freq to announce that Meacham and I were released to the LRP mission after refueling.

It took an eternity for the fuel to reach the top of the tank. It was 1205 when Wild Bill called Eagle Tower to announce a flight of two for departure to the west. When we were cleared, he barely had the aircraft light on the skids before he dumped the nose over. I could see the underside of 121 like I was lying under it. I quickly had 348 in pursuit. It was not how they had taught maximum performance takeoffs in flight school, but we were on the go, and no one was stopping us now.

Barry was calling out the torque as I demanded everything 348 had to give. "Forty-three, forty-four, forty-five, forty-six, forty-seven, forty-eight, forty-nine, hold it!"

The airspeed indicator was showing sixty-five knots before we had cleared POL. We had no more altitude than we needed to clear the barbed wire. Airspeed had risen to about 110 before Wild Bill brought the nose up to a 120-knot attitude. I commanded 348 to mirror the maneuver. The needle on the gauge settled at 120, with the torque still sitting at fifty, and caused the vertical speed indicator to point to about fifteen-hundred feet per minute. The altimeter began to wind up quickly; the power wouldn't be reduced until the aircraft were high enough to establish communication with Eklund or the team.

Scratchy noises coming from the Fox Mike radio indicated that someone was talking, but we weren't able to make it out until the altimeter was indicating about seventeen-hundred feet.

"Six, this is Two-Three. We are still in heavy contact, receiving intense automatic weapons fire. My ATL needs that damn medevac now!" To allow the more important transmissions to take place, Bill had not called yet. We heard no calls from a medevac. Bill cut in, "Linwood Teams Six, this is Kingsman Two-Five, we are about ten mikes out."

Eklund replied, "Kingsman Two-Five, this is Six. We have one wounded. I am over the area trying to pinpoint the pickup point for you. Do you have me in sight?"

"Linwood Six this is Two-Five. I have your LOH in sight."

"That's me. Situation is this, we have seriously wounded and intense small-arms fire in the area. The wounded man will have to be extracted by string."

McGuire extractions were dangerous by nature. Extracting a

wounded man that way was extremely risky. A man who was not fully conscious risked falling out of the rig. But there was no other way to get him out unless a medevac bird showed up with a jungle penetrator.

"Linwood Teams Six, this is Saber Three-Seven, I'm inbound to your location with a light fire team, maybe we can do something about that small-arms fire for you."

I strained my eyes to see ahead. I thought that I could just make out the silhouettes of the two Cobras about five miles in front of us. This was one time that they beat us to the scramble. I was glad to lose, the team obviously needed the Snakes desperately at that point. Later, I would learn that Jim Venable had been hit in the neck, arm, and chest while trying to guide Eklund's C & C bird with a signal mirror.

"Saber, this is Linwood Six. Roger we have plenty of work for you."

"Two-Three, this is Six. Gimme smoke."

"Smoke's out."

There was a pause in the radio traffic as everyone looked for the smoke. We had just passed Nue Khe, running as fast as we could.

"Two-Three, Six. I don't have your smoke," Eklund said.

The smoke was being trapped under the tree cover for so long that it would dissipate before escaping.

The LOH began flying crisscross patterns over the area where the team was. "Two-Three, tell me when I'm over you," Eklund called.

Contreros called to mark the position; as he spoke, the sound of automatic fire was clear in the background. Eklund dropped one of his favored willy petes to the west of the team to mark the position for the Cobras. "Linwood Two-Three, keep your heads down I'm bringing in the snakes." Break. "Saber, the friendlies are three zero east of the willy pete, everything else is yours."

The Cobras came back with, "This is Saber Three-Seven. Roger, I have Mr. Willy Peter in sight, stand back and leave the killin' ta us."

I looked over at Barry, keyed the intercom, and smiled, "Get some, Snakes."

Wild Bill set up on final to the ridge. I said to Barry, "You have the controls. Orbit out of everyone's way while 121 goes in for the wounded."

"Roger, I have the controls," was his response. The important part now was to get the NVA off the team's back for a while. A couple of Snakes was just the thing to keep Mr. Charles otherwise occupied. The Cav guys made a couple of runs, then the LOH went back into position, hovering directly over the team to mark its position for Bill. Then the LOH moved off to allow 121 to take his place. Meanwhile, the Cobras continued to make passes on both sides of the hovering Huey. The sudden dose of 2.75-inch FFARs seemed to have cooled the bad guys' interest; only sporadic fire was directed at Meacham's aircraft.

When Meacham departed, the NVA renewed the assault on the team. I whispered a prayer for Venable as I watched 121's tail grow smaller, en route to Two Two Surg. The Cobras began making their passes slower and tighter. They were passing directly over the team slow enough to do pedal turns to keep their fire on target. These guys must have flown LOHs or Charlie-models before. It was the kind of coverage we were afraid that we would never get from the Cobra. Wild Bill called Eklund while the Cobras plied their trade. "Linwood Teams Six, Kingsman Two-Five. Are we going to pull the team after the medevac is complete?"

"Negative, Two-Five. Division is sending a reaction force!"

"Roger, Six. You want us to go get the reaction force?"

"Negative. Division says they are sending Blues for the reaction team. The Cav will insert them."

"Linwood Six, this is Saber. We have to break off to rearm and refuel. We have requested more fire support for you. Saber Six will have it out here as soon as he can."

"Six, Roger."

"Linwood Two-Three, this is Six. Cobras are going to rearm and refuel. I got to let LOH have some go juice too or I'll be down there with you shortly. You have 105 mike mikes on standby at Brick and Spear, call sign Red Leg Four, on 38.75. You copy?"

"Affirm, Six." That meant that the team had two artillery batteries on standby.

"Two-Three, you also have Kingsman One-Eight orbiting out here, and Two-Five will be back shortly."

"Roger."

I looked at my map then called Meacham on company UHF. "Two-Five, One-Eight on Uniform. I will be orbiting at the west end of the valley to remain clear of arty."

He replied, "Roger, I'll be back out as soon as I can. I'm going to land at FSB Brick and get this guy inside so I don't lose him."

I keyed the mike. "I figure, if we have to, we can remain on station till 1400 and land at Eagle with five minutes of fumes."

"Yeah, me too."

Something was wrong with Meacham. He never let me make two decisions in a row uncorrected. "One-Eight this is Two-Five. I smell something worse than *nuoc mam* out here, partner."

"Yeah, me too."

We knew the LRP business well enough to go out with one of the teams if we needed to. We had even been invited. One thing that you never, never, never did with a LRP team was sit and defend a position in broad daylight. The team was down to ten by then. If they sat still for long, two regiments might just be enough to take them on. Two Hueys circled, four miles out, watching the artillery show for the next forty-five minutes. One important consideration in working artillery in close was that when you were surrounded by NVA, if you don't call it close enough, it tends to bring the enemy closer to you rather than drive them away. Now that's okay if you're driving them into force with the firepower to shoot them all. For a LRP team, using artillery is a fine art that must be executed with surgical precision. The Red Legs are very good at what they do and they're proud of their accuracy. But when you start calling rounds to within ten meters of your own position, they get real nervous. They like to hear things like "add five zero," meaning add fifty meters to the range. "Left one zero zero," meaning move to the left one hundred meters from the last impact. But their all time favorite is "fire for effect." That means wherever the last one went, blast the hell out of it. A small force that's pinned down tends to make numerous adjustments to wherever they're receiving fire from. When the adjustments are all ten meters, the arty guys know you are working close and get antsy. They're well aware of the amount of damage they can inflict, and they know it doesn't take much artillery to take out a whole LRP team.

It was around 1330 when Eklund returned. He brought four Cobras with him this time. (He done reeeeeal good.) Bill and I hung out for another fifteen minutes and watched the Cobras go to work. Unlike arty, gunship pilots can see what they are shooting at, so they are not quite so shy about working in close. At 1345, we split for fuel. We had about a forty-five-minute turnaround. By the time we got back, we'd been flying for five and half hours. The team had been in contact on and off for five hours.

Meacham keyed the mike, "Linwood Teams Six, this is Kingsman Two-Five. Are we ready to extract yet?"

"Two-Five, this is Six. Division still wants to develop the situation. They're saying, still, that they're going to provide a re-action force."

"This is Two-Five. I don't like this. Even with the Cobras, Charlie isn't going to stay away forever."

"This is Six. I don't like it either," was the mumbled reply.

"Two-Five, this is Six. What we need right now is to get out a bag of documents and maps the team has captured."

Meacham replied. "Roger, I can drop a McGuire rig rope, and they can tie the bag to it so we can haul it up."

Wild Bill came to a hover over the ridgeline and dropped a rope down to the team, but the rope hung up in the thick canopy of trees and wouldn't drop through to the ground.

Eklund got quiet; we knew he was probably on another frequency arguing for extraction. That was not the way it was supposed to work. Once the team was compromised, they got extracted. Some fool was changing the rules that day, and it didn't give any of us a warm fuzzy feeling. The Cobras were coming in regular intervals now. The artillery had the fire missions down to routine, so they were quickly able to fill any gaps in the Cobra support.

It was shortly after three when it happened. The Cobras were making rocket runs over the team in box patterns when suddenly a bunch of vegetation flew up in the air, just under one of the Snakes. It was followed by a dense cloud of black smoke.

Eklund excitedly called, "Two-Three, this is Six. What happened down there?"

There was no response.

Again he tried, "Two-Three, this is Six. Over."

Still no answer.

"Linwood Teams Two-Three, this is Linwood Teams Six. What's going on down there?"

I started to get a sick feeling in the pit of my stomach. What Bill and I had worried about all day had come to pass.

"Linwood Two-Three, this is Six. Answer me damn it."

Fphoooooooooot. There was the sound of breaking squelch. *Fphoooooooooooot*. It came again.

The voice came weak and strained, "Six, this is Two . . .

Three, we've been .... hit, everybody ... everybody's down, I ah ... ah ... think I'm the only one ... ah ... left."

There was a pause then, "No ... no, I'm not the only one. There's Indian."

Meacham jumped in, "Six, we'll call medevac for you. One-Eight, call Dustoff. I'm gonna go take a look."

Eklund jumped in with, "Two-Five, do more than take a look; go ahead and extract the team."

I didn't acknowledge the transmission, just nodded to Barry, and he grabbed the controls again. I changed the radio frequency and called Dustoff.

There was no answer. I looked up at the instrument panel, and we had already begun to climb. More altitude would give us better radio reception. I gave a thumbs-up to Barry; it was nice to have the other seat thinking. The helicopter climbed to twenty-three hundred feet, and I heard, "Kingsmen One-Eight, this is Dustoff control. Go ahead please."

"Dustoff, this is Kingsmen One-Eight. Requesting medevac. We have ten urgents at grid Yankee Charlie 845 876."

"One-Eight, this is Dustoff Control. What is the nature of the wounds?"

"This is One-Eight. I don't have all the information yet, I just know that there are ten, and they're bad. They'll have to be extracted by penetrator."

"This is Dustoff. We need to know the nature of the wounds."

"Dustoff, I'll get back to you; just get your crews going; we need them bad! One-Eight out."

I was afraid they wouldn't come if I couldn't give them the information. I didn't even know if anyone could actually load the wounded in the jungle penetrator. I later found out Mike Reiff, Art Heringhausen, and Terry Clifton were already dead. Contreros had a head wound, Souza had a hole in his back the size of a volley ball and was missing some ribs and a lung. Bacon, Czepurny, and Linderer were all hit in the legs or feet and were unable to walk. Bacon was barely able to stay conscious on the radio. Walkabout was wounded in both hands, and Cox was hit everywhere. Walkabout was the only one mobile, but unable to use his hands. Cox had a broken arm that was folded back in the middle. He tied it back, so that it wouldn't flop around and stop him from being able to shoot back. The tiny perimeter had five hands and two legs to fight off a lot of NVA. I tuned the Fox Mike back to LRP frequency. As I looked up, Wild Bill was going for the ridgeline, and Barry was setting us up to follow. There were now Cobras all over and they were working over large areas of the ridgeline. The Fox Mike was busy with traffic; Wild Bill and Eklund were directing Cobras. There was no way I could get detailed information for Dustoff. I tuned back to the Dustoff freq. "Dustoff, this is Kingsmen One-Eight, are you ready to copy on the wounds?"

The response was immediate. They must have realized that I wasn't fooling around the first time, "Send it, Kingsmen."

"Roger, Dustoff. We have four sucking chests, three traumatic amputations, and three head wounds." Barry shot me a funny look, and then he immediately recognized what I'd done. I'd been at war long enough to know what got immediate attention. So I gave them wounds that they would respond to instantly. If they found out I had lied, they could court-martial me later; meantime, the wounded LRPs were going to get prompt attention.

As I tuned back to LRP push, Dragon Six came on the radio and made his announcement.

"This is Dragon Six. I'm on the scene and am taking command of the situation here."

We could see some ARA birds orbiting about a mile away. Eklund must have had enough of being pushed around by then. "Dragon Six, this is Linwood Teams Six. This is my operation, so you can just get the fuck off the frequency and get the hell out of here. Or I'm liable to turn these Cobras loose on your ass."

Later we found out that Lucky Eagle, the division commander, was monitoring the push at the time. He had smiled and gave a thumbs-up to his staff when he heard Eklund's response.

As we made our overflight of Wild Bill as he hovered over the team, we could see that much of the overhead vegetation had been blown away. It no longer looked like the same ridgeline. The bad guys were shooting at us, the Cobras, Wild Bill, and the C & C bird. Maybe the reason why the enemy had not yet made a truly serious attempt to overrun the team was they figured that maybe they would get some helicopters out of the deal. Well, they were getting helicopters, but not the way they wanted them. Cobras have a really nasty bite. The entire ridgeline was littered with NVA bodies.

Wild Bill dropped his McGuire rigs. They just sat in the tree tops; the vegetation was still thick enough to hang them up. Bill was taking fire from all sides. The crew hauled the rigs back up, and he called to me. "One-Eight, I can't get the rigs to drop through the canopy. You give it a try."

I maneuvered 348 into position with the same results. The rigs would not drop through the cover. It did not matter, there was nobody down there that was really capable of riding the McGuire rigs much less getting in them.

I stepped on the floor button and called to Meacham, "Two-Five, One-Eight. Dustoff is on the way. What is the status of the reaction force?"

"No word yet."

"Two-Five, this is One-Eight. This is bullshit, let's go get some LRPs to reinforce the team."

"This is Two-Five. What does Eklund have to say about it?"

Eklund's LOH had left for Eagle to get more fuel, but he was still in radio range. I didn't have a chance to answer before he said, "This is Six. Great idea. Do it!"

Barry immediately lowered the nose and pulled in more power as he turned toward Eagle. The airspeed began to climb toward 120 knots. I knew 121 would be falling in behind for the trip back. Later on, Meacham told me that while he was hovering over the team, Tom Turk, his crew chief, had seen Riley Cox almost cut in half by a gook with an AK. Riley then rolled over and fired his shotgun into the dink. The combined effect of Cox's shotgun and Turk's M-60 left only two arms and legs hovering in a pink mist for a moment. Cox then calmly shoved his own intestines back in place and packed his boonie towel in the wound to hold everything together. Wild Bill called Saber Three-Seven, who was back on the scene, and told him he had the helm till Linwood Teams Six returned.

It took us only just over ten minutes to get back to Camp Eagle, yet when we arrived, the hillside above the Acid pad was covered with LRPs. They had obviously monitored the radio and knew we were coming. The whole company had turned out. They didn't look like LRPs, the faces weren't painted. They weren't all dressed in tiger stripes. Some wore flower-power cammys. Some wore tigers. Some were hardly dressed at all. Tony "Ti Ti" Tercero wore army issue, olive-drab boxer shorts and shower shoes. Of course, he had his weapon, LBE, and several bandoliers of ammo. He obviously didn't want to be overdressed for the occasion. It wasn't just LRPs either; the company clerk, Tim Long, was there; the supply sergeant, Phil Mueller, was there and ready to go. It was one thing to fight hard when things got hot, but these guys were climbing over each other to go on a ten-minute flight into hell. Nobody would have ever questioned a company clerk or supply sergeant who just sat the fight out in the orderly room. Those guys had buddies in trouble, and they were going to do something about it. It made me instantly proud to have the privilege of being associated with this bunch.

As the two Hueys touched down on the pad, the waiting LRPs rushed the aircraft. The heels of 348's skids had barely touched the ground when it was loaded so fast that the rest of the aircraft was dragged from the air with a thump.

I looked over my shoulder. There were at least eighteen people on board. No way that Huey was going to make it into the air with all those people and the ammo they were carrying. They had plenty of ammo.

I had to lighten the load, I saw a LRP sitting in the right doorway of the aircraft. Due to a screwup in his orders, he was several days past his DEROS. He was in shorts because one leg was in a half cast. He was an easy selection. I pointed to him and said, "You, off!"

He pulled the charging handle of his CAR-15 back and let it go, chambering a round, then yelled, "No, sir!"

So I pointed to the man next to him and said, "You, off!"

After running off five more, I called Meacham on the UHF. "Two-Five, you ready?"

His reply was simply, "Go."

Barry made the call, "Eagle Tower, Kingsmen One-Eight, flight of two, Acid pad, on the go."

Tower said, "One-Eight, hold for traffic."

Barry responded, "Sorry, Tower, we got a hot one and we're on the go."

Tower said, "Roger."

The Huey struggled into the air like we were hauling an overload of Cs. "Count noses again will you? I got ten."

Barry struggled around in his seat, then turned back and smiled at me and said, "twelve."

I said, "Twelve?"

Loser chimed in with, "That's right sir, twelve."

It took forty-seven pounds of torque to get the thing off the ground at Eagle. Now we'd have to hover on the side of a mountain twenty-two hundred feet up. This was not going to be fun.

The warm feeling of pride began to fade as I got back to the business at hand, and we headed back out to the Roung Roung.

It was just after 1530, and the team had been in contact for seven hours. My determination to get help to this team was overriding any sensation of fear that might have welled up during the flight out. I had friends out there, and I'd let them down today. The least I could do was to try to get their shattered bodies out alive. About halfway out there, I realized that Wild Bill had just fallen in behind and hadn't insisted on taking the lead as he normally would. He was as intent on fixing this as I was. I called just to make sure he was still there. "Two-Five, One-Eight. I guess we'll just do a standard heavy-team insertion in the original LZ?"

"This is Two-Five, heavy is right, how many you got?"

I knew that I'd screwed up and had set myself up for a bad time in the LZ. I meekly replied, "Twelve."

"This is Two-Five, I got eleven. Better tell 'em to get out fast when you get in the LZ."

"Roger that."

There were no wise-ass remarks passed back and forth for this one. I told the crew chief and gunner to make sure that the reaction force knew that it would be important to get out fast in the LZ. They didn't usually have to be told, but I wanted them to understand that this time it was important for us too. We wouldn't have the power to hover on that hillside, and there was no place to land. If we didn't unload fast, the Huey would settle to the hillside and roll down the mountain.

The first medevac was picking up wounded from the ridge-line. "This is Dustoff Niner-Four. I am receiving heavy ground fire from the left front.

"I am now receiving intense ground fire from the right and left rear."

Then simply, "I'm staying!"

Everyone thought those of us that flew for the LRPs were nuts. Here were unarmed medevac birds sitting in the middle of the hornet's nest we had broken open and ignoring the hornets.

The Cobras were working furiously to cover him, and the gooks were still shooting at him. Eklund was now working F-4s on the surrounding ridgelines, and the gooks were shooting at them also. These gooks were either beaucoup *dien cai dau* (very crazy), or they had all of North Vietnam out there, and we had stepped in the middle of it. Eklund was back in the air ahead of us. He had traded his LOH for a Huey. That meant the LOH was probably too full of holes to fly anymore. He called the team, "Linwood Teams Two-Three, this is Six. We've got a Romeo Foxtrot en route."

Dustoff Niner-Four departed with Contreros and was immediately replaced by Dustoff Two-Two, who extracted Souza and headed for the hospital.

There was a new voice on the radio, "This is Two-Three. Roger. If they aren't here in ten mikes, don't bother; we won't be here either." Linderer was on the radio; Bacon had gone into shock. We found out later that Walkabout and Linderer planned that if they got overrun, Linderer would shoot all the remaining LRPs and then himself. LRPs were not popular with the enemy, and wouldn't be well treated as prisoners.

We inserted the reaction force in an LZ about 150 meters down the ridgeline from the team. It didn't look like the same area, much of the foliage had been blasted back by the numerous assaults of the Cobras and 105 artillery. It was no longer necessary to trim the vegetation to get in. The LZ had a steep slope to it, but now the trees were low enough for us to get close to the ground. Close enough for a LRP with a cast on his leg to jump without injuring himself as John Sours had. The ridge formed a finger that pointed to the west. Just beyond it was a finger that pointed east. While on short final for the insertion, I could see that the F-4s had been dropping napalm and high explosives along that ridge.

Once in the LZ, I could see that it would be too steep to land, so I told Barry to clear the rotor blades in front for me. I would descend until there was a danger of the rotor blade striking the ground, or the toes of the skids touched down. That meant a pretty steep hill. The angle exceeded a line from the skids to the tip of the blades. As I tried to stop the aircraft at a hover, Barry began to call out the torque readings. When he said "Fifty" we were still descending; I was going to have to overtorque the aircraft to get out of this one. Then the aircraft began to shake from side to side as LRPs jumped from the skids. I held the power where it was, and almost immediately we began to climb with an empty bird. I looked up through the greenhouse, and an F-4, less than a hundred feet over our heads, was releasing napalm canisters that were impacting on the next ridge. The jets were breaking to the left. I decided to turn to my right and break downhill to get airspeed quickly and get out of Meacham's way. When I came around, Wild Bill was hot on my heels on short final to the LZ.

The fuel gauge read just over 250 pounds, about twenty-five

minutes remaining. It was 1620. Hard to believe that it had been over two hours since the last refuel stop. The twenty-minute warning light would come on about halfway back to Eagle, even with the cyclic pressed almost against the instrument panel in the go-fast mode. I started reducing power as the airspeed climbed through 110 knots. I called Bill and asked so he wouldn't think I was trying to take over, "Two-Five, One-Eight. How 'bout some gas?"

"Sounds like a good idea to me."

During the flight back, Barry had the controls again. I sat back and fished for a cigarette. As I lit up, I noticed that the mountains had already begun to cast their long, eastbound, violet shadows on the thick jungle in the valleys below. It had been over seven hours since we cranked up that morning. I began to wonder if we had any oil leaks. I was about to tell Barry that we would pick up more LRPs after we topped off when we heard a Cav bird calling Linwood Teams Six. They were en route with the reaction force. Well, it was certainly good to know that speedy help was on hand.

With a moment to relax, I could suddenly feel how wound up I'd been. The adrenaline had started to leave my system. A drained and tired feeling washed over me. Barry looked like a limp rag as well. But we still had a lot of flying to do.

My thoughts were interrupted by the UHF radio. "One-Eight, this is Two-Five. Did you hear that the Blues are on the way?"

"Yeah, I hope we didn't disturb their vacation." I knew that they were most likely not at fault for the delay, but they were a target of opportunity.

At the hot fuel point, when my turn came to get out for a stretch and to relieve my bladder, I gave 348 a quick lookover. One can't do much of a preflight on a running helicopter. I looked in the engine compartment for signs of oil leaks, near all the gearboxes for the same, and underneath for anything running out the hell hole. Inside the cargo compartment, there were two small, round, Plexiglas windows on the transmission island, one on the front for checking the hydraulic filters, and one on the right side for checking the transmission oil level. I couldn't check the level with the aircraft running, but if the windows were covered with oil or hydraulic fluid, it was a good indicator of trouble. The bird seemed to be all right.

While we refueled, the Cav inserted twenty-five blues into the new LZ. When we got back into the action, we found Dustoff Niner-Four was back to take Bacon and Czepurny out. Another

agonizing twenty minutes passed before medevac came back for
Linderer and Walkabout. It was 1720. It had taken two hours
and fifteen minutes to get everyone medevacked. The only ones
left from the original team were Clifton, Reiff, and Heringhausen. They weren't in a hurry.

When discussion on the radio turned to how to get the bodies
out, I became fully aware that we had lost some LRPs. Since
there was no LZ that we could land in to load the bodies, it was
decided that one of the Cav birds would lower a rope and sling
them out. I didn't like the procedure, but the alternative was to
leave them behind.

During the hour it took to get all that accomplished, we got
to sit back and watch the F-4s and Cobras do their stuff. We had
to be doing a *job* on Chuck. They kept coming though; it made
you think of the human-wave attacks the Chinese had used in
Korea. It wasn't that they were being mowed down in walls, but
they were relentless in the face of the awesome firepower of the
Cobras and fighters. About six pairs of F-4s had been used. I
lost track of how many pairs of Cobras. The biggest problem
the reaction force had in reaching the team was climbing the
hill; they kept slipping in all the blood and gore. They also complained about having difficulty climbing over the dead enemy
soldiers. At 1840, the decision was made to extract the reaction
force. Wild Bill and I had to extract them all, the Blues as well.
In order to accomplish it all, we had to refuel again.

It was 1850 when the flight of two settled to the ground at
hot fuel. The steel gray of dusk had started to fill the sky. It
was going to be another hot extraction at night. I was tired, it
was a lousy LZ, and there were about five billion bad guys out
there. Boy, these LRP guys sure knew how to show an aviator
a good time. By the time we started west again, God had
dropped the big velvet cloth over the lighting system. In the fifteen minutes that we sat on the ground, Nui Khe mountain had
become just a shadow. As we approached the mountains, I
couldn't make out the ridges or valleys. Meacham had assumed
the lead again as we left Eagle. I followed as 121 climbed to altitude and headed in the right direction. I hoped that as my eyes
"dark adapted," things would become more visible. When we
were about five miles out, Meacham called, "Linwood Teams
Two-Three, this is Kingsmen Two-Five. Give us a flare."

There was a short silence as though there was some confusion
on the ground. "Two-Five, this is Two-Three. We don't have
any."

I realized that everyone out there had been sent out in hurry and under pressure. No one had planned this mission.

"Two-Three, this is Two-Five. What have you got?"

"This is Two-Three. I got a Zippo."

"Say again, Two-Three. You got a *what?*"

"I got a Zippo lighter."

Thus the "M1A1 Zippo Landing Zone Lighting Device" was born. Amazingly, it was so dark that I was able to spot it right away from five miles out! We were right on course, a five-mile final.

I called to Bill to make sure. "Two-Five, One-Eight. You got the light?"

"Yup!"

"My, aren't we the blabber mouth this evening!"

"Yup."

We were both feeling a little better now that we were able to perform our mission the way we knew how. I began to slow the Huey down to allow Wild Bill the spacing he would need for a ladder extraction. At about two miles out the light went out. If you've ever used a Zippo for continued illumination, you undoubtedly remember how hot it gets after a while. Not only that, but once it's hot, it doesn't want to light again till it cools off some. Ti Ti Tecerero was on the end of the lighter.

"Two-Three, this is Two-Five. What happened to the light?"

"It burned my hand, and I dropped it, man."

They finally used two or three different lighters in rotation. That was enough to keep us on course. Between the LRPs and Blues, there were forty-eight troopers to be pulled off that hill. Using ACL of six, it was going to take eight sorties to get them out, four trips each. Pushing the birds as fast as they'd go, the turnaround time to Eagle was thirty minutes. On short final, we could look over to the next ridge, the one that had been pounded with napalm and high explosives by the F-4s that afternoon. The NVA were still coming. The whole mountain was dotted with pinpoints of light. They were using flashlights! They were coming after us, and they didn't care about the cost. The Snakes were still having a picnic. Chuck was actually marking the target for the guns.

It was 2130 when we picked up the last two loads. I was last to go in. As the final six scampered up the ladders, I told the crew chief to count noses. He counted six and asked if he was cleared to fire. I said, "Wait one."

I yelled to the guy sitting next to the radio pedestal. "Is the LZ clean?"

He yelled back, "What?"

"Is the LZ clean? Damn it."

He yelled, "Yes!"

I keyed the intercom mike. "Fire it up."

Both 60s responded instantly, and were joined by the M-16s from the Blues on board.

The radio came to life, "One-Eight, Two-Five. You are receiving heavy fire."

"Two-five, are you sure? We just started shooting." Sometimes at night, if you glanced too quickly, tracers going away from an aircraft could look like they were inbound.

Meacham came back, "Unless you're shooting at yourself. Somebody is awful pissed at you!"

"Well, if that's the way they're going to play, let's go home." We were finally getting out of there, and the relief swept over us in a rush.

I broke right and down the hill as I had done that afternoon. I wanted airspeed to build fast. It wasn't as abrupt as it had been in the daylight. I couldn't see enough detail, but I wanted out of there. Once we were clear, I was glad to surrender the controls to Barry for the ride home. I sat back in the seat and tried to relax. I drew hard on the cigarette I had lit with my own LZ Lighting Device. I stared out the window into the darkness to the west. There was nothing to see except the reflection of the red lights from the instrument panel in the cockpit. With another puff, I silently told God, "I know you're out there somewhere, 'cause you let me pull off another one. Now that you're not so busy with us, would you mind looking after the guys that got hurt out here?" He must have thought I had some nerve. He just saved my butt again, and I wanted another favor. Sometimes I think it's good that you don't hear His answers.

The reaction force had got the wounded out. Six more LRPs and several of the Blues had been wounded during the action. None seriously.

"One-Eight, this is Two-Five, on Uniform." Wild Bill had yanked me back.

"One-Eight. Go."

"When we drop this load off at the Acid pad let's reposition to the Castle and get these birds put to bed for the night." With this much flying there was bound to be at least some overdue oil samples.

"This is One-Eight. What about the debrief?"

"This is Two-Five. I'll make a deal with you. If you help both crew chiefs, I'll go back for the out-brief."

"You got it, you old turkey." Wild Bill would tell me about the debrief in the morning. I knew 348 would just need some oil samples taken, but I had no way of knowing if 121 needed an MOC after an intermediate inspection. When we parked the aircraft in the revetments, Meachem took off before the aircraft were shut down. It was 2145 at shutdown. We had been flying for 12.4 hours; most of it under fire. We took some oil samples and buttoned up the birds for the night. As we started down the hill, I realized that we hadn't eaten since breakfast. Loser came over and handed Barry and me each a C-ration meal. He was reading my mind again. He and the crew chief had sneaked in some chow during our many orbits.

21 November (118 days to go, 32d day in a row on LRPs). It was about 0500 when the CQ woke me. My eyes had trouble focusing. It'd been about 2330 when I hit the rack. I looked down at my watch, I hadn't taken it off last night. I thought, I had five and half hours sleep and not too much to drink, I should feel better than this. My head swam; my body felt like I'd been asleep for about ten minutes. As I struggled to sit up, I saw that I still had on my fatigue pants and socks. I sat on the bunk and scratched my head. The memory of the day before flooded back. The feeling of invincibility had been punctured. We'd lost some LRPs. I sat there with my elbows on my knees, head hung low. My eyes began to burn with the tears welling up in them. Clifton, Reiff, and Heringhausen were gone. They were dead because I wasn't there when they needed me. How would I be able to face the rest of the LRPs? I fought down the feelings; there was work to be done, and I was a Kingsman. There was no room for tears here. I pulled on my boots. Yesterday's shirt would complete the ensemble. I figured I'd have an extra cup of coffee to make up for not shaving.

The coffee had begun to wake me up by the time we'd completed preflighting the aircraft. I was wide awake by the time the birds touched down on the Acid pad. After shutting down, it was apparent that the dark gray cloud hovering over me was going to follow me around. I could suppress my emotions all I wanted, but the numb feeling inside my head wasn't going to go away. Wild Bill hadn't talked to me yet about the debrief. Since he looked as bad as I felt, I assumed he wasn't prepared to. We entered the LRP operations and headed for the coffee pot. When we'd settled down, Eklund brought us up to date.

"The weather's still bad out in the Roung Roung. We aren't planning on pulling Burnell's team today."

His eyes dropped to the floor. He said, "Yesterday . . ."

He hesitated, cleared his throat and started again, "Yesterday, we . . . eh, had some heavy contact. You already know that we had three of our guys KIA. I'll give you a rundown on what we know about the rest of the wounded.

"Souza lost a lung and three ribs. The doctors said he probably wouldn't make it till this morning. Cox had multiple shrapnel wounds, a broken arm, and multiple bullet wounds to the stomach. He also wasn't expected to live through the night."

He stared down at his feet again, shifted his weight. There was a wet shine to his eyes. He began once again. "Venable was hit in the neck, arm, and chest, he's not expected to survive either. Contreros was hit in the head. He had a small hole just over his right ear and a large exit wound on the top of his head. They say he might make it but . . ." His voice trailed off. He mumbled, ". . . but he'd be a vegetable."

I was stunned, my head felt numb, my whole body felt numb.

Eklund's voice came back to my ears. "Linderer was hit in the legs, Bacon was hit in the right leg, and Czepurny was hit in the feet. They're expected to be all right. Indian was wounded in both hands but should be released today. Sours has two broken ankles and should return to the company in several weeks. I'll be going over to the hospital later to check on them. Contreros has been sent out to the hospital ship *Repose*. The others are still at Two Two Surg.

"Here's a rundown of what went down on that ridgeline, as best as I have been able to piece together." He paused to clear his throat. Ken Eklund was managing to put his professional mantle back on. He was soon back to being commander, Company F, 58th Infantry. "At approximately 0935 on 20 November, a heavy team from this company ambushed a small force of NVA while patrolling a ridgeline of the Roung Roung Valley. The results of that ambush were nine confirmed enemy KIA and one probable. The KIA include what we believe to be three nurses and a field-grade NVA officer.

"Division passed the decision to have the team hold in place while a reaction force was mounted to further develop the combat situation. The reaction force was delayed for some reason, and the team was required to stay in place. At approximately

1200 hours, the ATL, Sergeant Venable, was hit by small-arms fire. He was subsequently medevacked.

"At about 1505, the team was hit with what we believe to have been a forty-pound Chicom claymore. There was some question at the debrief last night that they may have been hit by the Cobras, but a three-quarter-inch bolt was removed from Frank Souza's chest cavity during surgery last night. The last we know, Cobras don't shoot those." He recounted the wounds received by each member of the team. Then he described the actions of the Cobras and the aircrews involved. Then he turned to what had occurred on the ground.

"Bacon was going into shock but continued to operate the radio. Linderer, Czepurny, and Cox were unable to move but continued to secure the perimeter. Billy Walkabout was the only one able to move around, but he was unable to use his hands. When the medevacs arrived and sent down the jungle penetrators, they slid down the hillside in the direction of the enemy positions. Each time, Billy ran down the hill, unarmed, among the enemy positions, and retrieved the jungle penetrator. He then dragged one of the wounded over to Linderer, who could use his hands, and Linderer would strap the wounded into the penetrator. There was some great courage displayed on that hill yesterday."

His eyes fell to the floor again. The official part of the briefing was over. He looked up at Meacham and said, "Bill, would you fly me over to the hospital in Phu Bai; we need to be able to get back in hurry since we still have teams out."

Meacham replied, "No sweat."

I piped up, "Can I come along? I mean if we gotta go out, Barry can have 348 cranked by the time we get here, and we wouldn't lose any time."

We landed 121 at the 22d Surgical Hospital pad and parked off to the side in case they had any medevacs come in. The doctor briefed Eklund that Cox, Souza, and Venable were still hanging on and that his prognosis was improved for all three. That made me feel a little more hopeful. When we got on the ward, I saw Souza sitting on the end of his bed. For someone who was supposed to be dead this morning, he looked pretty good. As we walked over, he smiled. We found that he'd been sitting up for the nurses to change his bandages. While we visited, he complained to the orderly that he wanted orange juice. The orderly told him that due to his wounds he could only have fluids by IV.

Frank looked up and said, "We kicked ass on those gooks, didn't we?"

Eklund responded with, "You bet we did, Frank!"

"It wasn't the Cobras that did us, was it, sir?"

Eklund said, "No it wasn't. We think it was a forty-pound Chicom claymore."

"I'm glad to hear that."

Just then, a rather attractive nurse walked by. Frank said, "Check this one out; ain't she somethin'?"

I began to wonder about the doctors; it was obvious that this LRP wasn't almost dead.

Next, we moved two beds down on the same side of the ward to where Jim Venable was. He was apparently not feeling quite as feisty as Souza, but then neither was he acting like a man on his last legs. He was having difficulty trying to talk with the wound in his throat.

"We really dealt with them fuckin' gooks, didn't we?" His voice was weak and scratchy, but the pride in F Company's performance was clear as a bell.

Our next visit was with Riley "Bulldozer" Cox, across the aisle from Venable. I looked at him from the foot of the bed. The Dozer looked like a mummy. King Tut eat your heart out. He was bandaged from head to foot. All that was visible of Riley was his eyes, nose, and mouth. One look in his pained and drugged eyes quickly erased the boost that seeing Souza and Venable had given my feelings. I had to concede that the doctors may have gotten one in three right. Wild Bill moved to head of the bed to talk to Dozer. He leaned over to be able to hear the weak voice.

"Sir, was it the Cobras that shot us up?"

Bill responded, "No it wasn't, it was a damn forty-pound Chicom claymore, partner."

He then echoed Venable's words like he was reading a script. "We really dealt with them fuckin' gooks, didn't we?" The corners of his mouth slowly turned up into a smile. It was clear that it wasn't without great effort.

Meacham said, "You bet your ass we did!"

The tears were welling up in my eyes as I thought, He already did bet his ass.

After we got back to the Acid pad and shut down the aircraft, I went over and told Barry about our visit to the hospital. We all sat down on the hill at the edge of the pad.

I said, "I don't even know what to ask God when I pray for

Contreros. I mean, if he survives, he'll be a vegetable. I can't pray for him to die; but I don't think he'd want to live like that."

I finally decided in my own mind to just ask God to do what was best for Al. Later that afternoon, we got the word that Contreros had died. I felt relieved; God had made the decision. I'm sure He was really pleased to know that I approved of his work. I knew that I wouldn't have wanted to be left alive in the condition Contreros was in.

The next morning, shortly after we'd landed on the Acid pad, Captain Eklund informed us that Meacham, Walkabout, and I would be required to report to division headquarters in one hour. He told us that he'd been told that it was for an award ceremony, but that was all he knew. I suddenly realized that I hadn't bothered to shave again, and I needed a haircut. There wouldn't be time to get a haircut. I mooched up a can of shaving cream and headed for the shower shack. This time the K-bar would have to do the job. Once again the big knife was sharp enough for the task. With only a few minor nicks, I had a presentable shave.

At the division headquarters, we were lined up with about a dozen other Screaming Eagles outside the TOC. A major briefed us that Maj. Gen. Melvin Zais, the division commander, would be presenting the awards in person. I had the feeling that the major wanted to say something about my haircut, but didn't dare run me off with the CG expecting me there. The last three in the line were Walkabout, Meacham, and me. After he finished handing out awards to all the starched and polished staffers, he came to the three ragamuffins on the end. He pinned a Silver Star on Billy and shook his hand. He said, "Son, that was a very selfless and courageous act you performed on that mountain the other day. Soldiers like you have made and kept the reputation of this division. This Silver Star is only a small token of recognition of your bravery."

He then moved to Wild Bill and presented him with a Distinguished Flying Cross. He returned Bill's salute, shook his hand, and moved in front of me and pinned on a Distinguished Flying Cross, also. I saluted, and he returned it. As he shook my hand, he looked back at Bill and said, "I want to thank you gentlemen for making sure those boys got off that hill. Your resourcefulness saved us all from a bad situation."

I could feel the tears well up in my eyes. I felt he really meant the things he said to the three of us. Once again, he had shown a personal interest in F Company. Meacham and I went back to the LRP company area with Billy in Eklund's jeep. Ken stayed at division for briefings and meetings and a trip over to the hospital. Later, Ken told us that after the award ceremony the general had called him aside. General Zais had said, "Captain, I read the recommendation you made for a Distinguished Service Cross for Walkabout. I have thought it over, and I want you to rewrite it." Ken told us later that he wondered what he had done wrong.

Then General Zais said, "I want it submitted for a Medal of Honor. What that boy did on that hill deserves nothing less. That kind of courage and love for his buddies is what the Medal was designed for."

Ken told us he'd considered it when he was writing it up, but didn't think it would get support at division. We all agreed that Billy's actions were Medal of Honor stuff. Again I felt a warm surge of pride at being part of the operation. LRPs displayed that kind of guts all the time, but it took a serious incident to bring it to light. This made the fourth time that Ken Eklund had submitted me for a DFC or Silver Star. Each time, I hadn't seen my performance as any more than doing the job I had agreed to do. None of us knew at the time, but that fourth recommendation would set in motion the wheels that would cause F Company to lose me as a pilot.

23 November (115 days to go, 35th day in a row on LRPs, 51 days without a day off). I inserted Burford's team that day; it had been a fairly quiet day on the Acid pad, but I was still tired when we returned to the Castle. As I parked 348 in the revetment, I called ops. "Kingsmen Ops, this is One-Eight. Destination, termination. Over."

"One-Eight, this is Ops. Report to the ops tent as soon as you shutdown. Do not, repeat, go to your hootch first. Acknowledge."

"This is One-Eight. Roger."

It was a strange directive. If they wanted to chew my ass, why were they in such a hurry? I shut the aircraft down and did the postflight. If they wanted to jump on me for something, they'd have to wait. I took my time walking up the hill. I went into operations, and the ops officer was there waiting for me.

"Grant, you've been transferred."

"What?"

"You've been transferred to HHC, 3d Brigade, Aviation Section."

"Naw, bullshit, sir. I'm scheduled to fly LRPs again tomorrow."

"No, you're not. You're getting on 350 and being flown to Camp Evans today."

"I gotta get my stuff."

"No, your stuff is already packed on the bird."

"What?"

"You're already packed. Just get your ass on the bird and go."

I couldn't believe it. I went to my hootch. All my stuff was gone. My ammo-box furniture, my stereo, everything was gone. The mattress on my bed was rolled up. It was like I'd been killed in action. I was in a state of shock. I walked back to the flight line.

Dave Poley was waiting at 350 for me. As I walked up, The Dave said, "I'm sorry man."

I looked in the back of the bird and there was all my stuff. "I know it's not your fault, Dave. Fuck it. Don't mean nothin', man."

The shock was wearing off. I was getting really pissed. I'd been screwed. This time they didn't give me any chance to talk the new commander out of it. I had a team in the field; that was unfinished business for me. Also, the bastards had done it so I couldn't even get to say good-bye to my friends. I became aware later that whoever made the decision may've been concerned that I was on a collision course with death. It also occurred to me that Bill Meacham and I were potential witnesses to Walkabout's recommendation for the Medal of Honor. And someone may've wanted us to stay alive for that very reason. I found out years later that during Meacham's last month they were constantly finding him jobs to keep him out of the cockpit. When they did let him fly, it was always a low-risk mission.

The flight to Camp Evans didn't take long. I asked Dave not to unload right away. I went to the headquarters company and reported in and was sent to see Major Wallace, the aviation section commander. "Sir, WO1 William T. Grant reporting as ordered."

He returned my salute and said, "Welcome aboard, Mr. Grant. We're glad to have you. We need Huey aircraft commanders, and you have some heavy combat experience that you can share with the newer pilots here."

"Sir, I . . ."

Major Wallace held up his hand. "Son, I think I know what you want to say. This decision was made for us. We have no say in the matter. Even if I wanted to send you back, I couldn't. And I don't want to, 'cause we need you here. We've got a good bunch here; if you give us a chance, I think you'll like it here. Lieutenant Taylor here is our operations officer and will find you a room and help you get settled."

I saw no point in arguing with the man and getting off to a bad start. I'm sure the frown on my face told him how I felt as I saluted and said, "Yes, sir."

Outside, Bob Taylor introduced himself and shook my hand. I was trying my damnedest to remain pissed off at the entire world. I found that, in spite of my attitude, I liked him right away. He seemed to understand that I felt I'd been hosed over and was making allowances. He helped The Dave and his crew haul all my stuff to a room. The crews lived in a long building. It was supported by heavy timbers. The walls were made of ammunition boxes filled with sand and stacked up. The roof was PSP, with several layers of sandbags stacked on top. The individual rooms all had doorways to the outside, with a wooden porch that ran along in front of the doors. Along the outside of the porch there was a stack of sand-filled ammo boxes in front of each doorway. My new home was a bunker. It had been built by the First Cav when they were at Evans. The 3d Brigade Aviation Section called it Thunder Motel.

26 November (113 days to go). It wouldn't take long to become an AC there. I flew one day of log missions for almost eight hours as my orientation. The next day I took my AC ride, and on 30 November I was again turned loose on the world. I was still angry; but once more I was back in the air and in my element. The new unit's call sign was Thunder. I took the call sign Thunder Five-Five. The parking area for the aircraft was known as the Storm Center. The missions would·be VIP, and ash and trash. There would be no LRPs, Special Forces, or CAs. I wasn't going to be happy without a good adrenaline hit once in a while. The log missions were the most satisfying; the grunts were always appreciative for the support.

CHAPTER 10
DECEMBER 1968

1 December (109 days to go). The boredom with the missions continues. I'd begun to know the feelings of the tiger caged up at the zoo. I was headed north along Highway 1, returning to Camp Evans for termination at the Storm Center. The skids were just inches above the road. I spotted a water buffalo standing alone in an open field on the right side of the road. Something about the scene caught my attention. Why this one water boo called to me over all the others I'd seen in country, I'll never know. I knew that the buffalo and I had to cross paths. I reacted without knowing why.

"Clear right," I called.

"Clear right," came the reply as I pulled back on the cyclic a little so that the aircraft would rise enough for the blades to clear the ground as I turned. With a small application of right pedal, the Huey responded and turned around blade ends, with the tips just three feet off the ground. In the turn, I moved the cyclic further to the rear and let the turn continue to dissipate our airspeed. As the speed dropped through forty knots, I leveled the rotor disk and brought the bird to a three-foot hover, facing the buffalo. It was a good-flying Huey and responded flawlessly. The buffalo stopped grazing and looked up at the helicopter hovering fifty feet away.

That was the day I was to find out that a water buffalo is just about as dumb as anything can be on this earth and still live. Lieutenant Taylor looked over at me and said, "What are we doing, Mr. Grant?"

"You got a date, LT? This won't take long." It was apparent that the water boo was accustomed to helicopters. He didn't run away afraid. I still wasn't sure what was about to happen. Then

I heard myself say to the crew chief, "Did I see a CS grenade back there somewhere?"

"Yes, sir."

I glanced over my shoulder to see the crew chief grinning at me. The idea seeming to be growing in both our heads at the same time. I checked the wind to make sure we were upwind of the water boo. I turned the bird sideways to the buffalo.

"Toss that sucker out to him." The grenade bounced along the ground, spewing pungent smoke. I moved the aircraft back a ways to observe the buffalo. The boo stepped toward the growing cloud, stuck his snout down, and took a big sniff. The buffalo immediately began an impression of a rodeo Brahma bull. He jumped, he spun, and he kicked. Finally, he calmed down. He looked at the aircraft. "Is he going to charge?" Lieutenant Taylor asked.

"Don't worry. He can't catch us if he does."

The buffalo lowered his head, went back, and took another snort of the CS. Again, he went through the same gyrations, spinning, turning, and kicking. Again he calmed down, looked over at the helicopter, lowered his head, and went back for a snort. I was laughing so hard I could barely keep the bird hovering upright. As I lowered the nose of the Huey to gain airspeed to leave, the buffalo was sniffing and pawing at the spent grenade, trying to get another snort. The whole crew burst out laughing every time we looked at one another or tried to talk. I was barely able to get out the required radio calls for landing at Evans.

It didn't take long for me to become aware of the fact that the best missions (while I was assigned to this section) would be the log missions. It was ironic that the most boring missions I flew in the Kingsmen should become the ones I would now most look forward to. The last hundred days were going to be hard to endure.

9 December (100 days to go). After the water buffalo incident, I knew that my only hope was to make my own excitement. Perhaps that was the message the water boo had for me and why I felt called to him as we flew by. W. T. Grant soon became the source of entertainment for the 3d Brigade Aviation Section. The lieutenants who Major Wallace expected me to tutor would learn far more than combat skills. I believe that lieutenants Taylor and Snyder actually looked forward to flying with me just to see what the next lunacy would be.

John Hightower, the new lieutenant who had witnessed my disagreement with Lieutenant Dipstick, had been sent to this unit before me. It was Hightower who I felt sorry for. I'm sure he was convinced that I was truly criminally insane and self-destructive. He wasn't happy to be scheduled on flights with me.

I spent most of my flight time on the deck when there were no passengers to scare the hell out of. Flight at over one hundred knots, just inches off the ground, is nothing less than exhilarating. Low-level flight was not quite enough to feed my addiction to adrenaline. Lieutenant Taylor and I had been flying a long 6.2 hours. We were on the way back to Evans and looking forward to a cool one. Several days of bad weather had kept us on the ground. It felt good to be in the air again. Taylor was flying, and we were skimming along the deck. His low-level flying was starting to show signs of improvement because of the extra practice I'd been letting him get that day. Evans GCA had a standing request that we take a GCA (ground controlled approach) any time we could fit one in. They were training new controllers. The incident on the FOB mission, coupled with the lousy weather we'd been having, made me a very cooperative customer. I called from about seven miles out and found that the radar was down. I was surprised, since it was such a beautiful day (radar usually waits till the weather is bad to break). Then an idea hit me.

"I have the controls." I said, excitedly.

Taylor said, "You have the controls."

His hands went up to show he had relinquished. He had a puzzled look on his face. I could tell he was trying to figure out what he'd done wrong that caused me to take the aircraft. I just smiled at him as I reduced the airspeed to about sixty knots and increased power. The result was that the Huey started to climb like it had been kicked in the ass. We rocketed past two thousand feet, then three, and were still climbing. As we got closer to Evans, I saw his hand reach down and tune up the tower frequency. He then reached to turn his selector to the number two position and make our call. I lightly slapped his hand and made a no-no gesture with my index finger. He still looked puzzled. I grinned a Cheshire-cat grin. I leveled off the climb at fifty-three hundred feet. As we got over the middle of the airfield, I made my call.

"Evans tower, Thunder Five-Five."

"Thunder Five-Five, Evans Tower. Go ahead."

"Five-Five is mile high for landing."

Everyone in the aircraft cracked up.

"Say again, Five-Five."

"Five-Five is mile high for landing."

"Uh, Five-Five . . . Uh . . . Say again request."

Now he knew what he thought he heard. At that moment, everyone in the tower was frantically searching the horizon trying to spot the aircraft that was only one mile out. I had started a circle so I could stay directly over the tower. Now, an airport traffic area is five miles in diameter and extends from the surface up to three thousand feet. Any aircraft entering the airspace is required to contact the tower. While not quite legal, in Vietnam aircraft would often be inside the five miles when they called. The men in the tower weren't expecting a call from *above*. By having me repeat myself, they weren't expecting to hear anything differently, they were just stalling to try and spot the aircraft.

I repeated the request with more clarity, just as I would be expected to do. "Thunder Five-Five is one mile high for landing at the Storm Center."

I had certainly given enough information for them to decode the riddle. The controller still refused to hear correctly.

"Five-Five you are not in sight. Say altitude."

"Five-Five is mile high."

It was getting hard to talk on the radio without laughing. Especially since the entire crew now had tears running down their cheeks from laughing so hard.

"Five-Five, you are not in sight. Evans altimeter is three zero one five. There is no other reported traffic. You are cleared to land at the Storm Center." He still had heard, but not listened to, what I'd said.

"Five-Five. Roger."

I put the Huey in a steep bank and reduced power, moving the pedals only slightly to insure that the bird would be out of trim. The onboard giggling ceased as soon as we started falling. While the altimeter unwound, I explained to a white-knuckled Taylor about breaking the radar lock of antiaircraft weapons. As we passed through five hundred feet, I gingerly coaxed the Huey out of its fall, at the same time telling the lieutenant of the pitfalls of drastic control movement while conducting that maneuver. We zoomed along the runway from north to south, at about fifty feet, level with the tower, and made the turn into the

Storm Center. It wasn't until the next landing from one mile up that the tower caught on to what the deal was.

The brigade aviation section had the only aircraft stationed at Evans at the time, so the controllers knew each of our voices well when they heard us over the radio. It became harder to put anything over on them, but it was always fun trying. It got to the point that they were always looking for something suspicious in my calls. That alone was a victory for me. The game was enjoyed by both sides, me trying to put one over on them, and they trying to catch me. The unwritten rules never allowed the bounds of safety to be crossed, and the game was never played when the tower was busy.

10 December (99 days). Wow! Double digit midget. I made sure that everyone around me knew about it. I had lots of opportunity, the weather was bad, and we sat on the ground all day.

11 December (98 days to go). Ernie Navarrete and I were scheduled to fly in support of the S-3 shop. A major by the name of Hero wanted to go out and recon some areas out west. I started the day thinking of a VR like the ones we used to fly with the LRPs. I shouldn't have gotten my hopes up. The guy was so confused and disorganized that he wasn't sure what he wanted us to do. We spent a lot of time with him telling us to turn left, turn right, go here, go there. In the end, he got the crew so confused that we had to climb to altitude in order to find our way back to Camp Evans. Another exciting mission completed.

It was that night that we started the "Great Wall." Ernie and Bill Tharp shared a large room that had been made by combining two of the bunker's individual rooms. They both had their bunks on one side of the room; the door on that side had been closed off. A half wall stood where the original dividing wall had been. The second room was used as the living room. Because of the spacious arrangement, their room was often used as a gathering place. That night Rich Wideman, Eric Rairdon, Tharp, Navarrete, and myself were there. We were emptying great quantities of beer cans and tossing them on the floor in the living room. The discussion got around to the fact that some of us were getting pretty short. It would be a shame if we were to leave country and not leave something for those that followed us.

It was then that the Great Wall was conceived. The large

twelve-by-twelves that supported the roof would form the perfect framework. There was about ten feet between the center post and the rear wall. I don't even remember whose idea it was, but we started stacking beer cans along the floor, on their sides. The bottoms of the cans faced out toward the room. It was going to take a lot of cans to cover the ten-foot wall to its height of eight feet. It wouldn't be easy, but we were all prepared to make the sacrifice and drink the required amount of beer to complete the project. By the evening's end, there was a start that made us all pleased with ourselves. The Great Wall was about four feet long and two and a half rows high, and no one even had to puke for it yet.

Friday, 13 December (96 days to go). It began raining in earnest. I had flown 8.6 hours on the twelfth. It would be another week before anyone would be able to fly again. The weather had been getting worse, but it wasn't until Friday the thirteenth that I understood how bad monsoons could be. It rained so hard that it sounded like a freight train going by right next to the hootch. For six solid days. Twenty-four hours a day. The only way to sleep was to drink enough so you could pass out. At least our bunker-style building muffled some of the racket.

I thought of the Kingsmen living in their tents on wooden frames. How much rain could the plastic ammunition wrappers keep out? Everything was damp. Even the clothes you had just put on felt soggy and mildewed. Not even bread that had been toasted for breakfast felt dry. The bunker held the dampness like a cave. Only the parties that started about three each afternoon helped dispel the depression.

The worst part was waiting for the attack we were sure would come. If I were Charlie, I certainly would take advantage of the gunships' being grounded. Between the noise and the tension of waiting for an attack to come, tempers grew short. The depression began to mount by the third day.

16 December (93 days to go). The fourth day of rain. No let up, not even for a minute. Everything was damp, and there was no way to get warm. The temperature was in the mid-fifties, but with everything being wet, it seemed much colder. Out of sheer boredom, I began rearranging my room. I swept out the room, and then began moving the ammo-box furniture around. I was dragging the bunk further toward the back of the room when one of the legs caught in front of my left ankle. I tripped, and the bunk leg folded up, with the support brace catching my thumb and index finger as I lost my grip on the bed. I sat up and pulled the leg back to the extended position to free my already throbbing fingers. I looked down at them and saw that the thumb was cut, down past the fatty tissue. The tip of the index finger had been sliced off in a large oval pattern about a quarter-inch deep. I could see well into both wounds that it wasn't far from reaching bone. Then the bleeding came. The blood poured out of both fingers. I grabbed a clean towel and wrapped it tightly on the hand. It began to instantly turn red. Something told me that a Band-Aid wasn't going to fix this. By the time I walked down to Ernie and Bill's, the whole towel had turned bright red. I stuck my head in the door. Ernie was there reading a book.

"Hey, Ern, I got a boo boo. I'm headed over to the medics."

He looked at the towel wrapped hand. "Whadya do, blow your fuckin' hand off?"

"Naw just cut the fingers bad."

"Better get over there before you bleed to death. Besides, if you die here you'll stink up the whole area. Want me to come with you?"

I looked out at the rain. "No sense in both of us getting soaked."

By the time I got to the aid station, the rain and the blood had completely soaked the towel. The mess ran out of the towel and down the front of my shirt and pants. I did in fact look like my hand had been blown off. The medics at the aid station had obviously been bored all day; no one wanted to brave the rain, even if they were sick. One medic was sitting in the corner, reading. The other had a hypodermic in one hand and an orange in the other. He was injecting something into the orange. He told me later it was vodka. It was a way for them to drink screwdrivers on duty and not get caught.

By the way they both leaped into action, I could tell they thought I'd been seriously wounded. When they pulled the towel off, I could see the bleeding had slowed. One soaked me in disinfectant for about twenty minutes, and then stitched me up. After he wrapped and bandaged the hand, he asked questions about how it happened as he filled out the paperwork. He then thrust a form for a Purple Heart in front of me, for "bleeding in a combat zone."

That was the second Purple Heart I refused. While at Camp Eagle with the Kingsmen, I'd fallen down drunk during a rocket attack and cut open the palm of my hand. Infections were so rampant in Nam that I had gone to the medics and had it cleaned up. They removed the gravel, disinfected it, and offered me the same paperwork for a Purple Heart.

I just shook my head and got up to leave. As I got to the door, he said, "Sir, come back next Monday and see me again. And don't forget to get on a flight down to Eagle when the weather breaks and see the flight surgeon."

I thought, Sure, I'll run right down to the flight surgeon and have him keep me from leaving on R & R. By Monday my ass is in Hawaii.

They gave me a bottle of the large Darvons to kill the pain. No one had heard of Karen Anne Quinlin at that time, so I was drinking and taking the Darvon. Still, even they only allowed me about three hours' sleep before I woke with somebody pounding on my fingers with a five-pound hammer.

It continued to rain for six days. I was beginning to be afraid that the weather would keep me from getting to Hawaii.

Thursday, 19 December (90 days to go). The weather finally broke. Hallelujah. I had a special mission to fly. Somehow Wild Bill Meacham had managed to get a 3d Brigade aircraft scheduled to fly him to Phu Bai on his DEROS flight.

I didn't care how much the fingers hurt, I wasn't about to pass up that mission. The pain had subsided enough to allow me to get off the medication, but I was still applying liberal doses of alcohol to help me sleep at night. Taylor was going to fly with me. It wasn't until we strapped in that I realized that I couldn't put a flight glove on my left hand. We got cranked and headed south. A large part of the enthusiasm I felt for the mission was that I would get to call Eagle tower for landing at the Castle once again.

We landed and were quickly airborne again. Wild Bill borrowed the crew chief's flight helmet. "Hey, junior, I see you've managed not to kill yourself without me around to supervise you."

"You ol' turkey. It was you that was trying to get me killed."

"See if I ever teach you to fly again. Put the UHF up on guard will you."

I flipped the switch. "You're up."

Bill turned the selector to number two and pushed the button. "Good morning, Vietnam. Be advised this is Kingsmen Two-Five. No holes, no alterations, no ventilation, destination, termination, rotation. I'm goin' home y'all. Merry Christmas. Kingsmen Two-Five, over and out."

On Christmas Eve, Wild Bill Meacham boarded a bright green Braniff jet and headed home.

The next day I made the flight to Phu Bai, as a passenger, on my way to R & R. I waved good-bye to Bill Tharp after I hopped out of the Huey at the airport. As the Huey lifted, a moment of panic set in. It had been so long and I had seen so much, would Jackie be able to accept me as I now was? I paused in front of a mirror in the terminal. The moustache was new, so was "the look." It was the first time that I noticed it in myself. There were tired lines under my eyes, but more, I could see the hardness that had grown behind the eyes. I whispered to Jackie, "I hope you'll still be able to love me."

At the R & R center, I took my first hot shower in three months. The soap lathered up and turned brown from the filth imbedded deep in my pores. I showered for a full twenty minutes before I was satisfied. The damaged fingers had begun to throb again. I didn't want to take a chance of being hospitalized now, but I didn't want to risk losing my fingers. I went by the aid station that was run by the air force. A medic unwrapped my fingers and made a face.

"Who did this job on you sir?"

"Medic at Camp Evans."

He just shook his head and picked up a forceps. "These fingers are infected. Didn't they clean you up?"

"They soaked me in disinfectant."

He just shook his head again. He carefully snipped a couple of stitches out of the index finger and then rolled the forceps along the tip. I nearly went through the roof. Puss oozed out in large globs. He repeated the process, and it still hurt like hell. He got me cleaned up and rebandaged.

"Sir, you're not going anywhere for the next couple of days, are you?"

"Uh ... oh no, not me."

"Good. You need to come back and see me tomorrow so I can check on those fingers."

"Uh ... sure, okay. No problem." I thought, "In a pig's ass I will." Nobody was going to stop me from going to Hawaii at this point.

During the process of getting settled for my night at Camp Alpha, I ran into a lieutenant whom I'd met in Phuoc Vinh while I was there in September. He was the recon platoon leader and was also on his way to Hawaii to meet his fiancée. We buddied up, and he invited me to go to dinner with him at the Bien Hoa air force officers club. He told me that the food was pretty good. We set up our khakis with the shined brass that we'd wear on the flight the next day before we left.

Then we went to the club and had a steak dinner. It was a great meal. We even ordered a bottle of wine with the meal. I was clean and well fed; it made me feel almost human again. The excitement was building; I tossed and turned all night.

Saturday, 21 December (88 days to go). It was a bright sunny day; the weather matched my mood perfectly. By the time they had us all processed and lined up for the flight, it was late afternoon. I was worried about when we would get there till the lieutenant reminded me that the flight would take off on the evening of the twenty-first, fly thirteen hours, and arrive on the morning of the twenty-first. We clambered aboard the plane and sat down. I immediately and instinctively fastened my seat belt and reached over my head for the flight helmet that wasn't hanging there. The recon lieutenant asked, "What was that you just did?"

Embarrassed, I replied, "Uh . . . ah, oh, nothing."

He let it go.

I couldn't sleep more than a few minutes at a time. I read a book. As I became more tired, I got the feeling that the whole thing was just a trick. When they opened the door we'd be back in Bien Hoa. When the big Pan Am DC-10 finally landed in Hawaii, it was daylight again. As I stepped onto the tarmac, it dawned on me that the World was really still out there. I started getting very nervous.

For a change, the army had been very efficient. We were processed quickly and were on the bus to Fort De Russy. A sergeant briefed us on the way about the kind of behavior that was expected of us and how we were expected to be back on time. Somebody mumbled something about getting sent to Nam for being late, and even the sergeant had a good laugh. When the bus stopped at the R & R center, I leapt to my feet, in a hurry to get off the bus. Of course, there were fifty other guys on the bus with the same idea. I strained to see out the window. I couldn't see her. Then I got scared that I'd seen her and not recognized her. I'd been gone so long. The line to the door seemed to take forever to move; each soldier stopped at the top of the steps looking for his loved one. The sergeant was now in charge of moving embracing couples off to the side so the rest of us could get off the bus.

When it was my turn on the steps, I stopped and stared like the others. I still couldn't see Jackie. The butterflies in my stomach began attacking my heart. She missed her plane; something went wrong with the reservations. Then I saw her. The red hair and the green eyes that I'd missed so deeply. My love wasn't something I'd imagined. I dropped my bags, and we threw our arms around each other. I wanted that moment to never end. In a flash, the war had disappeared, and that was just fine with me. Everyone said that Hawaii was a paradise. I now knew it was Heaven.

After a while Jackie noticed the bandages on my fingers. I told her what happened, and she wouldn't believe me. Every so often, for the rest of the day, she'd ask, and I would again recount the story. She persisted in not believing me. So I told her that what really happened was a bullet had hit the collective control in the aircraft. When it had burst open, the shrapnel had cut up my fingers. She accepted that with no problem. (I let it lie till I was about to go back, and forced the truth on her.)

Jackie's mother had a schoolmate who worked in the gift shop of the Reef Hotel. Her name was Malia; her Hawaiian husband was called Petty. We stayed there, and Malia and Petty did everything they could to make sure our stay was perfect. Our room was ready when we arrived at the hotel, and a rental car was waiting. Each day, Malia advised us on things to see and do. It was the honeymoon we didn't get to have when we got married during flight school. We loved, we ate, we drank, we danced for six glorious days. It was like a dream. The war was a million miles away. Almost.

It hung between us like a dark cloud. As wonderful as each moment together was, each one brought going back that much closer. We tried to set it aside and just enjoy the time we had. We didn't talk about it, but we both knew it was there. We only talked of the war in generalities. She asked no questions, and I offered no more than I did in my letters.

I ate like food was going out of style. I had steaks for dinner and steaks with eggs for breakfast. And potatoes, baked potatoes. No one was going to slip me any of that powdered stuff. After dinner, we went out dancing. Through it all, there was no one else in the world but us. It was like falling in love all over again.

One night, we took the catamaran dinner cruise offered by one of the hotels. We sailed, and I gazed into Jackie's eyes and watched the wind blow through her hair. The whole thing was like a dream.

In celebration of Christmas, firecrackers were being set off on the beach. The echo across the water made it sound like an M-60 in the distance. Each time one went off, I automatically turned to check out the situation. It wasn't that I was jumpy; it was simply the combat sense making sure all was well. As much as I was enjoying myself, there couldn't be a total let-down of my combat instincts. Finally, as I turned toward the beach still one more time, a woman seated next to Jackie asked, "Is there something wrong?"

"Oh no, ma'am. Its just that the firecrackers sound like a pig . . . eh machine gun echoing across the water."

"Vietnam?"

"Yes, ma'am. I'm on R & R. I have to go back in couple of days."

"Oh, you poor thing."

It was one of the few times that a stranger expressed concern over my service in Nam. We chatted with the lady and her daughter during the rest of the cruise. After the boat was out a few miles, they started serving a delicious punch. The salt air made everybody thirsty, and the punch was very popular. Soon Jackie started getting tipsy. It turned out the punch was Leilani Rum and passionfruit juice. Everybody on board had enough to make sure that all were having a good time. The concerned lady's teenage daughter had her first drink that night, and she was plowed. It took her mom, Jackie, one of the crew from the boat, and myself to get her on the dock. Her mom and Jackie helped her walk along the pier, while I followed and picked up the shoes that she kept walking out of.

That night, we took a walk on the beach. We hardly said a word. We would stop and stare into each other's eyes for a while, then go on walking. I think more was communicated that night than on all the others. Most nights, we'd go to a place called the Merry Monarch and dance till one or two in the morning. Afterward, we would go back to the room and lie in each other's arms for the rest of the night.

We saw the Don Ho show and the Polynesian Cultural Center and the Pali Highway. All sights of Hawaii were beautiful, but all paled next to the woman who'd come there to meet me.

* * *

Friday, 27 December (82 days to go or maybe 80). The dreaded day came all too fast. It was time to go back. Part of me wanted to book a flight to San Francisco and keep on going. But I couldn't do that any more then than I could've two years earlier when I'd enlisted. The redeeming fact of the return was that the flight would leave Honolulu on the afternoon of the twenty-seventh and arrive in Vietnam on the morning of the twenty-ninth. Thank you, date line.

The tearful good-byes were kept to a minimum by the rush to get everything accomplished for both of us to leave. Jackie's flight left shortly after mine. During the rush through the airport, I remembered that I'd packed all my cigarettes in the suitcase I'd just checked. I spotted a vendor, and we both scrambled to come up with change to feed the machine. I dropped a quarter and a dime in, pulled the handle, and down came a pack of Marlboros and about thirty dollars in quarters. We both kind of stared at each other for a moment. Jackie asked, "What are we going to do?"

"There's no time to fool around. Gimme your purse!"

It was only a moment's respite from the good-byes. We arrived at the gate. There could be no more stalling; the time had arrived. Once more, I would have to leave my love and go to war. The kiss was long and lingering. It would have to last me for eighty more days. I stared after her as she left. She turned and looked at me one more time. I mouthed, "I love you." When she turned the corner, I wiped the tear off my cheek, turned, and headed for the plane, trying to get my combat face back.

Once on the plane, I found myself sitting again next to the recon lieutenant. As I sat down, I buckled in and reached for the flight helmet again.

"This time I know I saw you. What the hell are you doing?"

I knew I was caught this time. Embarrassed, I said, "I was reaching for my flight helmet."

"What?"

"Force of habit. I strap an aircraft to my ass, I automatically reach for my flight helmet."

He shook his head and opened a book.

It was about four in the morning when we arrived back in our Asian paradise. We shuttled back to Camp Alpha and got to bed. That afternoon when they rounded us up, it was too late to do anything with us, so they cut us loose for the rest of the day. I figured I'd better have the fingers checked so I swung by the air force aid station. As luck would have it I got the same medic.

"Sir, you didn't come back and see me when I told you to."

"You got to be kidding me. You didn't honestly believe I was coming back did you?"

"Shame on you, sir." He laughed. "Officers aren't supposed to be deceitful you know."

"Gee, I'm sorry, Sarge, didn't they tell you that army guys lie?"

He checked the hand, and I was healing up just fine. Oh well, so much for him keeping me there for awhile. I wasn't afraid of getting back to the war, but a couple of days wasted here and there would sure make my final days in country go faster.

30 December (79 days to go). I was having lunch with the re-con lieutenant before I realized it was my birthday. I was twenty-one. We decided that now I was old enough to vote and maybe even drink, or maybe even to go to war and kill people. By the time they had us out-processed, there were no more flights north, so I was forced to stay another day.

New Year's Eve (78 days to go). Once again, the flights were all filled up. The lieutenant and I figured that we would ring in the New Year at the air force officers club. We got to the club around 1630 and ran into 1st Lt. Doyle Struman from the Kingsmen. After introductions all around, we ordered dinner. The place was kind of strange. In a war that had all kinds of odd occurrences, this place was still unique. All the air force people wore civilian clothes. There were round-eyed women. The recon lieutenant said that many of them were the wives of air force officers.

There were a bunch of 82d Airborne lieutenants sitting in one corner. About thirty of them. It didn't take long for the harassment to start. They made cracks about puking chickens, and we made remarks about being almost Airborne. It was all in fun, and soon toasts were being passed back and forth. They would toast airmobile and we would toast the Airborne. As we got rowdy, I could see that the air force was finding us to be an embarrassment. We were certainly upset to see that was the case. So we got rowdier.

Somewhere around nine thirty, I was swapping lies with one of the 82d guys. Suddenly, Lieutenant Recon leaped up in the direction of Doyle. I turned in time to see him block a roundhouse that Doyle had thrown at one of the air force guys. The guy he had swung at was wearing civilian clothes. The man was tall and thin and had a flattop haircut which was half gray. I leaped up behind Doyle, slid my arms up under his and put a full nelson on him. Doyle was taller and heavier than I was. It was hard to control him. When he leaned forward my toes came off the ground. He was a wild man. As he struggled to get free, he cussed the air force guy up and down. "You air force motherfuckers don't know what combat is. Ya fly by so fast and high you don't even know what's goin' on."

I thought, Oh great, he's going to start a war here.

It might've been interesting, thirty-some airborne soldiers up against three times as many older flabby air-force types. Lieutenant Recon said, "Grant, we'd better get him out of here."

"I'm not trying to dance with the fucker."

He got behind me and started steering us toward the back door. I was along for the ride. I was able to keep Doyle under control, but I couldn't make him go where I wanted him to. Recon gave the bartender our hats and helped me shove Struman out the back door. He said, "I'm gonna get some transportation." He took off and left me holding the big Texan. We struggled all around the small vacant lot in back of the club. We fell down and rolled in the mud. Still, I held my full nelson on Doyle.

I kept telling him, "Doyle you gotta calm down, it's over. You can't go around kicking every REMF's ass."

An air force lieutenant appeared in the doorway and said, "Hit him, put him out."

I ignored him, and he said it again. I got pissed and let go of Doyle.

"You want him hit, you hit him yourself."

He quickly disappeared back into the club. I realized that I'd turned lose the wild man. I turned and looked at Doyle, fully expecting a fight. He stared at me blankly and began to tilt. He suddenly fell like a giant oak under the axe.

Recon returned and told me he had commandeered a jeep so we could get Doyle back to Camp Alpha. We dumped the unconscious Lieutenant Struman into the back of the jeep and hopped in. The air force sergeant driving asked if he'd been shot. Recon replied, "Yeah, he's had too many shots." At the gate to Camp Alpha, Lieutenant Recon slipped Struman's wallet out of Doyle's hip pocket and into mine. He whispered in my ear, "Keep his wallet, so the MPs don't know who he is to charge him with anything. Our story is we met him earlier here at Camp Alpha, but don't remember his name. We're just helping him get back to his bunk."

"Okay, sir, I guess you know what you're doing."

"I have to do things like this for the troopers in my platoon all the time."

Our turn at the gate was coming up. He winked and said, "Let me do the talking."

He stepped up to the gate and said, "Good evening, sergeant. Could we borrow your stretcher there?" He pointed into the MPs' booth.

The MP saluted, "Good evening, sir. Who's the drunk?"

"We don't know for sure, some sergeant, I think. We saw him here at Camp Alpha earlier, and when we ran into him this evening, we thought we'd get him back here and put him to bed."

The MP helped us load Doyle onto the stretcher and patted him down, looking for his wallet. "I don't know, sir; I'm not supposed to let anybody in without ID."

"Sarge, look at him. You can see he ain't no gook, and Mr. Grant here and I have ID, and we can vouch for him. At least, we can tell you that he belongs here 'cause we saw him this afternoon."

"He should be charged with conduct unbecoming an NCO."

"Well, I think you're right. But, I tell you what, Sarge, I'm willing to overlook it if you are."

After a moment the MP sergeant said, "Thank you, sir."

We hustled Struman off toward the NCO billets till we were out of sight of the MP, then we turned back to the officer billets. We stripped Doyle down and took him to the shower.

It was 2205, and we headed back to the gate with the intention of returning to the club. When we got there the MP said, "I'm sorry gentlemen, but it's after 2200; I can't allow you to leave the compound."

I said, "But we just want to go back to the New Year's party at the O club."

"I'm really sorry, sir, but the curfew is 2200, so I can't let you out."

Recon said, "You just let those guys in."

"Oh yes, sir, you can come in after 2200; you just can't go out."

I said, "Come on, Sarge, it's New Years E . . ."

Recon yelled, "Holy shit! Look at that," pointing over my shoulder.

The MP turned and looked, and so did I. The next thing I knew, something yanked hard at my collar, and I was out the gate. We were now outside. The MP turned toward us, a look of anger crossed his face, then he shook his head and started laughing.

Since we had left our hats and weren't exactly presentable, we opted for the rear door that we'd left by. I had cleaned off some of the mud that I'd acquired while wrestling with Doyle and reattached my wings to my shirt. As we retrieved our hats from the bartender, he told us that the guy Doyle had tried to punch out was a major general. He also said that Doyle had been sitting at the bar all afternoon, drinking double bourbon and Cokes. We were somewhat surprised at that, since he hadn't shown any signs of drunkenness till he tried to fight.

We started back to our table, and received a standing ovation. I looked around in surprise. The general came over, and I apologized for Doyle's behavior. He patted me on the shoulder and said, "Don't worry about it, Lieutenant. You did a fine job of averting a major incident."

His eyes drifted over to the 82d Airborne guys. I figured that he also realized that they would've given a good accounting of themselves.

"Sir, I have to admit that I was mostly trying to keep a friend out of trouble."

"That's fine, Lieutenant. I believe in loyalty to one's friends. Now, Lieutenant, what are you gentlemen drinking? I'd like to buy you both a drink."

I could see out of the corner of my eye that Recon was about to bust a gut trying to keep from laughing every time the general called me lieutenant.

"Bourbon and Coke, sir. Eh . . . General . . . there's something I've got to say."

"What is it, Lieutenant?"

"Sir, if you don't stop calling me lieutenant, I'm going to have to hit you."

He gave me a puzzled look for a moment, and then he took a closer look at my bar. I explained that I was a warrant officer. He smiled and said, "I'm sorry, son. I didn't mean to offend you."

The general called the waiter over and talked to him. Lieutenant Recon and I rang in the New Year at the general's expense. He picked up our tab for the entire evening.

CHAPTER 11
JANUARY 1969

On New Year's Day, there was only a limited number of flights going back north. The sergeant at the desk stamped my orders that I had showed up, but no flights were available. Lieutenant Recon wasn't able to get a hop to Phuoc Vinh, so we spent the day bar hopping around Bien Hoa. I got a flight back north on the second.

4 January (74 days to go). I turned over and felt like I'd overslept. The ever-faithful, self-winding Seiko told me that it was almost eight. I leapt from my bunk in a panic; the CQ hadn't woken me, and I'd overslept. My first day back flying after R & R, and I couldn't get back in the groove.

A peek out the door revealed low ceilings and poor visibility—no flying! Somebody had actually used his head that morning. It must have been an enlisted man.

I had breakfast and headed for operations with coffee in hand. Once again, I was thankful for the quality of the HHC mess hall. I was scheduled with Lt. Mike Snyder that day and knew I would likely find him in operations.

"Good afternoon, Mr. Grant. Did we have a nice nighty-night, or are we just still in Honolulu?"

"It's just that I'm getting so short I had trouble figuring out how to climb down from my bunk, asshole, sir." One good thing about our section was that all the RLOs were decent guys.

Lieutenant Snyder briefed me on some mission details that were not available the night before. We were to be flying on loan to a 2d Brigade operation, a log mission. They had called already and said that they were desperate. They'd made it clear that they would like us to take off as soon as we could. They had a jump TOC set up just about ten miles northwest of Evans, in the flat land at the base of the foothills. A jump TOC is a movable tactical operations center that's set up closer to an operation than the regular headquarters. In this case, the 2d Brigade TOC was at LZ Sally, farther to the south, so the brigade had set up a jump TOC at FSB Nancy. I went to the door of operations and looked out. The weather was about a hundred-feet ceiling, and a half-mile visibility.

I turned back to the room and said, "We'll give it a shot after coffee."

I saw surprise in Snyder's face.

"You're the one who said they sounded desperate, Mike. We'll probably only be able to get to the jump TOC anyway."

We made our way along at ten feet off the ground, keeping the airspeed below ninety knots to make up for the decreased visibility. When we landed outside the TOC, another Huey was on the ground, with the rotor coasting down. I looked at Snyder and said, "See, I'm not the only crazy bastard around."

During the engine cool-down period, a captain came over, saw the lieutenant, went to him, and told him they would like him in TOC right away for a briefing. Snyder just looked helplessly at me. I shook it off, told him to join me after he shut the bird down, and climbed out of my seat. The captain looked annoyed as I joined him on the walk to the TOC.

"Isn't the lieutenant coming?"

"Oh, no, sir. I'm the aircraft commander." I grinned at him. He kind of shuffled. "Er ... ah I'm ... ah sorry I ah ..."

I smiled. He wasn't being a smartass, he just didn't know. "Don't worry about it, sir. We sometimes have to do things a little different in aviation."

Once inside the TOC, I saw that the pilot from the other bird was already there. The man who was to brief us on our mission had no trouble understanding that WO1s were aircraft commanders. I was surprised to see him there. It wasn't often that we were mission-briefed by a brigade commander. He shook my hand and thanked me for coming. I was starting to worry, the reception was a little too friendly. He walked over to the situation map and uncovered it.

"Gentlemen, here's the situation. Troopers from my brigade are making a sweep of this valley." He pointed to a valley running from northeast to southwest, and then to the west. It was labeled Rach My Chann. Blue rectangles indicated companies of

Airborne infantry in the valley. Red rectangles indicated suspected enemy positions.

"I believe that we have several battalions of NVA in the valley in front of this sweep. I have a blocking force here." He pointed to a green rectangle at the northeast end of the valley. "That's where you come in. I have two problems. One is, the blocking force hasn't been resupplied for several days due to the bad weather. The second is, they're ARVNs, and they're talking about walking out if they don't get resupply." He held his palms up toward us in a hold-your-horses gesture.

"I know you guys don't like to hang your asses out for ARVNs." His voice got lower and he came closer to us, leaving the map. "See, the ARVNs don't know that they're a blocking force. If they did, the bastards would probably walk anyway. If I can get them a few chickens, they will stay where they are till it's too late. Once the NVA get there, they'll have to fight long enough for the paratroopers to catch up and finish the job."

I liked his plan. It would be nice to see Marvin get in a real fight for a change.

He continued. "I know the weather is shit, gentlemen. All I'm asking is the old college try. If you can't do it, then fine. What happens, happens. It's just that I think we got a damn good operation going here, and I think we can kick some ass with your help."

It was a kind of pathetic sight, a full colonel practically begging two WO1s for help. How could we say no?

I said, "We'll give it a shot, sir."

He gave us the coordinates of the log LZ and set his people scurrying about to get the birds loaded and ready to go. The other W1 was from the sister company of the Kingsmen, C Company, Black Widows. He grabbed at my sleeve and pulled me aside. "I don't know if my AC will go for this."

"You're not the AC?"

"No."

"Why didn't he come in?"

"Well . . . uh."

Something smelled here. "Who is your AC?" I asked, under wrinkled brow.

"Pat McCrady."

"Really! I haven't seen him since our graduation party in flight school." I headed out to the aircraft. He made a move like he was going to stop me, then changed his mind. Pat was still strapped into the bird when I got there.

I stepped up on the skid. "Hey you son of a . . . whoo." I waved my hand back and forth in front of my face to dispel the aroma of booze and barf that was on his breath. He finally managed to explain through slurred speech that he was supposed to be off today. He had still been in the club when they came and got him to fly. I told him that I was glad to see that I wasn't the only one living up to our Irish heritage. He assured me that his peter pilot could handle the mission solo. I told Pat to try not to pass out on the controls, and he showed me that his shoulder harness was locked.

I got together with Pat's pete and Mike Snyder, and we came up with a plan. Since my aircraft had two conscious pilots, we would go first. If the weather proved to be too bad, the Black Widow bird wouldn't leave the ground. We would try hopping saddles to work our way into the unit. Navigation would be by FM homing. It was unlikely that anyone else would be stupid enough to fly, so if one of us stayed on the ground while the other went in, we were not likely to run into another aircraft. Then the first bird would work its way out by FM homing to the bird on the pad. While the first bird reloaded, the second would work its way to the LZ, and so on till we finished.

We took off with the load of live chickens and some rice. I let Snyder fly, while I followed the map and worked the radio. We had to cross several hills prior to being able to make contact with the unit on the ground.

"Red Unicorn Four, this is Thunder Five-Five. Over."

"Five-Five, Unicorn Four. Go ahead. Over." It was obvious that the unit had an Aussie adviser.

"Roger. Four, can you give us a short count?"

"Roger, mate. One, two, three, four, five, four, three, two, one. Short count out."

The FM homing needle indicated they were slightly to the left. We hopped another saddle. I was barely able to keep the trees in sight through the chin bubble.

"Gimme another short count, Four."

"Roger, one, two, three, four, five, four, three, two, one. Short count out. We surely appreciate your comin' out in this bloody awful weather, mate."

"Think nothin' of it, Four. Anything for our bleedin' allies." He chuckled at my imitation of his accent. When we found the LZ, he came over, stood on the skid and reached in to shake my hand.

"I can't tell how much I appreciate this. These silly blighters were about to pack up and go home. Woulda' sent our whole operation down the loo." I'd found something I could feel good about doing again. I was helping to salvage the operation and getting to screw over Marvin at the same time. I was having a good time. But my heart sank every time we crossed a saddle and the trees disappeared for a second or two and we were surrounded by clouds.

We worked our way back to the TOC by FM homing to Black Widow 17. While we loaded up, they went in to the LZ. It continued that way through a refueling and for three hours of flight time. The weather remained about the same. Finally, during one of the fights into the mountains, I was on the controls. As we crossed one of the saddles, we punched into the clouds. My heart nearly stopped as the seconds ticked off. One thousand one, one thousand two, one thousand three . . . I lowered the collective a hair, knowing it was the wrong thing to do. One thousand four, one thousand five . . . then I saw a tree and another. We broke out into the valley and landed in the LZ. I told the Aussie adviser that this would be my last trip.

I landed back at the TOC and told Pat, who had sobered up some, that I wasn't going back in. He replied that it was a good thing. I was starting to scare his peter pilot. I told him I would go in and explain to the colonel. McCrady's peter pilot walked in with me. He was going to make a good AC. He flew smart and had the courage to face the brigade commander with me.

The colonel kept pumping our hands and thanking us. "I'm going to see that you both get DFCs for this."

I looked over at the other pilot. "Sir, I would rather you left me off of that recommendation."

"Why, Mr. Grant?"

"Well, sir, this wasn't a big deal. If I accepted a DFC for this, it would be an insult to the other awards that I've been put in for."

The idealism of youth, or was I afraid that if another award got submitted, I'd get sent somewhere where they had flush toilets.

5 January (73 days to go). I was flying with Lt. Robert Taylor. It was a log mission, the best mission that I could hope for during those days with 3d Brigade. Log mission at least meant a long day with plenty of flight time, thus making the days pass more quickly. We'd been flying for about four hours when the Mayday call came over the guard frequency on the UHF radio. We were unable to make out all of the transmission, only that a Marine helicopter was going down seven miles southeast of Camp Evans. We'd just taken off from Evans headed toward the west. Taylor looked over at me with a question in his eyes. My nod told him to turn the bird back to Evans. I called the unit and told them that we would drop off the passengers at Evans and respond to the Mayday.

Once in the air again, Taylor pointed the Huey southeast and lowered the nose, allowing the airspeed to build to 110 knots. In only two minutes, I could see thick black smoke rising ahead, never a good sign with a downed aircraft. In just over five minutes, we were on the scene. Taylor was carefully setting the aircraft down in sandy soil that was covered with thin grass. I surveyed the scene. A crashed CH-34 was burning furiously. A medevac was lifting off as we touched down. A half dozen grunts headed toward our aircraft carrying two wounded. I scanned the area for potential enemy activity. There was no sign of any. I checked the sky for other aircraft. There were none. It would've made me happier to see a Cobra or two circling. Again, I checked for activity in the direction of the village. The fact that there were no curious civilians headed our way made me a little nervous that maybe there were VC in the area.

The grunts were Marines. The two men they were carrying wore one-piece Nomex flight suits, obviously crewmembers from the 34. They threw the first guy in the bird like they were handling a sack of potatoes. I could see the second man's right arm was hanging by tendons and ligaments. They tossed him in the same way. The grunts clearly thought they were dead. The gunnery sergeant in charge jumped up in the bird and leaned over my seat.

"Don't get in a hurry with these two, sir, they're gone."

He jumped down from the bird, leaving a bloody handprint on the inside armor plate of my seat. I looked in the back, both men had no hair on their heads. The exposed skin was pink and peeling from the fire.

"I have the controls."

I picked up the Huey and lowered the nose. I pulled enough power to let the aircraft accelerate to max speed. I turned toward Camp Evans where the nearest field hospital was located. I didn't waste time by climbing to altitude. I held the Huey down on the deck, the airspeed quickly rose to 120. We'd make the hospital pad in less than four minutes.

Bob Taylor asked, "Those guys are dead, aren't they?" His voice sounded a little weak.

"Yeah, L T, I'm afraid they are."

"Why are we beatin' feet then?"

" 'Cause if we're wrong, I don't want to be the one that gave up on 'em."

"Oh." The lieutenant was just staring straight ahead out the windshield. It must have been the first time he became aware that some of our own got killed in the war.

"Evans Tower, Thunder Five-Five. Two miles southeast for the medevac pad."

"Roger Five-Five. Your traffic is Dustoff just lifting from the pad. Winds are calm, altimeter is niner niner eight. You're cleared to land medevac."

"Five-Five has the traffic."

I made a hot approach and touched down like it was for real. The medic rushed over and looked in the back. After one look, their pace slowed without even checking for a pulse. They threw both men on the same stretcher the way butchers might handle slabs of bad beef. I felt silly for my rush, but didn't regret it. I'd seen plenty of dead bodies and was pretty sure about these. Still, I was not about to make the final decision. If it made me look silly to the medics, then so be it.

I called the brigade log pad. "Logmaster, this is Thunder Five-Five."

"Five-Five, this is Logmaster. Are you on your way back?"

"Logmaster, Five-Five. Believe me, you don't want us back till this bird has a bath. We're going to take a break. We'll be back as soon as possible."

"Roger, Five-Five. Take your time. We only have a few more sorties for you. Was it a bad one?"

"Yeah." He knew better than to ask "How bad?" on the radio. I called the tower for reposition to the Storm Center.

I shut down on the maintenance pad. They had a fire hose that we used to wash down the bird. The sooner the blood was washed out the better. If you missed any, it let you know after a few days.

As the rotor coasted to a stop, I noticed that Taylor had not moved or said anything. I looked over at him. One hand rested on the instrument panel glare shield, and the other held the leather handle on the door. He was staring straight ahead. I looked in the back one more time. The cargo floor was covered with congealed blood, and blood had run out the doors into the slip stream, causing it to splatter back inside onto the bulkheads and the crew chief and the gunner. I pictured the two Marines.

They were aircrew; that was too close to home. My stomach started to remind me of what I had for lunch. As I pulled off my helmet, the crew chief was opening my door. I jerked my head toward the lieutenant and said, "If you don't mind, I'm going to pass on helping you clean this one up. I'll take the L T and get him a cup of coffee."

He smiled up at me. "No sweat, GI. I understand." Then more quietly, "The L T gonna be all right, Mr. G.?"

"I think so, he just don't need to be here right now."

"I can dig it, sir."

"Thanks."

Taylor got out with his helmet and gloves still on. We went to operations, and I had him wait outside while I went in. Lieutenant Snyder was behind the counter.

"When I go back out, maybe you'd better send another pete with me. I think Taylor could use a break."

"It was bad, huh?"

"Messy. They haven't washed it out yet if you want to go look." I jerked my thumb over my shoulder for emphasis. I was feeling better already and couldn't pass up the opportunity to mess with him.

"No, W. T., I think I'll take your word for it. By the way, Mr. Tharp is on the way in from his mission so I'll have him fly your last few sorties. Then you won't have to go back out either."

"In that case, I'll find Taylor a drink instead of some coffee. Tell the crew chief to come get me when he wants the bird moved to the revetment." I could see what he was thinking. "Don't worry, I'm gonna have coffee."

I drew two cups from the pot in operations, went outside, and rounded up Taylor. While we walked back to the hootch, he began to look a little less like death warmed over.

"W. T., you seen a lotta that shit?"

"More than enough."

"Guess you're pretty well used to it then, huh?"

I stopped and turned to face him on the narrow path between the building and the outer blast wall. "L T, if you ever really get used to it, then it's time to start worrying about yourself. I usually just make sure I drink enough that night to make the image fuzzy. By the next morning, it gets a little easier to live with."

We started walking again. "Does it ever go away?" he asked.

"Not yet it ain't."

In my room, I poured a double shot of bourbon in his coffee. He sipped it slowly. "Aren't you gonna have some, W. T.?"

"Later. I still gotta park the bird."

"What about the mission?"

"Tharp's gonna finish it."

That night, he got the image real fuzzy.

Monday, 6 January (72 days to go). Bad weather held us to only two hours of flight time.

Tuesday, 7 January (71 days to go). The weather was terrible, but we flew six and half hours of log mission anyway.

Wednesday, 8 January (70 days to go). The weather was even worse than the day before, but we managed 7.3 hours of flight time. The mission was part log and part ash and trash, hauling people back and forth from Evans to Eagle.

9 January (69 Days to go). The weather was really atrocious. The 101st Aviation Battalion staff duty log for the day showed that Ken Roach had called in and reported the weather as 180-foot ceiling and a quarter-mile visibility. I was limited to 1.3 hours. The poor visibility accounted for a mishap. A Huey from the 101st Battalion was flying south to get back to Eagle. There was large radio tower just outside of Hue. The UH-1H, traveling a mite too fast for the conditions, came upon the tower as a surprise. The aircraft commander, seeing the impending danger, flared the bird and turned at the same time. In a steep bank the aircraft hit the guy wires with the skids first. Unbelievably, the Huey didn't crash. The guy wire absorbed the impact and drew back like a bowstring and shot the helpless aircraft away from the tower. The only damage to the aircraft was to the skids. The tower, however, did have a permanent bow to it from then on.

10 January (68 days to go). I found out that HHC had an allocation for an R & R to Hawaii that no one wanted. I was told that I could have it if I was willing to take leave to go. I jumped on the opportunity. It would be another week off my tour and a chance to get away from the boring missions that I couldn't stand. I wrote home to Jackie to tell her she would have to tolerate another week in Hawaii. I would be there the nineteenth through the twenty-fifth of February. When I returned, I would have less than three weeks to go.

Monday, 13 January (65 days to go). The weather was still stinky, rainy and cold. I'd been prepared for the rain during the monsoons. The cold had been unexpected. Each day was something to be endured. I found the rain, the cold, and the missions all depressing. I was scheduled with L T Snyder. It was to be a log mission into the mountains near FSB Rakkasson, where a unit hadn't been resupplied in over a week. They were out of food and almost out of ammo. There'd been sporadic contact over the past twenty-four hours. The battalion commander was afraid that Charlie was getting ready to mount an attack. The company wouldn't be able to withstand serious contact.

I made the choice, we'd have to make an attempt. I knew full well that the unit's location in the mountains would be above the cloud layer. I told the log pad NCO to go ahead and load us up with some ammo. They put on about half of what we'd normally be able to carry. I figured that I might have to hover around to make this work out. If that was the case, it would be best not to have a full load. I took the controls from a worried Snyder.

"L T, we're going to have to make a good try at this. If we fail, that whole company could get wiped out tonight."

The plan was for them to walk out the next day if they didn't get my resupply. That plan would leave them open to ambush every inch of the way. They'd been in contact on and off, so Chuck was well aware of when they were last resupplied. The minor contacts were likely planned to drain off their ammunition. If I had been the enemy commander, they wouldn't get to walk out. The probing would continue during the night, until it became obvious that they were conserving ammo. Then would come the real attack.

When we arrived at the ridgeline, as expected the clouds were well below the level of the unit. I knew that saddle hopping and FM homing were not going to work the way it had the other day. I began to circle, talking to the unit as I did.

"Gallant Rover Six, this is Thunder Five-Five. Over."

"Thunder Five-Five, this is Gallant Rover Six. Go ahead."

"Six, this is Five-Five. I've been briefed on your situation. I have a load of ammo for you."

"Five-Five, this is Six. I don't think you can get to us. We are solid in the clouds here."

"Six, this is Five-Five. I'm circling along the ridgeline in your vicinity. Can you hear the aircraft?"

"Yes, I can."

He sounded puzzled.

"As I circle, tell me when we sound the closest."

As we made our circles, my mind was busily trying to come up with something that would work to get this ammo up the mountain. My thoughts were interrupted by the radio.

"Right there! You sound closest right there!"

I quickly picked out a reference point on the side of the hill. I then circled to the east trying to come up with something. I wanted to ask how far up in the clouds he was, but realized that he'd have no idea. Then an idea hit me.

"Six, this is Five-Five. Do you have flares?"

"Uh . . . yeah, we do."

"What do you have?"

"We got trip flares and star clusters."

"Okay, here's the plan. I'm gonna FM home to your location. When I start to sound real close, gimme a star. When I get closer, gimme a flare."

This time, he sounded really skeptical.

"Five-Five, you are sure you wanna try this?"

"Six, do you want this damned ammo or not?"

"Yeah . . . but . . ."

I didn't really want to do what I was about to attempt. I was risking the aircraft and crew on something that wasn't an accepted procedure; I kept thinking of how the whole company of infantry might not make it till morning. Snyder didn't look at all happy with my brilliant idea; I didn't tell him I wasn't too happy with it myself. I told Mike to monitor the homing needle and keep an eye on the attitude indicator. I brought the Huey to a hover over the reference point and started hovering up the ridge into the clouds. It scared the hell out of me. I panicked, turned, and dove out of the clouds. I circled around, came to a hover again, and asked for another short count. Once more, I started hovering up the mountain. I kept the trees in sight through the chin bubble of the aircraft, occasionally glancing at the instruments.

"Five-Five, it sounds like you're getting close. Star cluster coming up."

Snyder said, "I see it. Turn a little left."

"Trip flare coming out."

I could see the glow off in the fog. Then the LZ was under us. We kicked out the ammo and headed down the mountain. I flew us back to the log pad and got another load. We continued for four trips. They'd have enough ammunition to kill gooks all night long and into the next day. As I lowered the nose and dove out of the clouds into the valley one more time, I called.

"Gallant Rover Six, this is Thunder Five-Five. Will that hold you a while?"

"Roger. Thanks a lot, Five-Five."

"No sweat, GI."

That was a lie. My shirt was soaked with sweat. The operation had scared the hell out of me.

"Five-Five . . . uh . . . did you know that we've been out of chow for two days?"

I looked over at Snyder and smiled. I should have known this was coming. The company commander was well aware that we were hanging it out for him going in there. He wasn't about to *ask* us to do it again. That, however, did not preclude hinting.

"Roger, Six. I'll bring you one load."

I landed the Huey at the log pad and told the sergeant to put on fifty cases of Cs. That would give them two days' food. By this point, I'd made the run up the mountain enough that I could recognize many of the trees along the way. We kicked out the load and headed back to Evans. It was easy to tell the commander understood the risk we had taken and was appreciative.

At Evans, we picked up a major and took him out to FSB Jack. We shut down and waited while he visited one of the units there. Back to the taxicab service. I stretched out on the floor of the bird and thought about Hawaii. Soon I was enjoying the memories too much and had to think about something else. A while later the major came back and we cranked up. Just after takeoff, he plugged in his headset and said, "Take me up to Alpha company."

I asked, "They're the ones on the ridgeline aren't they?" I knew the answer already. The question was to give him the opportunity to change his request.

"Yes, they are."

"I don't think we can get in there, sir. They're socked in."

"But you made five trips in there already."

"We'll take a look, sir, but I don't think we can get in there."

I knew damn well the weather hadn't improved, but maybe a look would satisfy him. When we arrived, if there'd been any change at all, the clouds hung farther down the mountain.

"Sorry, sir. We can't get in there."

"You did it before; you'd better find a way."

I'd found another flamer. I was now almost sorry that I'd hung our asses out to get the ammo in.

"Different reason, sir. That was an emergency."

"Well, you'd better make this an emergency. I need to visit that unit."

"L T, you have the controls."

"Roger, I have the controls."

I turned as far as I could in the seat and looked him in the eye. "Sir, I am not in the habit of risking my aircraft or the lives of my crew for visits. I'll be glad to take you up there when the weather breaks."

"Mister, I'm giving you a direct order to fly up that mountain."

I turned back to the front wondering why I attracted so many assholes. I stepped on the mike button on the floor. "I'll tell you what I'll do, Major, we'll land at Jack, you can hand receipt this bird, and you can fly the motherfucker up the mountain, 'cause that's the only way you're goin'."

"Take me back to Evans!" I thought sure he was going to blow out a jugular from the look on his face.

When Snyder landed at Evans, the major leaped out and tore into the lieutenant that ran the log pad. I could see that the lieutenant was trying in vain to explain to him that he couldn't override my decision in the aircraft. He finally stomped off in a huff.

We were released with a total of five hours of flight time and no further complaint from the major. Back at the Storm Center I told Snyder that since he witnessed the whole thing as the ops officer, I wasn't going to write up the incident. The major hadn't bothered us any more, and I wasn't looking to get him in trouble. Mike told me he'd tell Major Wallace about it just to cover our asses, but wouldn't report it to brigade unless the guy made trouble about it.

One day, I was flying in support of the ARVNs near FSB Nancy. Like many other American soldiers, I had come to distrust the ARVN soldier. Much of the problem may have been a bad rap, but most of us felt we had justification to feel that the ARVN was not capable of fighting his own war. There never seemed to be even the slightest comparison between the fighting ability of the American soldier and the average Vietnamese soldier. The allegedly reluctant U.S. troop fought aggressively, with no stake in the outcome. The ARVN, who was fighting for his country's survival, seemed not to care.

As we flew a routine log mission, we did all the things we'd do with a U.S. unit. C rations were hauled, soldiers flown to the rear, and replacements flown to the field. On one sortie we landed at a field site, and an ARVN with a leg wound came hobbling toward the aircraft. Apparently his lieutenant had decided it was not time for him to be medevacked. The officer ran up to him and kicked him in the wounded leg. Unlike the U.S. Army, it was not uncommon for discipline to be physically administered in the Vietnamese army.

Later that same day, we landed in an LZ further out in the jungle. We were resupplying the unit with ammunition, as it had been in contact. We'd been told the unit had some wounded that would come out. The peter pilot had been flying, and as I looked out at the approaching wounded, one of them caught my eye. I could see that a round had entered alongside his nose, just above the left eye, and had exited on the left side of his head. Even though he was bandaged, parts of his brain were clearly visible. It was clearly a very serious wound, and unbelievably, he was getting into the aircraft under his own power!

Monday, 27 January (51 days to go). We had flown log all day, and it was getting close to the end of our missions. I was hungry and was looking to a good meal at the mess hall. We were directed to the brigade headquarters pad. When we landed, an MP came over and told me they had some prisoners to be flown to Eagle. I asked what kind of prisoners and he told me they were VC suspects.

"How many ya got, Sarge?"

"Eighteen sir. Two loads."

I looked at my watch and then over at L T Hightower in the other seat. At a hundred knots, it would take about fifteen minutes each way to fly to Eagle. That would mean thirty minutes round trip. It was already 1630. If I made two trips like they planned, the mess hall would be closed when we returned. It closed promptly at 1730. That would mean we'd have to eat Cs. I wasn't going to eat Cs because some VC was getting his first helicopter ride.

"Put 'em on."

"All of them, sir?"

"You bet."

"Sir, there are eighteen of them. Where will I put them?"

"They're VC, aren't they? Stack 'em like fire wood."

"But, sir . . ."

"Look, Sarge, if I make two sorties, I miss chow. I have no intention of going hungry for a bunch of VC fuckers."

"You're the boss, sir."

By the time they stacked the gooks in the back, there was barely room for the two guards to get in the aircraft. I knew that we'd be heavy trying to get off the pad, and there was a set of wires to clear at one end. We made the takeoff with little problem. After we cleared the traffic pattern, I called operations for flight following. "Thunder Ops, this is Thunder Five-Five."

"Five-Five, Operations. Go ahead."

"Roger, Operations. Five-Five is off Evans, en route Eagle with twenty-two SOBs."

"Five-Five, say again."

"Again." I smirked.

"No, no! I mean say again last transmission."

"Roger, Operations. Five-Five is off Evans, en route Eagle, with twenty-two SOBs."

There was a moment of silence. "Roger."

We headed for Eagle. On the way, I decided that there'd be enough time for my usual treatment for POWs. It was routine for prisoners to be transported with a sandbag over their heads and tied at the neck. I'd discovered that if I did a gradual cyclic climb, followed by a gentle pedal turn as the airspeed dropped through forty knots, it almost always resulted in barfing. Even experienced aircrewmembers would have trouble riding out the maneuver with their eyes closed. The VC on their first flight would be off-loaded at the end of the flight with their lunch dripping from the bag. I'd then tell the MPs that if Charlie wouldn't talk, just tell him that he was getting another helicopter ride. Of course, then he wouldn't shut up.

On my return to the Storm Center, I called down and was told to come right to operations. I told John Hightower to shut down and I'd meet him in the mess hall. When I walked in, Lieutenant Snyder was waiting for me.

"W. T., what the hell is this about twenty-two souls on board, en route to Eagle?"

"We needed to get back to make chow."

"You overloaded the aircraft to make the mess hall?"

"It's okay, sir; eighteen of 'em were little people."

I turned and walked out, terminating the conversation. I wanted him to know that I felt there was no need for further talk. I could feel his eyes boring into my back as I left, and restrained myself from laughing till I was out the door.

CHAPTER 12
FEBRUARY 1969

Monday, 3 February (44 days to go). The night before, we'd been drinking with the air force FAC (forward air control) pilots. We found out that they liked to sneak up on each other and say, "Rat tat tat" over the radio. They had fun dogfighting like that. They kept score on each other. It sounded like a fun game, and army aviators were always up for a good game. There had been some discussion during the evening about how we didn't feel their airplanes would be able to hold up against a helicopter in a dogfight. Needless to say the air force pilots seemed to have a different opinion. That morning one of the O-2s snuck up behind one of our Loaches and gave him the "Rat tat tat." I found out about it at lunch time. He had victimized one of the new guys. I explained to the Loach pilot that it seemed we were going to have to watch our asses from now on. I also told him there was absolutely no way that an airplane could turn inside a hovering helicopter. The OH-6 had no problem hovering at several thousand feet, thus an alert Loach pilot couldn't be "shot down" by any of the FACs. A fully loaded Huey might not be able to hover on command at altitude, but there were other ways to handle an airplane. I fully intended to seek revenge that very afternoon.

All afternoon, I watched the skies as I flew, looking for a chance to pounce on an air force O-2. I was on the way back to the Storm Center at the end of the day before the opportunity presented itself. The crew chief called out, "Sir, I got one at seven o'clock high."

They'd never get the opportunity to sneak up on all the eyes in a Huey. I looked over my shoulder, and there he was lazily circling about eight hundred feet above us to our left rear. He was hunting real targets. We were outside the circle he was flying, and he was turning away from us. There was no way he could see us. The FAC airplane was much faster than a Huey, and in the open sky there'd be no contest. But by being sneaky and staying fairly close to the ground, we had certain advantages. I called, "Clear left and up."

"Clear left and up, sir." The reply was sprinkled with laughter.

I pulled in max power and put the bird in cyclic climb to the left. With the altitude gap closing quickly, I lowered the nose to get my airspeed back. We leveled out nicely right behind the O-2 in his turn. Ernie Navarrete turned the UHF radio to the air force frequency and set my selector on two. I keyed the mike. "Rat tat tat."

On the intercom, "Clear left and down."

"Clear, sir."

I dropped the collective and headed for the ground. My turn brought us momentarily alongside the airplane. I heard over the UHF, "Ah, shit."

I laughed like a crazy man all the way back to Evans. I flew low level all the way, taking evasive action. It wasn't necessary. He had been totally had. Air force one, army one.

The next day, they caught one of our Hueys as he was coming out of an LZ, not looking for trouble from above. On the fifth, my door gunner spotted one trying to sneak up on us from behind at fifteen hundred feet. I turned toward him like I was trying to get around on his tail. He broke up and away, planning to slide in behind me for the kill. As soon as I knew he'd lose sight of me for an instant, I turned the opposite way and headed for the trees. We snuck away behind a hill and escaped. It's pretty hard to see a green Huey down among the green trees. The score remained air force two, army one.

The game was set aside for a few days till one of them tried the same trick on one of the more experienced OH-6 pilots that he tried on me. Rich Wideman saw him coming and brought the Loach to a fifteen-hundred-foot hover. As the airplane turned, trying in vain to get behind him, Rich pedal-turned, with his nose following the plane around. On UHF he said, Rat tat tat tat tat tat tat tat tat tat . . ." till the O-2 broke off in disgust and went home. Air force two, army two.

4 February (43 days to go). It was a good day of flying; I flew 7.3 hours of log mission. That night, we got together in the

party room. One room in the bunker row had been set up with a bar so we could raise hell away from anyone who might be sleeping. I think it'd been one of the lieutenants who thought of our using it.

With its scorched plywood bar, the room was very stylish. It seemed that anytime GIs wanted someplace to look special, anywhere in country, they took a torch to the plywood. I guess it didn't look like an official army room if the plywood was scorched.

L T Hightower was with us that night. He probably figured that he was due for spending some quality leadership time with the warrants. It was a hang-out-with-the-guys-and-gain-their-trust kind of thing. He may have wanted just to get to know us, but I always felt that he was uncomfortable around me. He arrived just as we were getting into drinking blue blazers. I've heard them called by many other names, but whatever they are called, it's a shot of your favorite liquor set on fire. The requirement is to pick up the flaming drink, toss it down and put the glass down empty but still burning. It's a simple matter of timing and practice. If you failed, you had to try again. Of course, the more shots one drank, the harder it was to get it right. I was one of the few who wore a moustache who was willing to attempt the drink.

John Hightower decided he would give it a try. I explained the rules to him, and he made an attempt. On his first, he exhaled as the shot got under his nose, and he blew out the flame. The second one he drank, but the glass wasn't burning when he put it down. After each attempt, I ordered one for myself and demonstrated the proper technique. The third he bumped and spilled on the bar. That made him nervous. On the fourth attempt his hand was shaking and he spilled a little on his hand and set it on fire. After he had tried to set the bar on fire, we made sure we had a wet towel handy, so we were able to put out his hand right away. I started to feel sorry for him, so I explained my personal technique to him. On his fifth try, he stared at the burning glass too long, and the shot glass got hot and burned his lip.

"L T, I think maybe you ought to hang it up and try again another night."

"Naw, W. T., I wanna get this right."

He ordered up number six. He got very nervous on that try, and as he tossed it down, he completely missed his mouth and set the whole right side of his face on fire. We told him that he couldn't try again unless he brought his own body bag.

Wednesday, 5 February (42 days to go). The right side of Hightower's face was red, his lip was blistered, and he had some blisters on his hand. We were flying a log mission. I'd just made the takeoff from the pad at LZ Sally when the Mayday came over the UHF guard frequency. It was fast and panicked.

"Mayday, Mayday, Mayday. Five miles east of sss . . ."

It was abruptly cut off. I couldn't tell if the last was part of the transmission or just radio noise. I turned the Huey east and nosed it over. If everyone who heard the transmission turned to the east and looked, someone had to find them. They had to be east of somewhere. I called the unit I was supporting and told them I was responding to a Mayday. I looked over my shoulder. We had two grunts, a large rope, a few cases of C rations, a sledge hammer, and an axe on board.

I told the crew chief, "Tell the pax what's going on, and tell them to keep an eye out for the downed aircraft. We might need their help if we find the bird."

After flying five miles due east, I found out where the aircraft was east of. It had not been radio noise, it was the start of the word "Sally." It had only been three minutes since the call had gone out. We were the third Huey to land on the scene. It was always good to know that Mayday calls received great reaction. As I touched down, an OH-6 and two Cobras started circling overhead. The crashed aircraft was resting in a rice paddy, on its left side, with one skid sticking up in the air. It was three-quarters of the way upside down. The rotor system was completely gone. The greenhouse window and the top of the windshield were gone. It was apparent that a rotor blade had taken a swipe through the cockpit. That was when I saw the headless figure strapped into the right seat. There was a bloody flight helmet lying below him. I turned away. It was one time too many. Someone was going to have to stay at the controls of the running aircraft; I decided that it would be me this time. I told the pete to take the crew and passengers and see if he could be of any help. It was a dirty trick, and I was using my position to help me cop out, but I didn't care. I was tired of the gore, and I was going to escape this once.

Several minutes later, the crew chief came back and plugged in and reported the situation.

"Sir, it seems they were flying low level and lost hydraulics and tail rotor control at the same time. They hit a rice paddy dike and cartwheeled in. The peter pilot was killed. The AC got out, and the gunner got out. The crew chief is pinned under the wreckage. The only part of him out of the water in the paddy is his nose and mouth. Another inch of water, and he'd be dead."

"What are they going to do?"

"We're going to take the rope and tie it to the skid. One of the Hueys will hook up and try to get the wreckage light enough to get the crew chief out."

"Be careful; we don't need anybody else hurt."

"Yes, sir."

He grabbed the rope and headed back to the wreck. They tied the rope to the skid and tried to lift the Huey. The rope went taut, the wreck started to move, and the rope snapped. Three attempts were made. Each time, the rope broke, and the crew chief remained pinned. It wasn't until the Chinook arrived that the aircraft could be lifted enough to get the crew chief out. He was removed and was in good shape. Amazingly, the only casualty was the pilot who was struck by the rotor blade. In less than a half hour, the entire rescue was completed, and we were on our way back to our mission.

Thursday, 6 February (41 days to go). I had the day off from flying, so I spent some time catching up on my letter writing and listening for Chinooks to land on the big pad. When one came in, I'd go up and wait to see if there was anyone I knew getting off. I was really waiting to see Joe Hall because he had given me the most grief back at Rucker about his going to Carson and my going to Nam. Now it would be payback time. The first big helicopter provided no joy. The second time I ran up the hill, I struck gold. There was Joe Hall, just coming off the back of the Chinook with his duffel bags. A wave of fiendish delight swept across me as I leaned against a telephone pole, lit up a smoke, and tried to look casual.

Joe looked every bit the FNG in his brand-new jungle fatigues. He stumbled and tripped as he half dragged, half carried his gear away from the noisy, windy blast of the huge helicopter. As the CH-47 lifted away, I slid around to the downwind side of the pole, turned my collar up and held my hat tightly. I didn't dared allow the grit going down my shirt to penetrate my aura of cool. The instant the wind let up, I shook my shirt twice to let out the sand, and put my hat back on. I'd recovered faster than any of the new guys. I straightened up, brushed my shirt, and smiled. They were still chasing hats and orders around the helipad. Hanging onto their heavy bags, some had been blown over. I knew I'd achieved the right image. The faded fatigues, the frayed baseball cap with embroidered rank and call sign, the fast recovery of dignity, all said "short-timer." As I casually strolled over to where Hall was still shaking sand from his shirt, I moved my facial muscles around to make sure I was wearing The Look.

"Hey, fuckin' new guy. What're you doing, dropping all your shit on my helipad?"

Joe was bent down over his duffel bags. He tilted his head up toward me with a look on face that said, "Why are you screwing with me?"

The recognition was immediate. Joe's familiar toothy grin flashed across his face. "Bill, how the hell are you?"

"Too short for any long conversations. In forty-one days I'm outa here, while you get to stay here and have your ass shot off and die. As a matter of fact, I'm so short, that sometimes I have to look up to see down."

"What do you mean di . . ." He stopped in midsentence as he remembered all the times in flight school he'd harassed me after we'd gotten our orders. "I'm going to Fort Carson to party, and you're going to Vietnam to die." He had said it so often. Now the shoe was on the other foot. I walked with him to his new company area, not offering to carry any of his belongings for him. I considered it punishment for the harassment of a year ago. Besides, I was a short-timer, and Joe was an FNG.

They were a new unit in country, but they were lucky in that they were moving into Evans. The Cav had left all its buildings for them. The 158th Battalion wouldn't have to endure leaky tents and the filling of sandbags. We talked for a while, and Joe introduced me to some of the guys in Company A. When word came that they would have a formation, I laughed and said it was about time for me to leave. The HHC mess hall would start serving dinner shortly, and I was getting pretty hungry. Joe asked me to come back later. I said that I would if I didn't get put on night standby.

That evening, I took a couple of six-packs with me to help ease the pain of the barbs I'd toss at those new guys. When I arrived, everyone was wearing steel pots and flak jackets.

"Hey, Joe. What's up? You guys playing army or something?"

"No. Haven't you heard? There's a yellow alert!"

I burst out laughing. I laughed so hard that I had to sit down; there were tears running down my cheeks.

"If you guys wear steel hats every time there's a yellow alert, you're gonna go home with flat heads. They don't even report the damn things in other units around here 'cause it don't mean nuthin'. Yellow alert means that it's dark out, and there's a war out there somewhere."

I soon found out that there were quite a few rules around that unit. They weren't allowed to wear flight jackets because snipers would pick them out and prey on the pilots. They were required to wear steel pots every time someone sneezed. It'd been quite a while since I had laughed that hard. I made a mental note to come over often and wear my flight jacket, no matter how warm it was.

It was then that their platoon leader came in. I was introduced to him. I shook his hand and said, "It's nice to meet you, sir." I could tell by the look in his eyes that he didn't approve of me. I felt he didn't want a warrant officer around who knew more about what was going on than he did. I wondered if their CO had been to Nam before. So far, everyone I had met was a rookie. No wonder they were being so silly about everything, it was an entire company of FNGs. I began to feel sorry for the Kingsmen that were sure to get infused here. I found out later that there was no crossleveling; the battalion began combat operations without any experienced aviators. It would cost them dearly to learn the ropes.

When the captain saw the beer, he told his pilots that they were limited to two each because of the alert. I assured him I would drink the rest so that he wouldn't have to worry about his people. He had a look in his eyes that said he wanted to have me sent to Vietnam.

I sat talking to Joe and some of the other pilots. They had lots of questions, and I even gave up the new-guy razzing to answer them. I could see that they were going to need all the help they could get. As we talked about CAs, log missions, and the like, an artillery battery on Evans was firing H & I fire and illum for the perimeter. I had to explain what harassment and interdiction fire was and explain about illumination. I had to explain that just because the arty was firing didn't mean there was any contact. The H & I was random and only meant to slow Charlie's movement, and maybe waste one once in a while. All during the conversation, the rounds went out anywhere from twenty seconds to a couple of minutes apart.

Finally Joe asked, "How do you know the difference in the rounds?"

I explained, "Well, Joe, if you listen carefully you hear that the illum rounds make less noise. They travel slower and have less propellant charge, 'cause they don't have to go as far. They also make a pop. So they go . . . *boom* . . . *whoosh* . . . pop. The HE rounds are far away when they go off; so all you hear is *boom* . . . *whoosh*."

One of the other warrants asked, "W. T., how do you know when to worry about the artillery? I mean you know when they're actually shooting at the enemy."

"When they have a real target, believe me, you'll be able to tell. The shit will be going out so fast you won't be able to count it. Still, there's nothing to worry about till you can hear the impact as loud as the firing. When it goes, *boom* . . . *woosh* . . . *boom*."

Joe asked, "What does incoming sound like?"

"That's the easiest difference. Incoming goes *whoosh* . . . *boom*. Outgoing goes *boom* . . . *whoosh*."

A minute later an outgoing round made its announcement. *Boom* . . . *whoosh*.

Joe Hall tugged at my sleeve and asked, "Is that incoming or outgoing?"

I explained again, "Joe, incoming goes *whoosh* . . . *boom*. Outgoing goes *boom* . . . *whoosh*."

A while later, he tugged again at my sleeve as the artillery fired an outgoing round. "Was that incoming or outgoing?"

"Damn it, Joe, I told you before, incoming goes *whoosh* . . . *boom*. Outgoing goes *boom* . . . *whoosh*."

He quieted down for a while, but still later tugged on my sleeve as a round left the tube. "Was that outgoing or incoming?"

I was starting to lose patience with him. These things were so basic that I never thought about them anymore, I just reacted as needed. I took a deep breath like an exasperated parent.

"Joe, let me see if I can explain it this way. When a round goes out it will go *boom* . . . *whoosh*, and you'll reach over and tug on my sleeve and ask again, 'Is that incoming or outgoing?' Of course, I'll reply, 'Joe, it was outgoing, outgoing goes *boom* . . . *whoosh*, incoming goes *whoosh* . . . *boom*. When the round is incoming, you'll hear *whoosh* . . . *boom*; you'll reach over to tug on my sleeve, and I won't be here. That's how you'll know the difference."

He never asked again.

It was sometime during February that I bumped into the Teenybopper at LZ Sally. It was good seeing him again. We caught up on things and as I was leaving he said, "W. T., wait. There something else I want to tell you."

I turned with a smile and said, "Roach, I've told you before, I don't care how much you love me, you're too young for me. Besides, I'm married."

"No, no, no! You gotta hear this."

I smiled at his excited manner. Ken was like a little kid sometimes. He got so excited about things.

"The other night I came out of the club, and when I got to the hootch Lieutenant Dipstick wasn't around. Over by his bunk was a pair of boots. I think he was in the shower. I couldn't resist. I pissed in his boots."

I burst out laughing. I never thought that Ken disliked Dipstick as much as I did. Ken went on, "It was great. I had terrific control. First, I pissed in one boot. Then I stopped in midstream and got the other boot. I couldn't believe it. As drunk as I was, I didn't get any on the floor. It all went in his boots."

"Teenybopper, I'm jealous. I'd trade in my AC orders to get to piss in Dipstick's boots."

Monday, 10 February (37 days to go). I didn't fly that day, and there was a formation at the HHC. All those not flying were required to attend. There was an awards ceremony. Major Hero from the S-3 shop, who was going home, was being given awards. He received a DFC for heroism during a flight. No one else was given an award. Afterwards, several of us went to see Major Wallace. Something wasn't right. Hero wasn't an aviator. If he had performed so valiantly during an aerial flight, where was the aircraft commander's award?

"Sir, unless the AC was killed or wounded, and Major Hero saved the bird, the AC should've received at least the same award. If not a higher one."

"You guys are right. If you figure out who it was, I promise the AC will at least get a DFC out of it."

Somebody had tried to fill up the guy's 201 file. The DFC would look good to his next promotion board. The guy wasn't even an aviator. But, at least one of our guys would get something out of the deal, and the lifers wouldn't be able to stop it.

That night, we had a meeting of the Huey pilots in Bill's and Ernie's room. The purpose was to make the Great Wall bigger and to figure out who had flown Major Hero on the "Great Heroic Flight." It took a few hours and more than one case of empties added to the Wall when it hit me. I started laughing. I laughed so hard I was rolling around on the floor. Bill Tharp sniffed at his beer and inquired, "Is there something funny in this shit?"

I was barely able to tell them, I was laughing so hard. "It was me."

"What was you?" Everyone had forgotten why we'd gotten together.

"It was me and Ernie, back when I first got here. Ernie, remember the day Hero took us out and got us lost?"

"Oh yeah, man, now I remember." Ernie burst out laughing, too. Soon he was rolling on the floor. Every time our eyes met, we burst out laughing again. It just struck us so funny that Hero had gotten a DFC for getting us lost out in the AO.

Bill Tharp wanted to know, "What's wrong with you assholes? You been smokin' wacky weed or something?"

"Naw, Bill. You don't have to smoke weed around here. All you gotta do is watch the lifers for a laugh."

Finally, I calmed down enough to explain. Still, each time I looked at Ernie, we'd start chuckling again. I told Bill how the whole description of the action in the award fit the flight we were on, except of course that nobody even shot at us. When I finished the story, everyone laughed. We knew that the major had probably even put himself in for the award.

Finally Tharp said, "Well, W. T., looks like you win the prize. You'll get the DFC that goes with it."

I then got very serious. "I don't want it."

"But it's yours."

"No. I won't take it. It's a bullshit award. Let's just tell Major Wallace that it was one of you guys who was the AC, or have him put Ernie in for it."

Ernie piped up with, "Hey, man, I don't want no bullshit award either."

"Look, you guys fly hard here and really work to support the grunts of this brigade. Just 'cause you don't get the kind of opportunities that occur in the lift companies doesn't mean that you don't deserve to be rewarded for your efforts."

Their youthful ideals were just as strong as mine. They would have none of it. We had figured out that I was the AC, and if I didn't take the award, no one else would either. The others even made me be the one to go back to Major Wallace and tell him. He advised me that I should take the award and that he might just put me in for it anyway. I gave him my coldest stare and warned him, "Sir, if I get to Fort Rucker and the CG pins a DFC on me for this, I will hand it back to him and tell him why."

Saturday, 15 February (32 days to go). My last day of flying before heading south to go to Hawaii again. I flew just over five hours, and as I was returning to Evans, I saw an O-2 entering traffic for the runway just ahead of me. I called the tower to follow him for landing at the Storm Center. The air force plane turned on his base leg with flaps down and gear down, his airspeed at a minimum. I knew it would be a dirty trick. I knew that it wasn't fair. I did it anyway. I smiled as I keyed the mike on the tower frequency and said, "Rat tat tat." All the air force guys protested. "You can't play in the traffic pattern."

I think they were mostly just embarrassed to be shot down by a helicopter on the tower frequency. Army three, air force two.

Monday, 17 February (30 days to go). I was headed south to Bien Hoa, happily on my way to Hawaii again. B. J. Hensley was my traveling companion, his Hawaiian R & R was to coincide with mine. I was glad to be headed back to Honolulu. I wasn't flying near as much as when I was a Kingsman, and on the ground, all I had to do was think about how much I missed my wife or get drunk. The more I missed her, the more reason I found to get drunk.

B. J. and I raised some hell in Bien Hoa. We had gone to the air force officers club. When we got back to Camp Alpha, B. J. was horsing around with his switchblade knife and cut me across the butt. I was really pissed at him for it. I didn't mind so much that he cut me, but that he had cut my khakis. I needed to wear that uniform the next day on R & R. I quickly got out of the uniform and washed out the blood. My handy-dandy GI sewing kit took care of the two-inch-long cut in the seat of the pants. Whenever I see the scar, I think of B. J.

I still found Hawaii to be an acceptable substitute for heaven. We hooked up with two other couples who were friends of B. J.'s. They were staying in another hotel. We met them in the bar of their hotel one night. Each of us ordered a drink, all but one of the guy's wives. The waitress ID'd us all. The wife who didn't want a drink was twenty. The drinking age was twenty-one. The waitress said she was not going to serve any of us because the one wife was under age. All the rest of us were twenty-one. B. J. went wild.

"What the hell do you mean you're not going to serve us?"

"I can't serve you 'cause there's a minor present."

It began to sink into the rest of us what was happening. It was dawning on us that, here we were combat experienced veterans, and we were being refused service because one of us had a wife who was under twenty-one.

One of the guys stood up. "You got to be bullshitting us, lady! You have the nerve to tell us after going to Nam and fighting for our country we can't get a drink on R & R."

His wife said, "We have two kids. If they were here, I suppose we couldn't have a drink either."

B. J.'s other friend joined in, "Maybe we oughta just bust this place up."

The wives calmed us down. They convinced us that we should just go somewhere else and forget it. We'd been told at the R & R center that some of the civilians on the island might give us some harassment, but this was the first I'd encountered. We got up and left. The waitress didn't get a tip.

Saturday, 22 February (25 days to go). After a big night on the town with B. J. and his wife, we all went back to our rooms. During the night, someone was setting off M-80s and cherry bombs in the alley between the hotels. The echo made the sound loud enough that it put my combat sense on alert all night. About two in the morning, there was a fire somewhere. The siren, combined with fireworks, woke me up with thoughts of a rocket attack. The next night at dinner, B. J.'s wife told Jackie and me that B. J. almost woke up when he heard the siren. He leaped from the bed and flung open the door to the room, racing down the hall looking for a bunker. His wife, not quite as quick to react to the attack, wasn't able to catch him till he was a good way down the hall. With a red face, she told us that she was glad it was so late and there was no one in the hall at the time, because they were both naked. B. J. sheepishly said nothing. He knew that I now had something to take back to the guys at Evans to get even for the cut on my butt.

Again, the time passed too quickly, and I once more found

myself looking into those loving green eyes and saying good-bye. The pain of it was only slightly tempered by the fact that I was so short. The return to Bien Hoa was depressing. My last twenty-two days would be long ones.

I bumped into John Burford in Bien Hoa. We talked and had a few beers together. We were walking across the parade ground; I tapped a cigarette out of the pack and held my Zippo up to it. As the first puff got started, John asked for my lighter. I handed it to him and he said, "I'll be right back, son."

He trotted across to the little Vietnamese plaque shop. John returned about five minutes later and handed me the lighter. On one side, the top had the initials W. T. The bottom had pilot's wings, and under it LRP. The other side of the top held my call sign "Kingsman 18." The bottom said "I deliver LRPS." A second look revealed the call sign was misspelled. It read "Kingsmam 18." I burst out laughing. John grabbed the lighter and said, "Son of a bitch! I'll make them fix this."

I said, "No, John, don't. It's just perfect the way it is."

"Yeah, but . . ."

"No, John, it says a lot the way it is. I wouldn't want them to screw it up any more."

I suddenly was aware how much of John was engraved on that lighter, how much that couldn't be said. I locked eyes with him and said, "Thanks, it'll be a treasured trophy."

I still have the lighter. I've lost it three times, and it has always found its way back to me. I lost it once during a field exercise in the Mojave Desert, and it found its way back to Fort Ord. It has been retired and doesn't light cigarettes any more. Partly because I no longer smoke. Mostly because I don't want to chance losing it.

B. J. and I had trouble getting on a flight back to Phu Bai. They told us it would be a couple of days before they'd be able to get us seats. I told the sergeant that was just fine with me. I remembered from last time about not being able get a flight if you showed up after ten in the morning. I decided then that I was going to spend some of my remaining days goofing off right there. It wasn't likely that I would be expected to fly when I got back anyway.

Friday, 28 February (19 days to go). I went by the Camp Alpha mess hall for lunch. The food wasn't great, but eating in the mess hall left me with more money for the club at night. I hadn't made any commitment to myself for any particular length of stay in Bien Hoa, but I figured that the money I had for the club would have a decided effect on it. I sat down at the last table at the end of the room. It wasn't empty, but the end I sat at was unoccupied. It was a long table that would seat about twelve. I sat at one end, at the other was a lieutenant and four FNGs. The lieutenant was directly across from me at the opposite end of the table. It was apparent that the lieutenant had been in country for a while. He wore his experience as obviously as the new guys showed their lack of it. I wasn't in the mood for company, so I paid little attention to the group at the other end of the table. While I ate, small bits of conversation filtered through the clatter of the mess hall. I caught enough to tell that he was in the 2/17 Cav. When I looked at him, I saw his name tag, and the name rang a bell now that I knew his unit. It was clearly the "veteran performing for the new guys." The hand gestures and tones indicating that he was telling war stories. I heard the word, "LRPs," and he had my attention.

". . . and the damn LRPs were mortared off the top of the mountain. There must have been a million fuckin' gooks out there . . .

"Then they reinserted the LRPs at the bottom of the mountain. Dumbest damn thing I ever saw."

This story was starting to sound familiar. If it was the one I was thinking of, he seemed to not know that division had made the decision to put the team back in. We had no choice in the matter.

"Well, bigger 'n shit, it gets dark, and the damn LRPs are in contact. Like it's a big fuckin' surprise. So we scramble out there in our Snakes, and the gooks are shootin' at everybody. The C & C stays high with the other bird, but this asshole goes in low level, with his nav lights on, to get the damn LRPs out. He takes fire from everywhere. I'm circlin' out there, and I figure for sure he's gonna get his ass blowed away, but somehow the dummy made it out."

I had heard enough now to know that this could be no other story. I couldn't pass this one up.

"Excuse me, L T."

He and four admirers all turned my way. The look in his eyes said the he did not appreciate the interruption. I smiled and continued.

"Let me see if I have this straight. You could see where the asshole in the slick was 'cause he had his lights on. Right?"

"Yeah."

"And you could see where the bad guys were from the muzzle flashes of their weapons?"

"Yeah." He was becoming annoyed at having to detail his story out to the dummy at the end of the table.

"And you could see where the LRP team was 'cause of the strobe they were signaling the asshole in the slick with?"

He got a puzzled look; he knew something wasn't right here. He hadn't mentioned the strobe light. "Yeah but . . ."

"Well, that brings me to my question. How come the Cobras never fired a shot?"

"What?"

"You could see were everybody was. How come the Cobras never fired a fucking shot?" I was now out of my seat leaning forward with my hands on the table.

"How could you possibly know that?"

" 'Cause I was the asshole!"

His jaw dropped so far his chin almost hit the table. I stood up, picked up my tray, and headed for the turn-in window. I could feel the rookies and the L T staring at my back. I smiled to myself; maybe what I'd done wasn't nice, but I was glad to have gotten in a shot. It kind of made up for the shots he'd never fired. I wouldn't have been so kind if we had lost anyone out there that night.

They had one seat on a 130 that afternoon for Phu Bai. I forced myself to allow B. J. to have the seat.

CHAPTER 13
MARCH 1969

3 March (16 days to go). I heard there was a Special Forces club in Bien Hoa. When I found out about it, I was already drunk, so I don't remember how I got there. I think a couple of SF NCOs made sure I got back to the SERTS (Screaming Eagle Replacement Training School) area that night. I went mostly because I remembered that I had my patch in my shirt pocket. It had a skull with red eyes, wearing a green beret. The skull rested on a yellow-and-black starburst. Under that was a scroll with FOB 1 on it, and below that crossed rifles, an M-16 and an AK. It was all on a blue background with a red border. It had been given to me when I was flying for Maj. Clyde Sincere and company out of Mai Loc. The guy who gave it to me told me not to bother sewing it on, just carry it, and if I was ever in an SF bar, just set it on the bar in front of me. I decided to give it a try far from where the patch had originated.

I walked into the bar. It was a large place but not very crowded. Strippers were performing on the stage, but memories of my R & R were too fresh for me to have interest in the show. I sat at the bar and ordered a drink and lit a cigarette. As I took the first puffs, I took the patch out of the breast pocket of my shirt and set it on the bar in front of me as I'd been instructed. I wasn't allowed to take my wallet out of my pocket the rest of the night. Nobody asked how I got the patch, or how it was that I had it, not being a Green Beret. My wings and having the patch said all that the SF troopers needed to know. That evening I felt that I was where I belonged again.

5 March (14 days to go). I finally got bored with Bien Hoa, and was running short of money, so on the morning of the fifth I made a serious effort to catch a plane back north. I knew I'd feel like a mooch if I went back to the SF club. I got on the first flight. I think the sergeant was getting tired of stamping my orders every day.

When I signed back into the company, the clerk told me that the HHC commander wanted to see me as soon as I got back. I went in and reported to the captain as directed. I figured he probably wanted an explanation of why I'd been gone for sixteen days on a seven-day leave.

"Grant, where the hell have you been?" Without giving me a chance to respond he continued, "If you'd been gone one more day I would have charged you with AWOL." He held up his index finger for emphasis and so the warrant officer would know what one more day was.

"Sir, flights back are hard to come by sometimes. If you'll look at the back of my orders they are stam . . ."

He interrupted, "I already heard that story from your buddy Hensley." I knew he couldn't do anything to me, my orders had been stamped indicating I had shown up every day trying to get a flight. "You are one sorry sack of shit, mister, but here, you can have this anyway." He started smiling as he tossed a stack of orders at me. The stack was pinned together with a CW2 bar. The orders were my promotion to CW2. He shook my hand and said, "Congratulations CW2 Grant. Now get the hell out of my office before I change my mind and have you shot at sunrise."

It was a promotion ceremony befitting a LRP pilot. I smiled as I saluted and scurried out the door. I'd forgotten about my promotion being due. I'd been a CW2 for a whole week already.

People from the HHC came around in the middle of the night, asking questions about high freq radios and the Green Hornet. It seems that someone identifying himself as the Green Hornet had been using a high frequency radio to contact Apollo Nine. The transmissions had been narrowed down as having come from I Corps in Vietnam. Someone in Saigon had figured out that the most common high freq radios were those that were mounted in some Hueys. A frantic message went out to find the Green Hornet and put a stop to him, he was interfering with NASA communications. I suppose that the reputation of warrant officers might have had a little to do with the search. I could picture one of my fellow aviators, bored to tears, flying circles while dropping flares that night. Playing with the HF radio, he discovers the NASA channel and sends the astronauts McDivitt, Scott, and Schweickart greetings from Vietnam.

The search came up empty, and the Green Hornet escaped undetected.

Friday, 7 March (12 days to go). I sat in my room, writing some letters and thinking about going home. Lieutenant Taylor stuck his head in my doorway.

"Just you in here, W. T.?"

"Yeah. Why . . ."

He was gone before I could ask the question. I leaped up and ran after him. I was willing to help him with shit burning if necessary, I was so bored.

"Hey, L T! What's up?"

"Oh, I need an AC for an admin flight."

Once again, he turned to go, since I was too short to fly.

"Let me get my helmet; I'll take it."

"But W. T., you're too short, and your records are already closed out."

"I've been screwed out of plenty of flight time already. What's a few more hours?"

"Yeah but . . ."

"Now wait a minute, L T. Didn't you tell me that you already have my DEROS flight scheduled for next week?"

"Yes."

"And who's going to fly me to Eagle?"

He perked up and said, "Mr. Tharp and me."

"Now, where will I be sitting on that flight?"

He looked puzzled. "In the back, of course."

"That's right. You expect me to risk my life by sitting in the back of that aircraft with you up front where you can get at the controls, and you think it's risky for me to fly today?"

He looked really hurt for a moment till he saw my smile. He'd come a long way in the last couple of months and had gotten to be a pretty good pilot. Soon he would be a competent AC. I was able to understand that combat flying hours were worth double in learning value. I also understood that the more desperate the combat, the more valuable the experience.

* * *

Monday, 10 March (9 days to go). One of the brigade's infantry battalions had just stood down. They'd been out in the jungles for nearly six months. I received an invitation to attend their standdown party. Being of a generous nature, I thought that it might be a good idea to go over to the 158th and invite Joe Hall to go to the party with me. Joe declined the invitation because he had to fly the next day. Lieutenant Jones, his section leader, wasn't so encumbered and asked if he might go along.

When we arrived, the grunts were just getting everything ready for the evening's festivities. They'd procured a large silver bowl from somewhere. Here we stood in a plywood and screen building with a corrugated steel roof, and these guys had come up with a silver punch bowl.

One of the grunt officers yelled, "Hey, Mr. Grant, glad you could make it. Come on in."

I introduced L T Jones around and watched as the punch was prepared. A quart of Bacardi light was poured in. Then a quart of Bacardi dark. That was followed by a quart of Johnny Walker Red. Next came a bottle of Jim Beam. About halfway through pouring the Johnny Walker Black, the lieutenant doing the pouring smiled up at me and said, "The order of the mix is very important you know."

"I bet it is, L T."

Vodka and gin were followed by tequila. The whole thing was topped off by filling the bowl to the rim with grapefruit juice that had been purloined from the mess hall. Now I really don't care for grapefruit at all, but that was the best damn tasting grapefruit juice I have ever had. Shortly after the sampling began, I noticed a lieutenant walking toward the bowl with about half a bottle of Jack Daniels in his hand. I stepped in front of him and said, "There are some crimes that are not pardonable."

He looked me up and down as I pointed at his bottle of Jack.

"I guess you're right, chief." That was the first time that someone had called me chief since I'd become a chief warrant officer two. They don't use the term in aviation mostly because aviators don't like it. I didn't make an issue of it, I just said, "I can keep an eye on that for you if you'd like. I'll make sure that nothin' bad happens to it."

He smiled and said, "Okay."

That was pretty easy. I was so impressed by his trust in me that I took care of his Jack Daniels all night, never letting it stray from my hand. As matter of fact, I even tasted it every once in a while to make sure that it hadn't gone bad.

That punch must have created an area of low pressure because I've never seen a drunk front move in so fast in my life. It was overcoming all but us professional drinkers. It must have been close to ten o'clock when one of the lieutenants announced, "It's time for bayonet training."

With that, they began to line up. Someone brought over a broom and handed it to the first one in line. They made him close his eyes and spun him around three times. After the spin he was released and he charged toward the door. Once outside, the man armed with the broom attacked the sandbag wall outside the door the way we were taught in bayonet training. Time and again the young infantry officers charged through the doorway growling and snarling. In their drunkenness, some tripped over their own feet or the low sandbag wall outside the door. Still they continued their assault. I calmly sat off to one side of the room, occasionally testing the Jack Daniels to see if it had gone sour. I'd already politely turned down the opportunity to participate.

The party ended some time later with me carrying Lieutenant Jones back to his hootch. I think he was praying to die as I left him in his bunk.

11 March (8 days to go). The weather had been bad for a few days. Once again, we were concerned about the possibility of a ground attack. It was midafternoon, and I was standing out in front of the Thunder Motel talking to L T Taylor when I heard the sputtering sound of an incoming rocket. It impacted before we could react. I saw the orange flame of the explosion only about fifty meters away. We both dropped to the ground. I felt a sharp rock jab at my hand as I landed. The next round was much farther away. We took the opportunity to make a run for the safety of the Thunder Motel. When we got there, I noticed that my hand was bleeding. Taylor took one look and said, "That's going to have to be stitched."

I was too damn short to take any chances on an infection that would keep me from going home. At the aid station, they cleaned out the dirt and decided it didn't need sewing. Then came the inevitable offer of the paperwork for a Purple Heart. It was right after the rockets landed so it was obvious how I got hurt. Once again, I refused. That made three Purple Hearts and two Distinguished Flying Crosses I'd refused. Now that I know some of the things people got similar awards for, it was probably a dumb thing to do, but we sometimes get smart too late. *Xin Loi.*

14 March (5 days to go). I was so short I could walk under a pregnant ant with a top hat on. I got word that day that Dave Poley had been killed. The Dave was gone.

On the ninth of March, Poley and the Teenybopper had been working for a Marine recon battalion up near Vandergrift. They were resupplying an element of the battalion when the weather closed in and both aircraft went into the clouds. Roach's bird broke out again. Poley told him to orbit until he was in the LZ. That was the last transmission Kingsmen One-Nine ever made. They flew into the side of the mountain and the aircraft burned. Killed with Dave were 1st Lt. Daniel O'Niell, Sp5. Charles Girard, and Sp4. Dennis Ormond.

Later that night I got drunk, and the feelings came. I got really pissed at The Dave for not going home when he had the chance.

16 March (3 days and a wake-up). I had worked it out that I'd get to spend my last night in I Corps with the Kingsmen at Camp Eagle. Gene Gillenwater and I would both leave the next morning for Bien Hoa to out-process. I could finally see myself making it home to my wife.

There'd be some serious celebrating to do that night. As I hung around the company area that afternoon, I began to realize how many new people had arrived since I'd left a few short months ago. I slowly became aware that I no longer belonged. A cloak of sadness came over me with the realization. Of course, that would make going even easier. Gene was on his way to pick up some uniforms at the PX laundry when he came looking for me. I was kicked back on a bunk in the FNG tent when he found me.

"Major Griggs wants to see you."

"I've been here an hour, and the CO is sending for me already?"

"Your reputation precedes you."

"Did you tell him that he can't have me transferred because I don't belong to him?"

"I don't know what he wants. Maybe he thinks you're trying to come back to the Kingsmen, and wants to tell you they don't want your kind around this neighborhood."

"I love you too, asshole." I swung my feet to the floor and started pulling on my boots. "Where can I find him?"

"He was headed to his hootch when I saw him."

"Okay, I'm on my way." I stepped outside the tent into the bright sunshine. The glare hurt my eyes. The heat was oppressive; there could be no doubt that the monsoon season was coming to an end. The commander's hootch was at the end of the company street. It was a small quonset hut. I knocked on the door.

"Come in."

I opened the door and stepped in. The air was cool inside. Air-conditioning was one of the privileges of command. It was small reward for all the bullshit he had to put up with from above and below. I saluted and reported, "CW2 Grant reporting as ordered, sir." It still felt strange being a CW2, but I was starting to like it.

The major smiled up at me as he sat on his bunk shining his boots. He pointed a boot toward a chair. "Have a seat, Grant."

As I sat down, he said, "Just for the record, you weren't ordered here. I do, however, need your help. Would you like a beer?"

I looked at my watch, not that it mattered. "Sure, why not?"

The boot jabbed again, this time in the direction of the small refrigerator along the wall next to me. I opened the fridge and took out a Schlitz. I looked over my shoulder and asked, "Can I get you one, sir?"

"No. No. Some us aren't so short that we don't have any responsibilities."

I thought he might be reprimanding me for accepting till I saw the smile on his face. I opened the beer and sat down again.

He began. "I would like to explain the reason I wanted to see you. I guess you've heard about Dave Poley?"

"Yes, sir."

"I'm sorry. I understand he was a friend of yours."

"Yes, sir."

"He was also a good and very brave pilot. I'm having a problem with another friend of yours. Mr. Roach. He wants very much to go out with the LRP team that's going to recover the bodies from 121. I don't think he should go. It would be a simple matter for me to just order him not to go. If necessary, I could have him locked up. I don't want to have to do that to him. It could ruin both a possible career and a man."

I could see that he was legitimately concerned for the

Teenybopper. I was sorry I hadn't gotten the chance to serve under this commander. "Where do I come in, sir?"

"Well, the way I hear it, Grant, Mr. Roach thinks just about as much of you as he did Poley. I'd like you to have a talk with him. See if you can talk some sense into him."

"I'll give it a shot, sir."

"Thanks, I appreciate your help."

"Dave Poley did a dumb thing by refusing to go home. I don't want to see Ken do something equally stupid."

I drained the last of the beer and got up to leave. "Grant, thank you again. I mean that."

"No sweat, GI." I smiled. "It's my business, too, sir."

I stepped out of the major's hootch into the heat. It seemed much worse after the air-conditioning. Looking for Ken Roach, I began a search of the company area. I caught up with him on my second pass down the company street. He didn't know that I was around, so he was surprised to see me.

"W. T., W. T. What the hell are you doing here?"

"I'm on my way south to out-process. I wanted to spend one more night with the Kingsmen before I went home. I hear you have plans to go out looking for The Dave."

Tears were welling up in his eyes. Ken Roach wasn't going to be easily sold on not going out.

"Teenybopper, you can't do this."

"I've got to. The Dave is out there."

"Ken, The Dave is dead."

"Yeah, but . . ."

"Yeah, but shit. Ken, you can't do this."

"I can't leave him out there."

The tears were thick in his eyes. I could feel my own eyes getting wet as well. I grabbed him by the shirt and shook him.

"Damn it, Roach, you dumb son of a bitch, you can't go out there. Dave is fucking dead. You can't do a thing about it. The Dave died the day he refused to go home. If we could bring him back, I'd go, too. He's gone, and sticking your ass out to go get his body back isn't going bring him back. What happens if you go out there and get wasted? Huh? Who do the LRPs call the next time they need an extraction?"

He just stared at me.

"Ken, you gotta promise me you won't do this. 'Cause if you do, I'll hafta come back to this godforsaken fuckin' place and kick your ass." I still had hold of his shirt collar.

"Okay, W. T., I guess you're right. But it's just it's The Dave out there."

"I know, Ken, I know." I didn't know what else to say, so I just threw my arm over his shoulder and walked back to his hootch with him. On the way, I asked him, "You wouldn't happen to have a cold beer in your fridge would you?"

He smiled, finally. "You bet, W. T."

I was glad not to have to tell him that Major Griggs was prepared to put him in irons if he had to.

That evening, Gene Gillenwater and I went to the club together. As we stepped in the door both of us removed our hats and Gene tossed his on the hat shelf in the corner. I hesitated and looked at Gene.

"Wait a minute, Water, this ain't right."

He smiled in response and we stepped back out the door. Both thinking along the same lines he said, "On the count of three. One. Two. Three."

We stepped back, leaving our hats on, and yelled, "Short," at the top of our lungs. The penalty for hats on was having to buy a round. We strode to the bar in thirty-inch military step and tossed our hats on the bar, violating a second rule. Then we went behind the bar and made our own drinks, for the third and fourth infractions. Once again in front of the bar, we each tossed a twenty-dollar bill on the bar. Gene reached under the right side of my jungle shirt and pulled my K-bar out of the sheath. He drove the big knife through the two twenties, nailing them to the bar. Breaking the rule about sticking your knife in the bar. We then told the bartender to let us know when the forty ran out.

The party was going strong, and everyone was having a good time on the free booze. One of the new guys whom I didn't know came up to Gene and told him he'd just been appointed the unit morale officer. The guy had been in the unit about a week. He said to Gene, "You've been through a whole tour. I was wondering if you had any suggestions for things I could do to boost morale."

Gene didn't have to tell me how new that cherry was. Gene replied, "All you gotta do to boost morale is to go around telling everyone how many days you have left."

Gene and I burst out laughing. The new guy looked at us as if he wasn't quite sure he got the joke. The look on his face made the joke even funnier, causing us to laugh all the harder. We had a lot to laugh about. We could now actually believe we were going home.

The newly remodeled club bore very little resemblance to the familiar old plywood walls, floor, and bar of the club I remembered. The black walls had white diamonds on them, with lighting behind them. The diamonds had been written on. On closer examination I realized that the writing had been done by Kingsmen departing the unit for home. Gene walked over and pointed toward the diamond with his glass. "It started just after you went north. As you leave, you sign out on the diamonds. Go ahead, you're entitled."

I thought for a moment, remembered my flight helmet and wrote, "Happiness is getting short, but it doan mean nuthin' till you're gone. Clear left, right, and overhead. Gone like a mutha. W. T. Grant. One-Eight."

As I wrote, one of the FNGs came over and grabbed my arm. "You can't do that; you're not a Kingsman."

I just glared at him with my best let-go-of-me-or-I'll-tear-off-your-FNG-arm look. I didn't say anything. I was slightly embarrassed that I would have to justify myself to this new guy. The Teenybopper came to my rescue.

"Hey, man, that's W. T. He can do whatever he wants around here." Ken led the new guy off, explaining to him how close he had just come to an unfavorable encounter with the criminally insane. I finished writing and went back to bar and sat next to Gene. Once again, a certain sadness came over me because I knew I no longer belonged here. I knew then that even if I didn't have Jackie to go home to, I couldn't stay there the way Poley had done. As I thought about him, I wished that I'd realized when he closed his locker door that he was going to refuse to get on his freedom bird. Maybe then I could have changed his mind.

It suddenly hit me that there was something I had to do. I pulled out my wallet and handed Gillenwater a twenty. "Water, take care of the tab for me for a while. I've got something I have to do."

I pulled my knife out of the bar and put it back in its sheath. As I put on my hat, Gene asked, "What's wrong?"

"Nuthin', man." I slid off my bar stool.

"Where ya goin'?"

"The LRPs."

He got a concerned look on his face. "Not gonna do something dumb are ya?" He was still worrying about me.

"No way, man. Jus gotta say good-bye," I replied over my shoulder as I headed toward the door.

"Want me to go with ya?"

I stopped and turned around. I knew that he really was afraid I would do something dumb. I guess even Gene thought I was crazy. Or, at least, I'd get crazy if I was left to associate with LRPs. I walked back to Gene.

"I just want to say good-bye. I would've done it this afternoon, but I didn't think I could. Now I know it's time to go. I'm not letting them down by leaving; it's someone else's job now. It's time to say good-bye, and I need to do it alone. Don't tell Roach where I went. I just got him calmed down. I don't want him starting in again."

He held out a padlock key. "Take my jeep, it's over by operations."

"No, I'd better walk. I'm gettin' pretty shitfaced, and saying good-bye at the LRPs will take some drinkin'. Besides, walkin' will give me a last look at good ol' Camp Eagle. Airborne!"

"You certainly have had too much to drink. Get out of here before Ken comes back and catches you goin' over there."

I stepped out of the club and took a look around. I took a deep breath. Yup, Vietnam still smelled like burning shit. I'd leave this place like I found it, smelly. I started off on the long walk over to the LRPs. It dawned on me that the hike might get pretty thirsty, so I went back into the club. As I got to the bar, Gene said, "That was a fast trip."

"Need some fuel."

To the bartender I said, "Gimme a six-pack of Bud." I grinned at Gene. I opened the first beer and chugged about a third off the top. I put the can back on the bar and told the bartender to top it off with bourbon. I pointed my index finger at Gillenwater. "Don't say a word."

He just smiled and shrugged it off and mumbled something about, "Alkies."

I tucked my six-pack in the cargo pockets of my jungle pants, lit a cigarette, and started off again, much happier. The boilermaker felt good going down, and I nursed it the whole way, as I had my last tour of Camp Eagle. Actually I'd get one more on the way back to the Castle, but I can't remember it for some reason. So I don't count that one.

I found Kenn Miller at the Ranger lounge. He was glad to see me. He told me that the Howlers were going out the next day to retrieve Poley's body. "I know. Where's Zo?"

"He's up at the hootch. I'll get some ammo, and we'll go find him." He got a six-pack, and we headed off to find Zoschak. We found him packing his ruck.

"Hi, asshole." I grinned.

Ray looked up. "Hey Mr. G., thought you'd forgotten about us."

"No way, man. I'm still having nightmares."

"Well, at least I haven't been airsick lately."

"It's felt good not to have some asshole sitting out in the jungle thinking up ways to get my ass blown off."

We sat and reminisced. Ray didn't drink much of the beer since he had a mission the next day. Kenn and I didn't complain; it just left more for us. LRPs whom I knew drifted in and out. Many of them showed up with still other six-packs. I felt at home with the men, yet I knew it was time to leave. No one expected anything less of me. In just a few short days, I'd be back in Jackie's arms, and that was all that mattered.

"Does everyone know I'm so short that I can sit on a dime and dangle my legs?"

Ray said, "Fuck you, sir!"

"I think that was insubordination. Don't you?" I asked the crowd in general.

"We didn't hear a thing," was the consensus.

"I guess I'll just have another beer."

It was shortly after that, I fell off the bunk I was sitting on for the first time. It must have been slippery. After the third drop to the floor, I announced that I'd better leave.

Ray Zoschak jumped up and said, "Wait a minute, we've got something for you. Come on, Kenn."

As they rushed out the door, I yelled after them. "Don't take too long, I'm down to counting minutes, you know."

When they came back, they had a set of flower-power cammies that they had scarfed up from the supply room. Ray handed them to me. "We want you to have these, 'cause you're one of us."

It was one of those gifts that had far more meaning than value. It hadn't cost them a dime, but knowing the reasoning behind it was what made it count. I still have that pair of cammies. Miller handed me a handful of the long-range patrol scrolls that they wore over their 101st Airborne patches. They were black with gold lettering. The tab was in the shape of a scroll with 101 at one end and DIV at the other, the middle read Long Range Patrol. He stood over me as I sat on the bunk.

"Mr. Grant, we expect that you'll have these sewn on your

uniforms and wear them home. If you don't, we'll have to hunt you down and kill you."

"I will," I promised.

They also gave me a couple of the 101st Recondo patches the LRPs wore on their black baseball hats. The arrowhead-shape patches were white and bore an embroidered 1–0–1. I said my sad good-byes, stuffed two cans of beer in the cargo pockets, and started my trek back to the Kingsmen club. I only know that I made it there because Gene Gillenwater told me I did.

The next morning, while Gene finished clearing and signing out of the unit, I headed for the tailor shop. I had a brand new pair of jungle fatigues that I'd been saving to wear home. They already had a new 101st Airborne patch on the left shoulder. On the right shoulder, which was reserved for combat patches, was the 1st Aviation Brigade patch. The nametags, patches and CW2 bar were all new. I was no longer afraid of looking like a cherry. When I got to the tailor shop, I had them install the LRP scroll over the 101st patch. I peeled off the faded shirt I had on and had another scroll put on that one. What were they going to do? Send my ass to Vietnam? I slipped back into the shirt that now proudly displayed the LRP scroll. I thought about buying a black hat, but didn't want to push my luck. I strode away from the tailor shop, walking tall with shoulders square so everyone would be able to see the scroll. I was just waiting for someone to tell me it was unauthorized.

When I got back, Gene was waiting for me impatiently. He'd completed his business and was ready to leave.

"Where the hell have you been? Are you planning on staying another year?"

"Nope, had to go by the tailor shop." I turned slightly toward him so he would have clear view of my left shoulder. He didn't notice.

"If I had to wait another ten minutes, you would've had to walk to Phu Bai."

"Bullshit, Gene, you wouldn't be able to find your way home if you went without me."

He laughed and said, "Get your stuff, and let's get the hell out of here."

"We gone like a mutha." As I used The Dave's phrase once more I thought of Zoschak going out after his body today.

I threw my bags in the back of the jeep and hopped in. Gene drove, and we both waved and yelled good-bye to everyone we saw along the way. There was something that didn't feel quite right as we drove to the Phu Bai airport to catch a C-130 south. We were unloading our bags after Gene parked the jeep when it hit me.

"Gene, how's your jeep gonna get back to the company area?"

"Beats the shit out of me. I don't care; I don't need it any more." He left the chain and padlock lying on the floor, and tossed the key to the lock on the seat. I knew it wouldn't be an hour before it belonged to someone else.

"Yeah but . . ."

"Look, W. T., the way I see it, the guy I stole it from four months ago is probably still looking for it. Maybe he'll come by and luck out."

We presented our orders in the terminal and sat down to await our departure. I watched the FNGs milling around, waiting for a ride to their new units, wearing fatigues as new as the set in my bag. I knew that even if I'd worn them, I wouldn't be mistaken for a FNG. There was no communication between the departing and the new. It would've been cruel to tell them just how short we were. Somehow, there was vast difference between the short-timer bragging we had done last night and our status that day. I felt pity for the new guys with three-hundred-plus days to go. I could still remember how insurmountable that figure had seemed just eleven months ago. As I looked over their clean, shiny faces, I realized that more had occurred in my life than the passage of a year. I'd seen and done things that would mean I'd never be the same again. The young kid who arrived in Cam Ranh Bay, wearing shiny new sterling wings, was now a competent and confident combat pilot.

I was surprised to find that there was a certain amount of regret in leaving. I knew I wouldn't change my mind. I wouldn't have it any other way. I was going home to my love, my wife. However, something told me that a part of me was being left behind in Nam. It made me all the more glad that I had Jackie. I feared that if I hadn't had her to go home to, I might have been dumb enough to stay for another six months.

We got a C-130 without seats in it. One more crummy ride on a cargo pallet before leaving country. We made two or three stops along the way to Bien Hoa. Each landing meant being piled in a heap as the cargo plane slowed. After arriving at Bien Hoa, Gene and I both swore we'd never again ride in one of those monsters.

They got us in-processed at SERTS (Screaming Eagle Replacement Training School). We were assigned to a barracks and got our bunks. Then it was off to the club.

17 March (2 days to go). Happy Saint Patrick's Day. Gene and I ran into Billy Walkabout. He was a staff sergeant. He'd only been a PFC on November 20. He told us that he'd been pulled from going out on patrols. Division didn't want him getting killed with a Medal of Honor pending. They had him working at SERTS, recruiting for the LRP company. We did some serious drinking that night. Gene left us early. By the time I left Billy, Vietnam had started the whirling phenomenon again. Billy came after me as I staggered back to my barracks.

"Sir, I want you to have this."

I looked down, and he was handing me his black baseball cap. The one with the 101st Recondo patch and his jump wings on it.

"Billy, that's got your jump wings on it."

"I know, I want you to have it, sir."

"Thank you. This means a lot to me."

"I appreciate you coming to get us all the time. Thank you."

He turned and started walking away. I called after him, "This doesn't mean we're going steady, does it?"

He just waved at me over his shoulder.

20 March 1969 (I'm outta here). The sun came up bright and hot. It was a perfect day for going home. I walked out of the hootch with my bags, set them on the ground, and looked around. The dust and the heat reminded me of the 90th Replacement Center in Camh Ranh Bay. Then the strangest feeling came over me. It seemed like such a short time ago. Yet, so much had happened, it seemed that it could have hardly been only a year. I tried to picture myself as a brand-new WO1 rookie just arriving in country. The image wouldn't form; I was no longer that person. I could never be that person again. It didn't matter. I knew that whatever I would now face in life, I'd be able to find a way to deal with it.

They loaded us on buses for the trip to Tan Son Nhut to be herded on the plane. We were issued our boarding passes and were shuffled into a covered waiting area to await our flight. There must have been close to a thousand GIs under the cover, waiting for their freedom bird. As a plane arrived and taxied up in line, the soldiers, sailors, and airmen were being lined up to board. The planes came one after another. Each plane disgorged its load of fresh meat farther down the flight line. Then it taxied up a way and refueled. After refueling, it would move up farther, load up with GIs, and depart. It seemed that we waited an eternity for our turn to arrive. Finally, they called our flight, and we headed toward the gate. Many rushed. I felt I'd spent so much time developing the grace of a veteran, that I'd maintain my dignity and not rush to the gate. The plane wouldn't leave until the last passenger was loaded. Running wasn't going to get me out of Vietnam any sooner. Gene seemed to feel the same way.

A cheer went up among the crowd of GIs. I stretched to see what it was they were cheering. It was the name of the airline that we were flying home on. Flying Tiger Airlines. The logo on the tail was FTA.

Some guys began to chant, "FTA all the way. FTA all the way."

Others chanted, "Fuck the army."

Gene and I just laughed. I wondered if any of those GIs knew Flying Tiger was a cargo and livestock hauler and that the plane they were riding on may have been converted from hauling cattle only the week before. I doubted anyone would turn down their flight home even if they had to share it with cattle. Then I wondered if the army had selected a cattle plane on purpose.

It seemed a lifetime till the pilot shoved the throttles forward on the runway and we started our takeoff roll. When the wheels broke ground and closed into the plane with a solid thump, for the first time, I really felt I was on the way home. Gene had a seat by the window; I was next to him. I stared across him for my last glimpse of Vietnam as we climbed through two thousand feet. I could make out hootches and paddies. Then I noticed the twinkling. It was the twinkling of muzzle flashes. You can only see them if they're pointed at you.

"Gene, the little motherfuckers are still shooting at us."

"What?"

"The little bastards are trying to shoot down our freedom bird. I can see the muzzle flashes." I pointed.

"I don't see them. We're too high for small arms anyway. Don't worry about it."

"That's not the point, Gene. The bastards are still trying to get us."

"W. T., relax. Its over. We're outta here."

I slumped back in my seat, wishing I had some way to call in arty on the sons a bitches. How dare they!

The desire to shoot up our attackers soon gave way to the boredom of the flight. For some reason, the eastbound flights seemed much longer than the westbound flights had been. We landed in Japan for fuel, and about a half hour later they announced that the plane had an engine problem. We ended up spending ten hours on the ground in Yokota. There was an entire plane load of pissed-off GIs. Everyone wanted to know, "Why didn't this happen on the way over?"

We finally boarded for the endless flight to Travis Air Force Base. Gene and I talked about what it would be like to get home. We wondered if there'd be demonstrators to greet us. As the plane descended to final, Gene looked over at me and said, "Hey, W. T., if there's any hippies there, whadda ya say we go back-to-back and take as many of them to the hospital with us as we can?"

I thought for a moment and gave him a thumbs-up. "You're on."

The news we got (*Stars and Stripes* and the Armed Forces Radio and TV) were certainly not the most liberal media. Still, the news was so full of war protesters that we expected even the air force base to have a welcoming committee. Gene and I had seats near the front, and we were the first ones to the door when it opened. We looked down the steps in surprise. No one was there to harass us.

We deplaned and processed through customs. The air force people told us we couldn't leave the base in jungle fatigues. Gene explained to them about the master sergeant who told us we'd be issued class A uniforms when we returned Stateside. The air force sergeant said that he knew nothing about that, only that we couldn't leave in jungle fatigues. Gene and I had a quick conference and determined that I had a pair of jeans and a civilian shirt, and he had a set of khakis but no brass to put on them.

I said to Gene, "I've got some brass; I'll give you the brass and put on my civies. At least we'll be able to get the hell out of here."

"Yeah, maybe when we get over to the Presidio in San Francisco we can find out about the uniforms."

We took a cab over to the Presidio. I looked around at everything. The freeways, the cars, the buildings, it all seemed so strange. The buildings were tall, and the cars weren't all green. It was like a dream, I was really back in the World. It wasn't like R & R. Hawaii was only a temporary reprieve from the war; this was permanent. I had survived.

When we got to the Presidio, the story was the same, no uniforms. Gene made sure that someone knew the details, including the name of the sergeant. A supply warrant came out from the back and asked what the problem was. I explained what had happened. He told me to come with him. He took me in the back and explained that often enlisted men who were ETSing didn't wait for their uniforms to be ready before they took off. Back on the unclaimed rack, he found a set of greens that fit me like they'd been custom tailored. They even had a 101st airborne patch on the left sleeve. The CW3 handed me the uniform and said, "You'll have to have officer's piping put on yourself."

"Thanks a lot. I kind of left myself in a bind, listening to that guy in Nam and shipping my uniform."

"Us warrants have to look out for one another. Just don't let this get around."

The PX tailor shop assured me they'd have the uniform ready to wear by ten the next morning. Unusually for the army, the out-processing at the Presidio was efficient and in almost no time at all we were cleared to travel.

As we had promised back in August, before he went home, I called Scott Wilson. He said he'd be right out to get us. While we waited for Scott, they paged Gene. It seemed they had come up with an early flight to Seattle, and he could leave that very afternoon. We'd have to hurry to get him to the airport on time. Gene looked at his watch.

"It's awful tight; I don't think we can make it."

"Sure we can, Gene. Scotty will be here in a few minutes to drive us."

"But I don't have brass for my uniform yet."

"Keep mine."

"But . . ."

"Gene, don't worry about it. I'll get some at the PX tomorrow when I pick up my greens."

"W. T., I feel like I'm leaving you behind in the LZ. You can't get a flight till tomorrow afternoon. What are you going to do till then?"

"Look, Water, this is *going home*. You can't wait around for me. Get on the plane and go home. I guess I'll just have to go out with Scotty tonight and get drunk for both of us."

I knew how he felt. There was still that last tug of Vietnam that held us together. As ugly as war is, it still makes brothers out of those who fight side by side. Wilson showed up, and we explained about Gene's flight as we hustled him back to his car.

They were closing the door of the plane as we ran up the ramp with Gillenwater. If the three of us charged a plane today the way we had that one, we would be mowed downed by security guards as terrorists.

After Gene was on his way to Seattle, Scott Wilson took me on a tour of his favorite bars. I don't remember much about my tour of San Francisco. I do remember that the last bar we stopped in was much like the typical corner bar back in New York. I had begun to very much envy Gillenwater his early flight. We closed the place down at 0230. We climbed in Scott's white Mustang and traveled about half a block when the flashing lights of the police car showed up in the mirror. He must've been sitting and waiting for the car that had the great parking spot in front of the bar.

The officer was administering the field sobriety test to Scott. I was impressed with how well Scott was doing, but felt it was my place to take action here. I couldn't sit there and let a crew chief just take the rap. I crawled out of the passenger door. As I stood up, the officer rested his hand on his gun and said, "Stay in the car please, sir."

I held my hands wide out in front of me to show him that I was not being hostile. I made sure I stayed where I was by the passenger door of the car.

"Officer, I just want to explain. This is kind of my fault. I just came back from Nam today, and Scott here had been my crew chief. He was just taking me out to celebrate my survival."

I knew that it was not a good reason, but it was the best that we had. The cop asked, "Crew chief? Were you a helicopter pilot?"

"Yes."

"You guys did one helleva job over there."

He addressed Scott. "Is this your current address on your license?"

"Yes, sir."

"That's only a couple of blocks from here. Is that where you're headed?"

"Yes, sir."

"Okay, if you guys go there, and promise me you'll stay there till you sober up, I'll let you go."

"You got it," we replied in chorus.

He followed long enough to make sure we were headed to

Scott's place. Once again a stranger had been understanding of our serving in Vietnam. As with the lady in Hawaii, I remember, since the instances were so rare.

The next morning Scott drove me back to the Presidio. I picked up my plane ticket and my uniform. The pants and jacket now had officer's piping and the jacket had a 1st Aviation Brigade patch on the right sleeve and, most important, a LRP scroll over the 101st patch. I went into the PX and bought some wings, bars, and warrant officer insignia.

Back at my BOQ room, I put the brass on the uniform and got dressed. I'd carefully pinned on the ribbons that I'd been issued in Bien Hoa on the jacket. As I stared down at the jacket lying on the bed, I felt pride at being a veteran Screaming Eagle. I was still officially a member of an Airborne division, so I wore my now well-shined jump boots with my greens. When I put the blouse on, Scott told me I looked like a good little lifer pig. I looked in the mirror and said to him, "Just let some fuckin' hippie spit on this uniform."

"If they got any sense, they won't be fuckin' with W. T.," Scott said.

Wilson drove me to my flight and, once again, we said goodbye. The six-hour flight to John F. Kennedy International Airport seemed like a short hop compared to the flight from Nam. It was a short hop compared to some of the Huey flights I'd made in the last year. I'd wanted to surprise Jackie when I got home, but didn't want to waste precious time taking a train out on Long Island from the airport, so I called and told her to pick me up.

When I got off the plane I strode through the airport with pride, deliberately feeling each footfall of my boots. Once again, there were no protesters around, just one hippie girl who gave me a glare. I stared back with my best thousand-yard stare, and she elected not to say anything to me. When I reached the waiting area, my eyes searched frantically for that familiar red hair. When I saw it, the hippies, the war, everything was gone. I ran to her and folded her in my arms, and I tried my best to crush her into my chest. I prayed that our lips would become stuck together. This was what I'd fought to survive for. Now I was truly and finally *home*.

REFLECTIONS

If we have to fight, we will fight. You will kill ten of our men and we will kill one of yours, and in the end it will be you who will tire of it.

Ho Chi Minh

Ho's prophecy to a representative of Charles de Gaulle in 1946 might well have been heeded by Lyndon Johnson in 1964. It was almost as though Ho had already seen the antiwar protests in the United States during the sixties.

In the beginning of this book, I noted that the troops serving in DESERT STORM won their war. I did not note that the veterans of Vietnam lost theirs. Because those who fought in Vietnam were not afforded that opportunity. It is only being recognized after twenty years that the war was lost by the politicians who sent the soldiers, the public which didn't support them, and the media which lambasted them for doing what they were asked to do. The Americans who were sent reluctantly to war fought with ferocity against a determined and elusive enemy. Contrary to the image portrayed by Hollywood, most came home and became pillars of their communities. Solid citizens, supporting the traditional image of working America. One of them, Raymond Zoschak, fulfilled his dream of having his own eighteen-wheeler. In 1972, on the New Jersey Turnpike, some cars were involved in an accident. Ray had a choice. He could hit the cars, or try to avoid the collision at greater risk to himself. Zoschak made his decision in favor of others; his truck rolled over, and he was killed.

In spite of all the lack of support at home, the young Americans sent to Southeast Asia fought courageously, and their true victory may lie in current events. The economic collapse of the

Soviet Union is largely attributable to their support over many years of puppets, such as North Vietnam.

Recently, I had the opportunity to renew friendships with many of the LRPs with whom I had the privilege to serve in Vietnam. I was pleased to find that Riley Cox, Jim Venable, and Frank Souza survived their wounds of 20 November 1968. There are many who suffer wounds much deeper than those that were inflicted by the enemy. Some of those wounds may never heal.

Normally, we tend to refer to those who are killed in combat during time of war as having made the ultimate sacrifice. These brave souls are tagged, shipped home, and buried with military honors. There is, however, another group who give so much to the service of their country that they can never come home. When they're done giving, there's nothing left for themselves, their families or their friends.

On 10 January 1992, Command Sergeant Major (Ret) John "Doc" Brubaker became another casualty of the Vietnam war. Doc gave seven years of his life to service in Vietnam. He gave almost thirty years to the service of the United States Army. I pray that God can understand old soldiers and can find Doc a place where he can no longer be at war.

Doc had asked me recently, "Why did you guys always come get us when we called for an emergency extraction?" The best answer I could give was, "Because you called." I only wish that Doc had let me know he was in "contact" the last time we talked, maybe one last extraction could have been arranged.

For all those other veterans of our wars who can't find their way home, remember that somewhere out there you have friends who care. It only takes a call to let them know you need help, and it will be there.

WHERE ARE THEY NOW?

Jim Bacon—Recovered from his wounds of November 20th and is now an Emergency Medical Technician living in Jefferson City, Missouri.

John "Honest John" Burford—Is a sales representative living in Marietta, Georgia. He has written three books, a two-volume set called *Long Range Patrol* and the soon to be published *Team Leader*.

Richard "Uncle Bernie" Burnell—Retired from the Army as a Command Sergeant Major and is now serving as a civilian observer with the U.N. peacekeeping force in the Sinai.

Larry Chambers—Larry's book *Recondo* was recently released. Larry writes for a living in Ojai, California. His favorite sport is chasing women.

Tim "Green Lantern" Coleman—Lives in Loxahatchee, Florida. He is a facilities supervisor for the Palm Beach County Fire and Rescue Department. He will soon be medically retired from the fire department as a result of injuries received in the line of duty.

Riley "Dozer" Cox—Survived his wounds of November 20th. He has undergone surgery fourteen times since then as a result of those wounds. Riley lives in Colorado with his new bride Linda and he is happy.

Ted "Wild Turkey" Crozier—Retired from the Army as a Colonel, having served in a number of positions in the 101st Airborne Division including a stint as Chief of Staff. He lives in Clarksville, Tennessee, where he served as the mayor for eight years. He is currently the president of the 101st Airborne Association and an honorary colonel of the 101st Aviation Regiment. This year he is involved in forming a museum foundation at Fort Campbell.

Ken Eklund—Ken is living in Concord, California, fighting earthquakes instead of VC. He was recently married and is working on several books.

Gene "H20/Water" Gillenwater "Kingsmen 10"—Gene lives in Seattle, Washington, with his wife of 26 years, Sharon. They have one son who is a musician. Gene is a senior buyer for the Boeing Aircraft Company. His wife writes historical romances under her maiden name of Harlow.

Don Harris—Works for the Postal Service in Merryville, Tennessee, where he lives with his wife and two sons.

Rod Heim "Kingsmen 29"—Rod is the base manager for a helicopter ambulance service. He and his new bride Jeanne are enjoying wedded bliss in Batavia, Ohio.

Gary Linderer—Gary lives in Festus, Missouri, with his wife of 24 years, Barbara, and four sons. Gary has written four books and is the executive editor of *Behind the Lines*, an up-and-coming special-operations journal.

William "Wild Bill" Meacham "Kingsmen 25"—Wild Bill is a retired Lieutenant Colonel living in Ocala, Florida, with his wife, Carol, and a small herd of German shepherds. Bill works part-time as a helicopter pilot on firefighting contracts.

Kenn Miller—Kenn lives in San Gabriel, California, with his wife and two children. Kenn is a translator/interpreter and a free-lance writer.

Phil Myers—Phil is still on active duty in the army. He spent many years in Special Forces and Ranger units before going to flight school to become a helicopter pilot. He is now a CW3 flying Apache gunships at Fort Hood, Texas. Phil flew Apaches during Desert Storm.

Bruce "Doc" Proctor—Lives in Antioch, California, where he is a corporate executive and a Command Sergeant Major in the Army Reserve.

Ed Regan "Kingsmen 24"—Ed lives in Alpharetta, Georgia, where he is a drug and alcohol counselor for the Norfolk and Southern Corporation. Ed is married and has four grown children and four grandchildren.

Ken "Teenybopper" Roach "Kingsmen 18"—Ken works for the Federal Aviation Administration where he is a supervisory aviation safety inspector in Windsor Locks, Connecticut. Ken is married and has a son and a daughter.

Ron "Mother" Rucker—Mother is self-employed and lives with his brother on Lake Bistineau in Louisiana where he spends all his spare time "catchin' fish" and hunting.

Barry Schreiber—Barry switched to the Air Force (we forgive you, Barry) and retired as a Major after 23 years' total service. He is currently Chief Pilot and General Manager of Soir Aviation. Mary, his wife of 23 years, Barry, and their dog live in Beaver Creek, Ohio.

Gordon "Snuffy" Smith—Snuffy is a cardiovascular intensive-care and trauma-care nurse. He lives in Chandler, Arizona, where he is a captain in the Army Reserve. Gordon is married and has five children. One of his sons is an Airborne Ranger.

John Sours—John and his wife run a special-education program for children in southwestern Missouri. He is an accomplished musician. John and his wife live on and work a medium-size farm.

Frank Souza—Frank has overcome his wounds of November 20th. Frank and his wife Karen live in Alaska, where Frank works as a plumber.

Jim "Sir James" Thompson "Kingsmen 22"—Sir James has been married to his lovely wife, Diane, for 20 years. They have two beautiful daughters and live in Saint Charles, Illinois. Jim owns and operates DMT and Associates Incorporated, a national direct-mail marketing firm.

Tony "Ti Ti" Tercero—Tony lives in Phoenix, Arizona, where he works for Arizona State University as an event coordinator. He also works on the "Keep Off Drugs" program for kids in the Phoenix area.

Jim Venable—Jim has recovered from his wounds of November 20th and lives in Alaska with his wife and daughter. Jim is a bush pilot.

Billy "Indian" Walkabout—Billy is alive and well, living in Oklahoma. Billy never received the Medal of Honor he earned on November 20th; he received instead a Distinguished Service Cross and medical disability pension for his wounds.

Darol Walker—Retired from the Army as a Command Sergeant Major. Since his retirement he has been in the life insurance business. He lives in Clarksville, Tennessee, with his wife. Darol has three children, one of whom is a West Point graduate and an Airborne Ranger.

GLOSSARY

(A)

AC—Aircraft commander.

ACL—Aircraft load. Generally refers to the number of troops a helicopter can lift on a given day. The performance is affected by temperature and humidity.

Admin—Abbreviation of administrative.

AFB—Air Force Base.

Airmobile—A unit that is able to move entirely by its own internal helicopters.

Air strike—A bombing mission directed at a specific tactical target.

AIT—Advanced individual training. The training a soldier attends after basic, which determines his MOS (Military Occupational Specialty).

AHC—Assault Helicopter Company.

AK-47—The weapon most used by the enemy. An assault rifle capable of automatic fire.

Americal—The name of the 24th Infantry Division.

Ammo—Short name for ammunition.

AO—Area of operations. The area a particular unit was assigned to operate in most often at the division level.

ARA—Aerial rocket artillery. Gunships that were heavily laden with 2.75-inch rockets and no machine guns. Often used to prep LZs.

ARVN—Army of the Republic of Vietnam. Frequently used to refer to individual soldiers of that army.

ATL—Assistant team leader.

Autorotation—The method of landing a helicopter after the engine has malfunctioned. The rotor system is designed to freewheel as the aircraft descends through the air. The energy in the rotor system allows the pilot to slow the rate of descent just before impact.

AWOL—Absent without leave. When a soldier isn't present for duty as required and has left his station without permission.

(B)

Bastogne—A famous battle from World War II. Used as a fire-base name in Vietnam. The 101st was very big on tradition, and most of the firebases were named after previous historical battles.

BDA—Bomb damage assessment. At times, a LRP team would be inserted into an area that had been bombed to determine the effectiveness of the bombing.

Beaucoup—French word for many. Used by the Vietnamese in their language. Many times pronounced boo coo.

Big-time—Slang. Meaning a lot of something or with much fanfare.

BOQ—Bachelor officer quarters.

B–17—World War II bomber.

(C)

CA—Combat assault. Moving troops into an area by helicopter usually in a flight of several aircraft.

CAG—Combat Aviation Group. A level of command above the battalion.

Cal.—An abbreviation of caliber.

Call sign—The name by which one is known when operating a radio. Names and unit designations weren't used for security reasons. Most aviation units had a nickname which was used in conjunction with a number.

CAR–15—A carbine version of the M-16 with a folding stock. Favored by special operations soldiers.

Carabiners—A metal oval used in mountaineering. It has one side that opens and is spring-loaded to the closed position, and it served a wide variety of purposes. Carabiners were used to attach McGuire rigs to the aircraft. They were also used by soldiers to attach themselves to a rope for rappelling.

Cav—A short name for the 1st Cavalry Division or any other cavalry unit.

Chalk—Refers to the position of an aircraft in a flight. Chalk One is the first aircraft, Chalk Five the fifth, etc.

Charlie—A nickname for the Viet Cong. It came from the phonetic alphabet words for VC, Victor Charlie. The names

Chuck and Mr. Charles were also used. The NVA were also referred to as Charlie.

CG—Commanding general.

CH—Cargo helicopter. A prefix used with the aircraft's numerical designation to identify its type. Such as CH–47, CH–53, etc.

Chicken plate—A bulletproof ceramic plate in a vest. They came with a front and a back plate. Most pilots wore only the front plate since the seat was armor plated, but the crew chief wore front, back and usually sat on another. The implication being that if you wore one, you were a chicken.

Chinook—The formal name of the CH–47 helicopter.

CID—Criminal Investigation Division. The military police version of the civilian detective. Often called Sid by soldiers.

Commo—Communications.

Company—Euphemism for the CIA.

Conex—A large metal shipping container.

Concentina wire—A roll of barbed wire used to provide some perimeter security.

CQ—Charge of quarters. An enlisted man who is given overnight duty to assist the officer of the day in handling problems.

Crew chief—The enlisted man charged with the responsibility of maintaining an aircraft. He also served as part of the crew of the aircraft by manning one of the door guns.

Crew members—Assigned members of an aircrew. The UH–1 had four in combat operations: the aircraft commander, the pilot, the crew chief, and the door gunner.

Crosstube—The tubular support for the helicopter's skids.

CS—A very strong version of tear gas. In concentration can actually disable troops due to vomiting.

C's—C-ration meals. Each meal came in an individual box. Most of the items were canned.

CWO—Chief warrant officer. During Vietnam, there were four grades of warrant officers, WO1 being the junior grade. The grades W2, W3, and W4 were all considered chief warrant officers. Known for having big watches and stealing jeeps.

(D)

DEROS—Date of estimated return from overseas. The date when a soldier's tour was over.

DFC—Distinguished Flying Cross. An award designed for valorous action during aerial flight. The fourth highest award for valor.

Di Di Mau—Vietnamese, also *di di*, meaning roughly to go away quickly.

Dien Cai Dau—Vietnamese meaning crazy. The Americanized pronunciation was "dinky dow."

Dink—Derogatory name for a Vietnamese, primarily the enemy. Interchangeable with gook.

DMZ—Demilitarized zone. The area between North and South Vietnam, into which no one was allowed to go. A no-man's-land.

Door gunner—The second enlisted member of a Huey crew. The door gunner's primary responsibility was maintaining the machine guns for the helicopter. He also assisted the crew chief in performing maintenance. Many gunners came from the infantry and were later trained as crew chiefs.

Dustoff—The call sign for medevac aircraft. The call sign originated with the 57th Med Detachment and later became used by all medevac aircraft.

(E)

EM—Enlisted man.

(F)

FAC—Forward air controller. Normally a small air force fixed-wing aircraft, most often an O–1 or O–2.

FFAR—Folding fin aerial rocket. A 2.75-inch rocket used by gunships.

Firebase—A small base camp for artillery. The places from where an artillery unit supports the infantry.

Firefight—When opposing forces engage each other with small arms.

FNG—Fucking new guy. The term used to refer to those newly arrived in Vietnam.

FO—Forward observer. Generally an artillery officer assigned to the infantry for the purpose of coordinating their artillery support.

FSB—Fire Support Base. See Firebase.

F–4—The numerical designation for the Phantom fighter plane. Used as both a fighter and fighter-bomber during the Vietnam war.

(G)

GCA—Ground controlled approach. During bad weather, a controller operating a GCA radar can give a pilot information to land his aircraft by vectoring him into the airfield. The controller provides both directional and altitude data.

GI—General issue or government issue. Actually refers to the government issued equipment a soldier is given to use. Most often used to refer to the soldier himself.

Gook—Derogatory name for a Vietnamese, primarily the enemy. Interchangeable with dink.

GP—General purpose. In the designation for army tents, they come in GP, small, medium, or large. It's a tent that might be used for almost anything, as opposed to one with a specific design purpose, such as mess tent.

(H)

Helipad—A designated landing area for helicopters.

HHC—Headquarters and Headquarters Company. These companies are found at battalion and higher levels. They are the unit to which all the staff of a battalion or higher headquarters are assigned. The unit serves the administrative needs of all the staff.

Hootch—A place to live. Originally refers to a Vietnamese dwelling made of straw, but used to mean any dwelling.

Hootchmaid—A Vietnamese maid who cleans your hootch, shines boots, and takes care of your laundry. Hootchmaids were nonexistent at Camp Eagle.

Hoverdown—An LZ that required the helicopter to hover straight down for a hundred feet or so.

Huey—The popular nickname for the UH–1 series helicopter. The army's formal name for the aircraft is Iroquois.

H–34—A Sikorsky helicopter used by both the army and Marine Corps in Vietnam.

(I)

IFR—Instrument flight rules. Refers to flying the aircraft solely by reference to instruments, such as in the clouds.

In-processing—A term referring to all the paperwork required to be filled out on arrival to a new unit. Leaving a unit requires a reverse procedure called out-processing.

IP—Instructor pilot. Teaches flying, also responsible for administering check rides to qualified pilots.

(J)

Jarheads—Derogatory name for Marines. May originate from their calling their headgear a lid.

Jodie—The guy back home who goes after your girl while you're away serving in the military.

JP4—The grade of jet fuel most used in the Huey.

(K)

KIA—Killed in action.

Kingbees—The call sign for a Vietnamese Air Force helicopter unit.

Kingsmen—The call sign for the 17th Assault Helicopter Company. The unit became B Company, 101st Aviation Battalion.

Klick—Short for kilometer. A distance of one thousand meters.

KP—Kitchen police. A duty assigned to soldiers to assist in the mess hall.

(L)

LBE—Load bearing equipment. The suspenders and other equipment used in carrying a soldier's equipment.

LBJ—The initials of a U.S. president and the initials of the Long Binh Jail. Neither were often held in high esteem by soldiers serving in Vietnam in 1968.

Lifer—A career soldier. Sometimes considered an insulting term, depending on the opinion the user held of the military as a career option. Universally insulting when the word pig is added as a suffix.

Loach—or LOH. Refers to a light observation helicopter, usually the OH–6A.

LRP—or LRRP. Long-range patrol or long-range reconnaissance patrol. Refers to a type of unit, also the soldiers in that unit. Pronounced Lurp.

LT—Abbreviation for lieutenant. Was used to address lieutenants. Pronounced as the letters individually (el tee).

LZ—Landing zone.

(M)

Mai Loc—A small Vietnamese village in northern I Corps. There was a Special Forces camp known as FOB I, outside the village, from which CCN (Command and Control North) missions were staged.

Marvin—Nickname for Vietnamese soldiers. Short for Marvin the ARVN.

Mayday—An internationally recognized distress call.

McGuire rig—A type of emergency extraction rig used to get soldiers out of the jungle when no LZ is available. Consists of 120 feet of rope with a nylon seat arrangement. Not a preferred means of transportation since the passenger has to ride 120 feet below the helicopter.

Medevac—A contraction of medical evacuation. The name of a helicopter ambulance.

Marmite can—An insulated can for keeping food hot. Mess halls would prepare hot chow in the rear area, and it would be flown by helicopter to the field to provide hot chow for the units in the jungle.

Minigun—A six-barreled, electrically operated machine gun. The weapon also had an electrically operated feeder and delinker to allow it to fire up to 2400 rounds per minute. On the Charlie-model Huey gunships, the guns were one on each side of the aircraft, on flexible mounts that could be moved by the pilot to aim the weapon. The Cobra could have two mounted in fixed positions on the wings and one in the turret under the nose.

MO—Maintenance officer.

MOC—Maintenance operational check. A run-up of the aircraft engine after the aircraft was worked on to check for leaks and proper operation of equipment.

Montagnard—Mountain tribes of Vietnam. A French term meaning mountain men. They were called *moi* (savages) by the Vietnamese and treated as second-class citizens. They were fierce fighters and valuable allies to the Special Forces soldiers.

MP—Military police.

MPC—Military payment certificate. Also called play money by soldiers. The money used to pay soldiers in Vietnam. It was meant to control the flow of greenbacks into Vietnam.

M–1—M–1 Garand rifle. World War II vintage, gas-operated, semiautomatic, .30-caliber rifle.

M–16—The fully automatic, 5.56mm assault rifle used by U.S. forces in Vietnam.

M–60—A 7.62mm machine gun capable of firing 750 rounds per minute. Also called Pig, referring to the rate at which it used ammo.

(N)

Nam—A shortened version of Vietnam used by GIs.

NCO—Noncommissioned officer. Senior enlisted leadership in the military. Generally responsible for making everything happen, once the decisions are made. Many times they make things work in spite of the decisions made by the officers.

NDP—Night defensive position. A position selected for its defensibility during the night.

Nomex—A flame retardant material used in the manufacture of flight suits to protect aircrews in the event of fire.

NVA—North Vietnamese Army.

(O)

O club—Officers club. Stateside, it was meant as a place to dine and socialize. The clubs in Vietnam were primarily meant for getting smashed.

OCS—Officer Candidate School. A six-month training course for college graduates to train them to be lieutenants.

OD—Olive drab. The color of everything in the army.

OER—Officer efficiency report. Once a year, a form is filled out by each officer's boss to report on the officer's performance. Many officers spend their entire career worrying about every word that goes on their OER.

OH–6A—An observation helicopter made by Hughes aircraft, known as the Loach.

Opera Non Verba—The motto of the Kingsmen. It means action not words.

Ops—Short for operations.

O–2—A two-engine airplane made by Cessna, used for observation. The aircraft is unique in that one engine is in the nose and one in the tail. This configuration makes it known as a pusher/puller aircraft.

(P)

Penaprime—A thick petroleum product that was poured on dusty areas to keep the dust down and firm up the soil.

Peter Pilot—(as in Peter the Pilot) Term meaning copilot.

Preflight—The inspection of an aircraft done by a pilot prior to flight. Its purpose is to insure that the aircraft is safe to fly.

PSP—Perforated steel planking. Steel planks measuring about two feet by ten feet. The planks have slots along one side and teeth along the other. This allowed them to be interlocked to form a large flat surface. Often used to make heli-pads.

PT—Physical training or pilot technique.

PX—Post exchange. A soldier's department store.

PZ—Pickup zone. The place troops are loaded on the aircraft to be taken to the LZ.

(R)

Recon—Short for reconnaissance.

REMF—Rear echelon motherfucker. A term used to describe support personnel who did not see combat. While it was recognized that their jobs were necessary, the attitude of some REMFs earned them disrespect.

Revetment—A protected parking spot for aircraft. Constructed of sandbags or sand-filled barrels and covered with PSP. The purpose was to protect the aircraft from shrapnel during rocket or mortar attacks.

RLO—Real live officer. Nonwarrant officers, most often used in reference to lieutenants and captains.

RTO—Radio transmitter operator. The army's name for the man who talks on the radio. Such titles demonstrate the need for acronyms.

Ruck—Short for rucksack or backpack.

RZ—Recon Zone.

(S)

Sapper—A specially trained enemy soldier with the mission to sneak into a base and plant explosive charges. Sappers would select targets to cause the most possible damage, either by trying to blow up barracks full of sleeping soldiers or some important equipment such as helicopters. Since it was unlikely that the sapper would escape, target selection was important. To cover his assault, the sapper usually performed his mission under the cover of a rocket attack or infantry assault.

Seabees—The navy's combat engineers. They'll build anything they can get the materials for, even under fire.

SFC—Sergeant first class. The rank of a platoon sergeant.

Short-timer—Someone who has little time left on his tour. The exact amount of time required to qualify as a short-timer was dependent on the perspective of the observer. Someone who was new in country might consider a soldier with two hundred days short. A soldier with only fifty days left would believe himself short unless he was around someone who only had ten days to go.

Sin loi—G.I. spelling for the Vietnamese phrase *xin loi*, meaning, roughly, too bad or tough shit.

SOI—Signal operating instructions. A small book that contains frequencies, call signs, and instructions to encode messages. The codes are simple, and the books are closely guarded. If one is captured by the enemy, everyone simply destroys their book and uses a new one. The simplicity of the system makes it fairly easy to secure radio transmissions.

SP—An abbreviation for specialist. Specialists grades were from E–4 to E–7 in 1968.

Spec—Another abbreviation for specialist. Pronounced speck.

(T)

Tac—Abbreviation for tactical.

Tac Air—A tactical air strike on a specific target, most often conducted by a fighter-bomber.

Tail boom—The long aft portion of the helicopter's empennage that supports the tail rotor and its drive shaft. The length gives the tail rotor additional leverage to counteract the torque applied to the main rotor through the transmission.

Tail rotor—The small rotor on the back of a helicopter. Its purpose is to counteract the torque applied to the main rotor through the transmission. Without the tail rotor, the fuselage would try to turn in the opposite direction of the main rotor at the same RPM. This condition not only makes it hard for the pilot to see where he is going, it also makes it impossible to keep lunch down.

Tet—The Vietnamese Lunar New Year. A holiday that would most likely have been ignored by most Americans, save for the offensive of 1968. The offensive of Tet '68 is considered the turning point of the war. It well could have been in our favor. The offensive was an act of desperation on the part of the enemy. He stood and fought, and tried to capture and hold territory. He was decidedly overwhelmed. The VC were virtually broken. Had we continued the bombing of the North and our counteroffensive of '68 and '69, even the Vietnamese have admitted that they would have been defeated. Instead, Tet was a turning point against our side. Even though it was a resounding defeat for the enemy, the news in the United States made it appear as a loss for us. The news coverage was the final straw in turning public opinion against the war and withdrawing their support for the troops.

TI—Technical inspector. His job is to inspect the work that mechanics perform on an aircraft to insure that it was done properly. His signing off of the work means that two men, the mechanic and the TI, have checked to insure correct maintenance procedures.

TL—Team leader.

TOC—Tactical operations center. The center for communications and formulation of the battle plans. Most military operations are planned and controlled from the TOC.

Toe popper—Small antipersonnel mine.

(U)

UH—Utility helicopter.

UHF—Ultrahigh frequency. A type of radio named for its frequency range.

Unass—Military term that describes the act of removing one's posterior end and all attached miscellaneous body components from somewhere.

(V)

Vandergrift—The name of a USMC fire support base.

VC—Viet Cong.

VHF—Very high frequency. A type of radio named for its frequency range.

Ville—GI slang for village.

VNAF—Vietnamese Air Force.

VR—Visual recon. A reconnaissance performed by flying over an area without placing troops on the ground.

(W)

WO—Warrant officer. Normally meaning a WO1, but could be used to mean any warrant officer. The warrant officer aviator is perceived differently as seen by:

Headquarters—A drunken, brawling, jeep-stealing, woman-corrupting liar, with a star sapphire ring, Seiko watch, and a survival knife.

Himself—A stout, handsome, highly trained professional killer and a female idol, who wears a star sapphire ring, carries a finely honed survival knife, and is always on time due to the reliability of his Seiko watch with GMT.

His wife—A stinking, foul-mouthed bum who arrives

home every twelve months or so with a bag of dirty flight suits, two flight helmets, a huge ugly watch, a survival knife, and a hard-on.

His commander—A fine specimen of a drunken, brawling, jeep-stealing, woman-corrupting liar with a ring, a knife, and a fantastically accurate Seiko watch.

Department of the Army—An overpaid, overranked, overrated tax burden who is indispensable since he will volunteer to go anywhere as long as he can drink, brawl, steal jeeps, corrupt women, kick dogs, lie, and wear dirty flight suits, star sapphire rings, survival knives, and a Seiko watch.

ABOUT THE AUTHOR

W. T. Grant enlisted in the U.S. Army in 1966. He is currently an MW4, still serving on active duty and stationed at Fort Eustis, Virginia. He was recently selected for promotion to the new rank of CW5.

He lives with his wife, son, and daughter in Newport News, Virginia.

He has flown other aircraft over the years, but is currently serving in a Huey lift company as the Aviation Safety Officer. The unit traces its heritage to Company C, (Phoenix) 158th Aviation Battalion, 101st Airborne Division.

W. T. Grant was awarded the Distinguished Flying Cross on three occasions in Vietnam. All three instances were in support of F Company, 58th Infantry (LRP). Among his other awards from Vietnam are the Bronze Star, nineteen Air Medals, and the Army Commendation Medal.